SIMPLY RED

W/o

SIMPLY RED

THE FUNNY BOOK OF MANCHESTER UNITED

JOHN SCALLY

BLACK & WHITE PUBLISHING

Published 2021
by Black & White Publishing Ltd
Nautical House, 104 Commercial Street
Edinburgh, EH6 6NF

1 3 5 7 9 10 8 6 4 2   21 22 23 24

ISBN: 978 1 78530 320 3

A CIP catalogue record for this book is available from the British Library.

Typeset by Iolaire, Newtonmore
Printed and bound by Clays Ltd, Elcograf S.p.A.

MIX
Paper from
responsible sources
FSC® C018072

Koller shares a hairstyle with Jaap Stam.
Of course, they have no hair.
JOHN MOTSON

The ageless Teddy Sheringham. Thirty-seven now.
TONY GUBBA

There's only one club in Europe that you can leave
Manchester United for – Real Madrid or Barcelona.
JOHN ALDRIDGE

My parents have been there for me since I was about seven.
DAVID BECKHAM

Wes Brown has stepped into the plate.
NIALL QUINN

Nobody is perfect but being a
Manchester United fan is close enough.
MAN UNITED FAN

To the memory of Ray Wilkins:

A Manchester United legend and a gentleman to his fingertips.

CONTENTS

FOREWORD

Ken Doherty

Winning the World Snooker Championship on 5 May 1997 was the summit of my career, but the icing on that cake came at Old Trafford.

After I won my world title, I asked my agent to see if he could swing it for me to go to Old Trafford and to walk on to the pitch with my trophy. I also told reporters that it was my greatest wish to do that, hoping it would improve my chances! Anyway, a few days later I got a lovely letter from Martin Edwards (the then chairman) inviting me to come and parade at half-time for the final match of the season against West Ham. When John Parrott won his world title he wanted to parade his trophy in Goodison Park because he is a big Everton fan, but they had already played their last match of the season so he paraded at Anfield when Liverpool played Spurs.

On the day I met Martin Edwards and he took me on a tour of the ground and brought me into the boardroom where I met Bobby Charlton, which was a big thrill. Then my big moment came when I walked on to the pitch in front of 55,000 people. It was like walking onto holy ground. After the match I met the players, which was nice because a lot of them are interested in snooker.

It was an experience I'll never forget and the perfect day in many ways. It was a real party atmosphere. It was the last game of the season. United won 2–0 and had the Premier trophy presented. None of us knew at the time but it was also Eric Cantona's last game for the club. The whole thing was a mind-blowing experience and a real fairy tale.

As a youngster my two heroes in life were Muhammed Ali and George Best. George produced many a laugh during his career. I have the videos of George's best matches for United and his finest goals. He was such an outstanding player – in a class of his own. I don't think he had any flaw as a player, though obviously he had his problems as a person, but he had to handle an awful lot of attention and very few people could live like that. After I won the World Championship, Joe Duffy did a radio programme about me and George rang in to congratulate me. I played him at snooker in town one evening. He wasn't half bad!

I have supported Manchester United since I was a boy. My favourite United player was Mark Hughes. Sparky was twice Players' Player of the Year (in 1989 and 1991) and although he had great power, there was much more to his game than that. He scored some fabulous goals from incredible angles – often with his back to goal. I especially remember the cup semi-final in 1994 against Oldham when Mark got a last-gasp equaliser with an incredible volley. Even by his standards that was a magic goal – probably one of his best. (A narrow-angled drive in the Cup Winners' cup final against Barcelona and a memorable looping 25-yarder against old rivals Manchester City following the signing of Eric Cantona in 1992, as if in answer to those who speculated his United career was on the rocks, are other worthy contenders for that distinction.) I firmly believe United sold him too soon – in the summer of 1995 to Chelsea for £1.5 million – because Andy Cole was not nearly as effective for a long time. Hughes always gave a hundred per cent and put his life on the line for the club and that is the quality I admire most in a player.

That's why I was also a big fan of Bryan Robson. Robbo was a great battler – a real warrior – and Roy Keane took on that role so well too.

Manchester United have produced many great players but also many great characters.

This book captures many of the laughs associated with Manchester United.

Ken Doherty
September 2021

INTRODUCTION

This book was conceived and written as Covid-19 struck the world with the ferocity of a tsunami. Apart from the global trail of illness, economic devastation and death it sparked a tidal wave of fear. It struck at something deep inside us and shattered many of our cherished certainties. We thought we were in control, but nature reminded us of our fragility, vulnerability and mortality not with a gentle whisper but with a primeval scream. The virus had echoes of a medieval plague, but our twenty-first century world struggled to find an adequate response to it. I knew things were bad when I saw in my local bookshop that all the books about the apocalypse had been moved from the back of the fantasy section to the centre of the current affairs section. Apparently, there are two factors at play: how dense the population is and how dense the population are.

I heard that everyone at John Lennon International airport had been quarantined. Imagine ... all the people? Appropriately enough, as this came at the start of the coronavirus, this news went viral.

I did learn some valuable life lessons: it is not advisable to cook fish fingers in the toaster. Or boil sausages in the kettle. I was depressed, though, that people were making apocalypse jokes like there was no tomorrow.

I worked hard on my fitness. Does going round the bend count as an exercise regime? I tried to grow genetically modified apples, but it all went pear-shaped. However, my other gardening skills improved massively. I planted myself on my sofa in the middle of March and have grown hugely with every passing week.

Finding myself older and wider, in response I decided to turn vegan. But that would be a big missed steak.

To make matters worse, football fans around the world were suffering withdrawal symptoms because they were badly missing their fix of the beautiful game.

The good news was that football continued in Belarus. Thanks to Sky Sports News I am now an expert in football there. For Manchester United fans, there was some reassurance in the frequent appearances on the channel of Gary Neville to give us a tiny reminder of what we used to call 'normal life'. Of course, Sky warmed the cockles of the heart with repeated showings of great moments from the past such as United's many title-winning moments.

As only they could, Sky got days in April out of the rumour that Manchester United were thinking of spending £200 million to buy Harry Kane. They also milked the story that Paul Pogba did not know who Graeme Souness was. Very unfairly I felt they also 'outed' Pogba. They revealed the shocking fact that he had supported ... Arsenal as a child.

Where will all this end? I sympathise with Mao Tse Tung. Sometime in the 1960s, he was reportedly asked, 'Chairman Mao, what do you think is the long-term consequence of the French Revolution?' The furrowed Chairman replied, 'The consequences of the French Revolution of 1789 to 1790? Far too early to say.'

This too will pass. It may pass like a kidney stone, but it will pass.

INTRODUCTION

When we went into lockdown my bins were going out more often than I was. I knew I was in a bad place when I went to clean the dishwasher and I was crushed with disappointment to find it was spotless. I tried to reassure myself that it was the situation that was abnormal – not me.

As the medical and scientific worlds desperately sought an antidote to the virus, I was seeking an antidote of my own. So where would I find it?

Jimmy Greaves famously said about football: 'It's a funny old game.' This book confirms the truth of his statement with hundreds of amusing anecdotes and memorable quotations. The world of football is constantly evolving and changing, but the one constant is that each generation produces its own legends and iconic names. Rather than focus on the universal game I decided to home in on perhaps the world's most famous club, Manchester United, to give the book a sharper focus, though I have no problem wandering off the reservation if a story catches my eye outside the theatre of dreams that is Old Trafford. Father Ted would have described this as an 'ecumenical matter'.

Martin Keown's observation about a sluggish Luis Suárez at the 2018 World Cup could have been applied to my inglorious career as a footballer: 'He looks like he's towing a caravan.' Given the severe limitations of my talents on the pitch, I acquired at a young age an enduring interest in the funny side of football.

Bill Shankly famously said that, 'Football is not a matter of life and death. It's much more important.' In professional sport today, and increasingly at amateur levels, the desire to win is the dominant force. Sometimes it seems that we have taken the sport out of sporting activity. In a small way this book attempts to act as a corrective to that tendency. It strives simply to celebrate the fun that is attached to sport and to give people a laugh or two.

It was 2020, so everyone had perfect vision. The pessimist says things are terrible and could not possibly be any worse. The optimist steps in and says: 'Oh yes. It could.' Manchester United fans learn that lesson the hard way. Now that my get-up-and-go has gone and left, I appreciate that even more.

A writer friend of James Joyce was dying after a traffic accident and someone insensitively asked him what dying was like and the writer with his final breath said, 'Oh, Campbell, it's terrible but at least it's not nearly as bad as writing a book.'

Although former United player Eamon Dunphy claims 'rugby is the new sex', in the football world the truth is stranger than fiction and often funnier. It can be a safety valve in the bleakest of situations.

A friend said to me once: 'My wife told me that I was a people person because although I didn't please her, I pleased others. She left me because she said I was obsessed with astronomy. What planet is she on? She always said that I have more issues than *Hello* magazine.'

In an effort to impress her he told her that he had a league medal.

'At what level?' she asked him coldly.

'At ground level,' he replied. 'That's where I found it.'

My doctor told me yesterday I was obese and diabetic. He could have sugar-coated it a bit. Some people get totally out of shape when they retire from playing sport. Not so me. I was never in good shape in the first place. I took up a running for a while, but the closest I got to a Marathon was to eat one of them – actually thousands of them. It is okay to tell jokes close to the bone, as long as it is a humerus.

However, I am part of a chosen few. There are four types of people: happy people, sad people, very sad people and then people who collect funny sports quotations and stories. I belong to that endangered species. My doctor agrees with this and has clinically diagnosed me as suffering from SAD: Sporting Anecdotes Disorder. Will a panacea cure my hypochondria?

Meanwhile my psychiatrist describes me as suffering from 'Football Foot and Mouth'. On the other hand, my mother claims I suffer from ASS: Addicted to Sports Syndrome. If you are thinking of another name for your mother, then mum's the word.

My condition keeps me awake at night pondering such difficult questions as: How do you recognise a downhill skiing race when everyone has to compete on a level playing field?

First a few words of warning. There are books of truth. There are books of fact. This is not one of them. This will not be a publication for anoraks because my aim was neither veracity nor accuracy. The author Quentin Crisp wrote: 'There are three reasons for becoming a writer: the first is that you need the money; the second that you have something to say that you think the whole world should know; the third is that you can't think what to do with the long winter evenings.'

My sole agenda was to try and put a smile on people's faces. I dedicated my time and energy to finding the funniest anecdotes. No story was too apocryphal for consideration if it was funny. My attitude was that if it was funny enough it just might be true enough!

Fake news watchers reared on a diet of the truth, the whole truth and nothing but the truth will despair at this book because in this context it was humour that was sacrosanct. It is often said that truth is the first casualty of war. In some cases, truth may have been a casualty in these pages as the agenda to entertain took precedence.

Many of the stories in this collection are strange but true. However, the veracity of some of the stories would not measure up to that expected in a court of law.

This book celebrates the great Manchester United comedians,

although much of the time their humour is unintentional. From time to time – to help younger readers in particular – I do give a little bit of historical context to help establish the bigger picture.

Many of the stories in this book are based on real events. Only the facts have been changed!

PART I

Manchester United's Miscellany of Funnies

My mother describes me as a 'quarter'. When I become twice as good, I will graduate to a full-blown half-wit. Nonetheless, for me, sport is more than just a game.

When Nelson Mandela walked out to shake hands with the players of South Africa and New Zealand in the moments before the 1995 World Cup final, it was a reminder of how powerful sport can be in symbolising friendship and forgiveness on a grand scale. Here was a former convict, standing in the middle of Ellis Park Stadium wearing the green and gold Springbok jersey and cap, shaking hands with the men who, for many, had represented the ideas of racial superiority that had excluded so many of his countrymen. It was probably the most moving moment in sport ever witnessed. To see Mandela, with the Black player Chester Williams standing at his side, walk out there and shake hands to congratulate captain Francois Pienaar and all the white players in the Springbok team, bore powerful witness to the power, intelligence and grace of the man who had united a nation after he had walked the long road to freedom.

Football is drama's first cousin. It is theatre without the script. There are times, though, when people take football too seriously.

In 1969, El Salvador and Honduras played each other at football in qualifying matches for the 1970 World Cup. The first match was played in Honduras. The night before the match a crowd of Hondurans gathered outside the hotel where the Salvadoran team was staying and set off firecrackers, leaned on car horns and beat on sheets of tin all night. The sleepless Salvadorans lost 1–0. The first casualty occurred when eighteen-year-old Amelia Bolanos, after seeing El Salvador lose on TV, shot herself in the heart. The following day the Salvadoran newspaper *El Nacional* said: 'The young girl could not bear to see her fatherland brought to its knees.' Amelia's funeral procession was televised, and the President and his cabinet walked behind the coffin. A few weeks later the Honduras team went to San Salvador for the return match. They were given the same type of pre-match treatment as their rivals, including having rotten eggs and dead rats thrown into their rooms. El Salvador won the match 3–0. As the Honduras side were taken back to their airport in armoured cars through crowds holding up pictures of their national heroine, Amelia Bolanos, the Honduras coach, Mario Griffin, claimed: 'We're awfully lucky that we lost.' The following morning a plane dropped a bomb on Honduras. Then came the news that the Salvadoran army was attacking over the border between the two countries. The football war led to the deaths of 6,000 people and more than 12,000 were wounded.

There are times when it is good to be serious. A case in point is Marcus Rashford's campaign which raised over £20 million to stop children going hungry during the Covid-19 crisis. Moreover, he singlehandedly forced the government into an embarrassing U-turn so that they were compelled to continue to provide food vouchers for children at risk of poverty. The result was clear:

Marcus Rashford – 1
Boris Johnson – 0

While Rashford – and the courage of his convictions – emerged as unquestionable winners, how much was in fact an own goal for BoJo?

Rashford's efforts were rewarded with an MBE in the Queen's Birthday Honours List. *The Sun* did a clever take on their front page with their headline:

Marcus
Big
'Eart

However, footballers are also renowned for their less than serious sides. At its best, the beautiful game has the power to make the heart miss a beat. Whatever your fancy, this collection recreates the unique excitement, drama and unpredictability of football in the words of Manchester United's practitioners. The result is a wry, idiosyncratic and sometimes bizarre catalogue of comic creations. For lovers of the absurd, outrageous and totally bizarre this *Simply Red* selection of stories and quotes will hopefully make the proverbial cat laugh or at least raise a wry smile. It is a guide or perhaps a travelogue around the strange ways in which people pursue football pleasure.

Above all, this kit bag of double entendres, quips and stories from the tongues of and about Manchester United's elite will provide reading pleasure for the madly mischievous and wickedly warped. Funny quotes and gaffes abound.

From golden balls to golden balls-ups anyone who is anyone is here: players, managers, commentators and fans including Ronaldo, George Best, Alex Ferguson, the Special One, David Beckham, Roy Keane, Ryan Giggs and Paul Pogba.

1

HUMOUR FOR ALL SEASONS

I was rude but I was rude to an idiot.
José Mourinho

The 2020–21 season was the strangest in the history of the Premier League because of the Covid-19 crisis. There were some constants. Marcus Rashford continued his journey from Red Devil to Saint in the eyes of the general public. Managers continued to have persecution complexes. Jürgen Klopp was complaining that Manchester United got too many penalties. A month later Harry Maguire was bemoaning that, in the wake of the Klopp criticism, Manchester United were not getting enough penalties. There were many VAR-ginal calls like when the ref refused to penalise what appeared to be a blatant handball when United played Chelsea.

Former Manchester United players continued to shine as pundits, with Dion Dublin leading by example: 'Sandro's holding his face, and you can tell from that it's a knee injury.' There was also the irrepressible Alan Brazil: 'City midfielder James Milner joins us to look ahead to yesterday's remarkable display.'

Other pundits continued to be nostalgic about United triumphs such as Matt Le Tissier's declaration: 'I don't think we'll ever see that again in the history of football.'

However, the pandemic seemed to affect football people in the most peculiar ways. To take one example, there was Jürgen Klopp's reaction after Virgil van Dijk was seriously injured against Everton, 'We will wait for him like a good wife who is waiting while the husband is in jail.' It was as puzzling as Barry Fry's remark after delivering his own granddaughter: 'Got a text from my daughter; she was having contraptions.'

Then there was the case of Burnley's assistant manager Ian Woan speaking of his boss Sean Dyche: 'He gets a lot of stick because he looks like a nightclub bouncer.' Things, though, were to get worse for Dyche. He was asked: 'Has someone ever told you that you look like Mick Hucknall?' According to reports, Dyche's skin colour immediately changed to Simply Red.

I hate it when people get well-known sayings wrong. Come on. It's not rocket surgery. Steve McClaren was explaining the importance of getting the balance right while dealing with players, 'It's like holding a beautiful white dove in your hand and if you squeeze it too tight, you'll kill it. And if you relax, the dove will fly away. You've just got to get the right amount of squeeze.'

FC Saarbrücken became the first fourth-tier team to reach the German Cup semi-finals. This was largely because of their penalty shoot-out win over Fortuna Düsseldorf, during which goalkeeper Daniel Batz saved four of Düsseldorf's efforts to add to another penalty save in normal time. He said, 'That's more than I'd saved together in my whole career!'

However, Saarbrücken vice-president Dieter Ferner made the more dramatic claim, 'This is the biggest sensation since the birth of Christ.'

Pelé turned eighty in October 2020. He was the subject of this glowing tribute, 'In Pelé's eighty years, the only thing that's missing is to land on the moon.'

Who was it that paid this lovely compliment? Oh yes, Pelé himself.

However, his vanity was topped by Colombian legend Faustino 'Tino' Asprilla who modestly remarked, 'In my room there is an image with the twelve Apostles and when I make love they applaud me.'

Two people who don't have self-esteem issues either are Mesut Özil and Piers Morgan. After signing a massive €350,000-a-week deal with Arsenal, Özil was frozen out and hadn't played for the club since March 2020 when he joined Fernerbahçe S.K. in January 2021. Özil tweeted, as he posed with a roll of toilet paper with Morgan's face on it. 'Piers, I took this with me from London to Istanbul to remind me of you! Although you probably knew that already before.' Morgan responded, 'Mesut, you're full of cr*p so I'm glad to be of much-needed use.'

It was claimed that over a million Fernerbahçe fans watched Özil's flight to Turkey to sign for the club on a special app. One uncharitable Manchester United supporter said the reason the journey got so many viewers was because all the Arsenal fans were watching just to make sure he had finally left the Emirates.

BT Sport's Paul Dempsey was in the middle of commentating live, from his home in Northern Ireland, on the Borussia Dortmund versus FC Schalke game that marked the return of the Bundesliga. Viewers wondered why Paul fell uncharacteristically silent for a couple of minutes, but it turned out that he had to mute himself because the delivery driver from Tesco was pounding on his door. Once Paul got his groceries in, he resumed his commentary.

Meanwhile, Porto manager Sérgio Conceição struggled with football games played out without crowds: 'It will be like being without the condiments to make a good salad,' he observed. 'Eating a salad without oil, vinegar and salt is not the same.' Spanish coach Luis Enrique had a severe dose of the lockdown blues, too: 'Playing matches without supporters is sadder than dancing with your sister. It's very ugly.'

For the first time in many years Rangers were outperforming Celtic. One fan gloated, 'The last time Celtic won a match, people in Glasgow were still allowed to visit pubs.' A Celtic fan countered, 'The last time Rangers won a trophy you could smoke in pubs.'

Danny Rose left Spurs for a loan spell at Newcastle. He faced real problems. 'I lived in London for thirteen years,' he reflected, 'and only found one good chip shop.'

The pandemic had a severe impact on the club's finances. Hence the most exciting thing that happened during the January transfer window was Harry Redknapp getting lost on his way to the Sky Sports studio on Transfer Deadline Day.

Manchester United played their unique part in this mirth and mayhem.

SUGAR-COATING IT

United got used to life without Ashley Young and reminded themselves of his days with the club and with England; as when Roy Hodgson said of him: 'I don't like to use the word "dropped". He just fell outside the twenty-three.'

EYE-CATCHING

Ole Gunnar Solskjaer paid an unusual compliment to one of his players after their great away win against Paris Saint-Germain in the Champions League. 'Scotty played the first half with one eye,' he said, 'that was the most impressive thing.'

In fact, Scott McTominay had lost one of his contact lenses rather than his actual eye.

WRONG SAID FRED

Meanwhile, Watford striker Troy Deeney was giving a less positive assessment of another United midfielder. 'Whenever you play against Fred,' he observed, 'you let him get the ball because he has to take three or four touches. He gets it facing the wrong way, turns and turns, chops, chops and he'll give you the ball three or four times a game.'

In times like this, United fans were nostalgic for Sir Alex Ferguson – who would always defend his players in public. A case in point was how he explained why a United player missed an open goal: 'Maybe it's not his best foot, obviously.'

NOBBY'S FLOSS-OPHY

In October 2020 United fans mourned one of their greatest legends, Nobby Stiles, who starred in United's European Cup triumph in 1968 and in England's World Cup victory two years earlier.

Nobby was almost as famous for the gap between his teeth as for his football. Hence the riddles:

Q: What did the dentist say to Nobby Stiles when he had to pop out to take a phone call?

A: I'll fill you in when I get back.

Q: Why does Nobby have a smartphone?

A: Because he likes to use Bluetooth.

But Gary Lineker drew on Nobby's teeth issues to pay him a lovely tribute: 'He had a heart bigger than the gap between his teeth.'

UNFORGETTABLE

Nobby enjoyed a few riddles of his own.

Q: What's the best way to forget about indigestion?

A: Take milk of amnesia.

Q: How do angels greet each other?

A: Halo.

Q: What would you do if your nose goes on strike?

A: Picket!

Q: How do you know Santa Claus was a man?

A: No woman is going to wear the same outfit year after year.

MISTLETOE AND WINE

Nobby had an endearing sense of self-deprecation. He told the story of how one Christmas he held up the mistletoe over his wife to give her a Christmas kiss. She was enjoying a nice glass of wine at the time.

She said, 'I love you so much. I don't know how I could ever live without you.'

Deeply moved, Nobby felt obliged to ask, 'Is that you or the wine talking?'

She replied, 'It's me ... talking to the wine.'

PAST PRESENT

Nobby had a very thoughtful side, too.

One day Matt Busby said to him: 'You should think of the future.'

Stiles: 'I can't. It's my wife's birthday and I'm thinking of the present.'

HATS OFF

In the end Nobby gave his wife a generous sum to go shopping. The next day she returned from her outing with ten new dresses.

Stiles rolled his eyes. 'And what would any woman want with ten dresses?'

His wife smiled beatifically. 'Ten hats.'

SHOCKING

Nobby also joked about his shortcomings in the DIY department.

'My wife said I'm hopeless at fixing appliances. Well, she is in for a shock.'

A FINAL SOLUTION?

The most famous Nobby story has subsequently been attributed to a number of other famous footballers, but it is Stiles who was the original of the species.

England were playing against Portugal, whose star player was Eusébio. His name features prominently in the canon of the greatest players of all time. It is a supreme compliment to Nobby that the England manager Sir Alf Ramsey trusted him to mark the legend.

In the dressing room before the game Alf called Nobby over and said, 'I need you to take Eusébio out of the game.'

Nobby nodded. Then he asked, 'Do you mean just for this game or for the rest of his career?'

OUT GUNNED

Arsenal were struggling. Jamie Redknapp stated: 'An Arsenal win would be a great fillet.'

Paul Merson described their habit of always playing out from the back and being devoured by the opposition, thus: 'It's like going to Woburn Zoo and walking into the lions' cage with a lorry-load of steaks. You're going to get eaten alive, aren't you? If you stay in your car you are going to be all right and that's what it was.'

In October, though, United lost 1–0 at home to Arsenal.

The press had a field day: 'Gunnar outgunned by Gunners.'

In the words of Bryan Swanson: 'There was total silence from Old Trafford, which means the alarm bells were ringing.'

Ole Gunnar Solskjaer was crestfallen. He was so thrilled when he won his next game that he threw the ball into the middle of the crowd.

He has been banned from the bowling alley for life.

NEW IMAGE?

In an effort to project greater authority Ole contemplated growing a beard. He sought advice from Roy Keane. Keano's response was encouraging, 'I didn't like my beard at first, but it's growing on me.'

FAST LEARNER

During that losing spree one fan observed that, 'Ole is learning from his mistakes. He can repeat them exactly.'

MISSING A BEAT

Trevor Sinclair had the scoop on United's losing streak: 'They took their finger off the pulse a little bit.'

HIGH ENERGY

Paul Pogba's form went into a dip. The United fans were not impressed with his work ethic. One claimed that he was writing a new book: *The A to C of Laziness*.

Lee Hendrie offered faint praise: 'He's a very special player who certainly can turn something into nothing.'

WHO IS THE MOST HANDSOME OF THEM ALL?

Another fan felt that the problem was that Pogba was too much in love with himself. He claimed that the United player spends the morning looking at himself naked in the mirror.

Eventually the employees in IKEA called the police to remove him.

KNOW WHAT I MEAN HARRY?

Harry Maguire also had his struggles at this time. Hence former Dutch international Rafael van der Vaart's comment, 'I think Maguire goes home every day and tells his wife: "I screw up, but I earn so much! They really believe I'm good!" He laughs at everyone!'

KEANE BY NAME

Roy Keane, settling comfortably into his role as pundit on Sky Sports, described Liverpool as 'sloppy' in a 3–1 defeat of Arsenal much to Jürgen Klopp's chagrin. In retaliation Liverpool fans recalled Jason McAteer's famous Keane story, when both lined out for Ireland against Norway in the 1994 World Cup finals in the United States.

Trigger describes how the Irish team played a unique version of Chinese whispers. Andy Townsend whispered into Packie Bonner's ear and each player whispered into the ear of the next person until John Aldridge was ready to whisper to McAteer. Jason was bracing himself for last-minute tactical instructions. He was taken aback when Aldo said to him, 'Row F. Look up at the girl with big breasts.' He did and was duly impressed. Then he realised that the person he had to whisper to was Keano. Thinking that Roy would not welcome this comment Trigger whispered, 'Keep it tight and don't give the ball away.'

NO ROLLING STONE

United fans responded by undermining Jason. They recalled the story that after one trip abroad with the Republic of Ireland, McAteer returned for a night out with one of his heroes, snooker player Jimmy White, who just so happened to be with 'the fella from the Rolling Stones, you know the one with all the lines on his face ... Keith Moon'.

FATHER AND SON

Keane also finds himself in the Sky studios with another former Liverpool player, Jamie Redknapp. His most memorable moment in punditry was the full truth: 'Peter Schmeichel will be like a father figure to Kasper Schmeichel.'

FROM COLE TO NEWCASTLE

Keano is clearly happier when they have special guests like his former United colleague Andy Cole. Perhaps the reason Cole is used as sparingly as a pundit goes back to his observation: 'I can learn as much from Darius Vassell as he can from me – but he can learn more.'

OVER THE HILL?

In December, United beat West Ham, managed by their old manager David Moyes, 3–1. One United fan speculated that Moyes's next job would be managing a bobsleigh team given his skills at leading clubs down the table.

DIAMONDS ARE FOREVER

Some players are generous. Joe Hart used to hand out bottles of shampoo to anyone who wanted them on the back of his Head & Shoulders deal.

Others less so. Discretion precludes me from revealing the United player who bought his partner a beautiful diamond for Christmas. After hearing about this extravagant gift Marcus Rashford said to him, 'I thought she wanted one of those sporty four-wheel-drive vehicles.'

'She did,' he replied, 'but where was I going to get a fake Jeep?'

What I love about this story is that most people think it's a joke.

THE INVISIBLE MAN

In marked contrast, Jesse Lingard thoughtfully bought Harry Maguire an expensive camouflage jacket for Christmas. The

United defender reluctantly returned it to the shop. He couldn't see himself wearing it.

HEAD AND SHOULDERS

On Boxing Day, United drew 2–2 with Leicester. After a Bruno Fernandes performance which mixed the sublime with the infuriating, Ole Gunnar Solskjaer joked that Bruno left him 'tearing his hair out'. Within an hour Ole's agent had got a call to offer the United gaffer a hair-raising sum to appear in a TV commercial for a well-known shampoo.

It's because he is worth it.

O, CHRISTMAS TREE

Before the game, United fans entertained themselves by telling the story of two best friends, a Liverpool supporter and a Manchester City fan who went deep into the frozen woods searching for a Christmas tree.

After hours of sub-zero temperatures and a few close calls with hungry wolves, one turned to the other and said, 'I'm chopping down the next tree I see. I don't care if it's decorated or not.'

HAPPY NEW YEAR

United fans went into the New Year in good form with Marcus Rashford scoring a late winner against Wolves in their last game of the calendar year to send them second in the league.

For the country at large it was an unhappy time as England found itself in a severe Covid-19 lockdown. People responded by reading more. What were they reading? The 1993 Booker Prize winner Roddy Doyle observed, 'Men my age don't want to read fiction generally. They just want to read about Hitler, Stalin and Wayne Rooney.'

THAT SINKING FEELING

Unlike United fans, Brighton supporters went into the new year in a bad place, as they headed into the relegation zone. Brighton very generously announced they would give a thousand free tickets to NHS workers for future matches, as thanks for their frontline work. One United fan asked, 'Haven't they suffered enough?'

9-9-9

In February, United were on cloud nine when they beat Southampton 9–0. It was only the third time in the history of the Premier League that such a result had been achieved. Southampton lost by the same score line to Leicester the previous season and in March 1995 United beat Ipswich 9–0.

As Southampton have an Austrian manager in Ralph Hasenhüttl, one of Ireland's favourite radio personalities, Manchester United fanatic, buyer of robots (long story) and king of the pun, Dave Moore, was first to joke that the score was: 'Nein nil.'

HAIR-RAISING

Newcastle forward Joelinton was fined £200 for breaching Covid-19 regulations after he posted a photo of himself getting a haircut. The club's £40 million record signing was investigated by Northumbria Police following the post he shared on Instagram. One Manchester United fan was impressed by the cut but observed, 'Pity he never looked so sharp playing for Steve Bruce.'

To be fair, Bruce scoffs at conclusion-jumping journos: 'People are putting two and two together and getting four.'

PUNBELIEVABLE JEFF

One of the most high-profile transfers during the transfer window was Jesse Lingard's loan move from United to West Ham. Lingard made a sensational debut for the Hammers scoring two goals away to Aston Villa. United fans had a new nickname for him: 'Messi Lingard'.

HOWLER

In February, United contrived to lose a lead to draw 3–3 against Everton. The finger of blame was pointed at David de Gea. He had already come under criticism for failing to save Everton's first, netted by Abdoulaye Doucouré, before committing a howler and allowing Dominic Calvert-Lewin to score the crucial equalising goal. United fans were furious at yet another mistake from the keeper. One said, 'David is so slow he needs two hours to watch *Sixty Minutes*.'

ERROR PRONE

Ole Gunnar Solskjaer was fuming with the referee after United failed to get a penalty against Chelsea despite VAR's intervention. Jermaine Jenas was sympathetic: 'The people behind VAR are making all the wrong mistakes.'

SIAN-SATIONAL

Other football personalities try to be more respectful to officials. Observe Paul Merson on Sian Massey-Ellis: 'Great decision by the lady linesman.'

A BATTERED SOLE

Marcus Rashford is not the only Manchester United legend who has shone during the Covid-19 pandemic. Lou Macari was a pocket dynamo in midfield during the mid to late 1970s and made 401 appearances for United before leaving in 1984. The 1977 FA Cup winning hero is the driving force behind the Macari Centre, a shelter for rough sleepers which is situated in Hanley near Stoke-on-Trent. The centre accommodates forty-eight people.

Lou jokes: 'The highlight of their week is when I come back from Old Trafford after a match and I bring them some pies. They love the Man United pies. But it's all they like about Man United, because most of them are Stoke supporters!'

Apart from Old Trafford the most famous building in Manchester is said to be Lou's Fish and Chip shop. Lou's favourite story involves driving a rental car along an old mountain road in Eastern Europe at night when he started having engine problems. Unable to get a signal on his mobile phone, he saw a light in a building not far off and made it there just as the car stalled. Getting out of the car, he knocked on the door. A monk in a brown habit opened the door.

'Good evening, brother!' greeted the monk. 'What can I do for you?'

'I'm very sorry to bother you, but I'm having trouble with my car and can't seem to get my phone to work. Would you have a landline I could borrow to call for help?' asked Macari.

The monastery did have a phone. Lou managed to get the car company to send a replacement but it would take a couple of hours to arrive. When the monk heard this, he invited him to stay for dinner.

'Please have a rest,' assured the monk. 'We're having fish and chips tonight.'

Lou accepted the offer with thanks and sat down to the best fish and chips he had eaten. Grateful, he asked if he could thank the cook in person. The monk obliged and went into the kitchen to convey his request. Shortly after, another monk walked out.

'Thank you so much for the fantastic meal!' exclaimed Lou. 'You must be the chip monk.'

'You're most welcome but no, that would be him,' explained the monk pointing at a third monk who was walking over. 'I'm the fish friar.'

MARCH-ING ON

March began slowly with the biggest news that Nigel Pearson had become the Bristol City manager prompting Simon Jordan to observe: 'Manchester has 550,000, Liverpool has 500,000. But Bristol ... that's got half a million!'

Gareth Bale finally found his feet in his second coming with Spurs. As Perry Groves claimed: 'Gareth Bale has been levitated to the status of one of the best players in the world.'

United seemed to be in a rut of 0–0 draws, but as a wise man, Paul Merson, insightfully observed: 'No one wins anything winning 5–4 every week.'

In contrast, former United manager David Moyes was riding high with West Ham. Steve McManaman spotted a pattern: 'The better West Ham have been, the better their performance has been.'

Moyes also earned plaudits for his memory: 'I remember my first game against Fulham – I remember it like it was tomorrow.'

Then came the perfect Super Sunday for United fans. It began by Liverpool losing their sixth consecutive home game against lowly Fulham. Even Jamie Carragher was dismayed, claiming that Liverpool had gone from being 'mighty monsters' to 'mighty midgets'. Former United player Darren Fletcher caught the mood on Merseyside perfectly: 'Jürgen Klopp with a handshake through gritted teeth.'

Liverpool's big stars were struggling, but Paul Merson wouldn't take off Mo Salah: 'Even if he's dragging his foot around, walking like Herr Flick out of 'Allo 'Allo, he's got to stay on for me.'

Then came joy unconfined as United ended Manchester City's 21-match winning run with a 2–0 victory at the Ethiad. As Mark Lawrenson pointed out: 'If you can make chances against Man City, you'll always have a chance to score.' And Pete Graves remarked: 'The Man United front three have been playing very well in tandem.'

City did hit the post and their fans made much of that. It was very much in the 'What If' school of punditry championed by (a) Trevor Francis: 'If that ball had dropped to a West Brom player, who'd put it in the net, that would have been the equaliser'; (b) Alan Smith: 'It certainly would have crept under the bar had it been on target'; and (c) Steve McClaren: 'If Villa hadn't conceded three goals, they'd still be in this game.' That approach doesn't mean much to philosophical Andy (or is it Andrew?) Cole: 'You know the woodwork, Kelly, it is what it is.'

Luke Shaw's United career has been hampered by injuries, but in the words of Russell Fuller: 'His back problem seems to be behind him.' Shaw produced a wonder goal to seal the win. Luke was Shaw-some.

The game was a reminder of Kevin Keegan's eyebrow-raising assertion: 'Manchester City are built on sand and I don't mean that because their owners are from the Arab countries.'

FOR GOD'S SAKE:

Former United star Zlatan Ibrahimović was recalled to Sweden's squad for the World Cup qualifiers, five years after retiring from international football. With characteristic modesty the 39-year-old, who often speaks of himself in the third person, took to social media to confirm the return, tweeting a picture with the words: 'The return of the God.'

SPLIT PERSONALITIES

United lost to Leicester in the sixth round of the FA Cup. In the words of Niall Quinn: 'They went out with a real damp whimper.'

It was left to Jermaine Jenas to break the bad news to the United trinity: 'They'll be absolutely fuming, Ole Gunnar Solskjaer.'

BULL'S EYE

Phil Neville left his job as manager of the English women's team to link up with his old United teammate David Beckham in Miami. It was possibly time for Neville to move on given one of his observations: 'There was a girl there that played without fear. She's literally a bull.'

BLITHE SPIRIT

Former United legend Steve Bruce was struggling as his Newcastle side hovered over the relegation zone. He was under no delusions: 'All this nonsense about the spirit in the camp ... I had *deluded* to it before the game.'

HAND-SOME

In April speculation was rife that Manchester United were chasing Erling Haaland ahead of a proposed £150 million move from Borussia Dortmund. Watching him in his role as a pundit Dion Dublin made a startling revelation:

'I can count on the fingers of one hand the number of touches Haaland had ... he must have had ten to twelve touches.'

TALKING OUT OF HIS ARSE-NAL

Meanwhile another United legend Rio Ferdinand was worried about the frailties in the Arsenal squad. He had an interesting analogy: 'Arteta must look at the squad like a promiscuous girlfriend ... he can't trust them at all.'

SUPERTROUPERS

The biggest talking point of the season was the announcement of the establishment of the soon to be aborted Super League. With remarkable insight Jermaine Jenas observed: 'It'll leave a sour taste in some fans' minds.' Whereas Leon Osman was in prophetic mode: 'I wouldn't say it's been coming but it's been inevitable.'

United fans asked: What's the biggest joke in the world?

Answer: The Super League.

THE GLAZING ISSUE

In May, Manchester United's Premier League game against Liverpool at Old Trafford was postponed following protests against the club's owners, the Glazer family. Hundreds of supporters got into the stadium ahead of the behind-closed-doors contest, which was originally scheduled for a 4.30 p.m. start before being delayed and finally postponed completely. The Manchester United Supporters Trust claimed the incident was:

> The culmination of sixteen years since the Glazer family's acquisition of the club. Over that period, the owners have taken £1 billion out of the club and we have witnessed decay and decline both on the field and off it. While the invasion of the stadium isn't something we expected, and it is rumoured a gate was opened for fans, but even if that is not the case we believe the vast majority of Manchester United staff are sympathetic with the views of the fans.

When it was reported that a window had been broken in the stadium one United fan saw the upside: 'At least we have Glazers here to fix it.'

IN TWO MINDS

Jermaine Jenas seemed a little confused by the owners: 'Under the Glazership's reign...'

However, Andrew Cole was firmly on the side of the protestors during the Old Trafford demonstration: 'I back protests. I protest against myself half the time.'

PAYING THE PENALTY

When informed that the club would face a penalty for the scenes during the demonstration one fan replied: 'No problem. Bruno Fernandes will score it.'

FAULTY TOWERS

The 2021 close season was an eventful one on and off the field. Wayne Rooney famously (infamously?) went partying with four young women in a hotel. One of them who did not recognise him – but knew he was famous – intriguingly kept calling him 'Wayne Clooney'. One United fan tweeted that given his antics with them in the hotel room he should have been addressed as 'Wayne Clowny'.

Having already signed England international Jadon Sancho for £73 million from Borussia Dortmund, Manchester United agreed a fee of £41 million with Real Madrid for defender Raphaël Varane. Ole Gunnar Solskjaer signed a new three-year contract.

Then, sensationally, two weeks into the new season it was announced that the prodigal son Cristiano Ronaldo was to return 'home'. To make it all the sweeter just that morning he had looked destined to sign for Manchester City. Such was the enormity of the news that the United website crashed under the sheer weight of the traffic.

Given the new signings and the new contract one United fan mused that Solskjaer would have an 'Oly Jolly' Christmas.

2

THE LETTER

If he was an inch taller, he'd be the best centre-half in Britain.
His father is six foot two – I'd check the milkman.
Alex Ferguson on Gary Neville

The year 2020 began in unfamiliar territory for Manchester United fans. The team's form was inconsistent, and they had a lack of fit strikers. It looked as if they were going to miss out on the Champions League (in fact, they rallied well to secure qualification) for a second consecutive year.

MORALE BOOSTER

United fans can be an unforgiving lot. January 2020 was a disappointing month for the team and one player was given a rare chance to play for them. It didn't go well for him and the side shipped a bad defeat. Afterwards one of his friends told him, 'Don't worry, it wasn't your fault. It was those f**king idiots who picked you in the first place.'

THE NUMBERS GAME

United fans were a little underwhelmed by the club's transfer activity. Even the normally hyper Jim White on Sky Sports News on Transfer Deadline Day was uncharacteristically reticent about United's singing of Odion Ighalo.

Odion had a major decision to make and when he finally made it to Old Trafford he announced, 'Number 19 was not available. When I was at Watford, I put on 24 – but 24 was not available. In Shanghai, Number 9, it's not available, so I said 24+1 is 25, so I said, okay, let me go for 25 instead of 19.'

Who knew that players brought such a mathematical sensibility to shirt selection?

DRY JANUARY

That month one dejected fan said he was going to start a new drinking game. Every time United won a game in the league he was going to drink a shot.

'How did you get on?' asked a friend at the start of February.

'Great – according to my doctor. I had a dry January.'

What really rubbed salt into the wounds of the United fans, though, was that Liverpool were flying. They were unbeaten in the league and looked like they were going to become the Invincibles. What was most alarming was that they looked on course to emulate Manchester United's historic treble in 1999. Who could stop them?

CONSPIRACY?

Manchester United don't do conspiracy theories but . . .

Many fans believe that the entire season was turned by a letter.

A young Manchester United supporter from Donegal wrote to Jurgen Klopp requesting that Liverpool stop winning matches. As part of a school writing project, ten-year-old Daragh Curley wrote to Klopp in late January asking that he make Liverpool lose their next match in order to give the Premier League chasing pack a chance. He wrote:

Liverpool are winning too many games. If you win nine more games then you have the best unbeaten run in English football. Being a United fan that is very sad. So, the next time Liverpool play please make them lose. You should just let the other team score. I hope I have convinced you to not win the league or any other match again.

Much to the surprise of Daragh and his family, Klopp responded with a signed letter outlining that while he would not be able to send his team out to lose, he admired the ten-year-old's 'passion for football'.

The Liverpool manager graciously wrote in reply:

Firstly, I would like to thank you for writing to me. I know you did not send me good luck or anything but it is always good to hear from a young football fan no matter what, so I appreciate you getting in touch. Unfortunately, on this occasion, I cannot grant your request, not through choice anyway. As much as you want Liverpool to lose it is my job to do everything that I can to help Liverpool to win as there are millions of people around the world who want that to happen so I really do not want to let them down. Luckily for you, we have lost games in the past and we will lose games in the future because that is football . . .

Take care and good luck, Jurgen.

MEDIA GOLD

The letter created a media sensation. Speaking at a Liverpool press conference, Klopp explained why he responded to the letter. 'It was just nice, it was cheeky,' he said. 'We had time that day, so I read the letter and I replied. I have no problem with supporters of other clubs. I think and hope and know it's a free world and we can choose our club. I don't think everybody has to be a Liverpool fan, but I like working for Liverpool and I like the rivalry we have.'

The Klopp letter did have an impact on Daragh. When he was interviewed by Shane Coleman on Newstalk Radio Daragh said, 'I would be disappointed now if Liverpool beat United by 5–0, but if they only beat them by 4–0 that would be okay.'

Later that night Daragh got to ask Roy Keane on Ireland's premier TV programme, *The Late Late Show*, what his ambition was as a ten-year-old. Not surprisingly Keano said it was to be a professional footballer. When Keane asked Daragh what his ambition was he was surprised with the answer, 'To be a professional rugby player.'

THE FALLOUT

Post hoc, ergo propter hoc. One thing follows another – so one thing must be caused by the other. Otherwise known as the post hoc fallacy . . .

The Daragh–Jurgen correspondence transformed the season. Liverpool could not stop winning in the time preceding the letter – but of the six subsequent games they played before the Covid-19 crisis shut down the season they lost four!

THE FAB FOUR

The football world was stunned on 29 February 2020 when relegation-threatened Watford beat Liverpool 3–0. Gone was Liverpool's chance to become the Invincibles. The Watford game coincided with the announcement that the British Prime Minister Boris Johnson and his partner were expecting a baby. Gary Lineker saw the funny side. 'Liverpool are getting a spanking and someone admits to sleeping with Boris Johnson. Bloody hell, these leap year days are weird.'

Better still from a United perspective, Liverpool lost to Chelsea 2–0 in the FA Cup. Atlético Madrid beat them twice in the knockout stages of the UEFA Champions League, the second time being a match in March 2020 played as the world was closing its doors to mass gatherings. So Liverpool's chances of emulating Manchester United's unique treble were dashed.

JOY TO THE WORLD

United fans took to social media to express their glee:

'Thanks to that letter the Invincibles have become the Invisibles.'

Another said, 'That boy is a magician. He must have gone to school in Hogwarts.'

ODDS ON

Antony Johnson was cruel enough to bet £3.30 at the start of the 2019–20 Premier League season on Jesse Lingard failing to register a single goal or assist. Finally Lingard scored ... eight minutes into injury time of the final game of the season. How much would Antony have won? £135.30.

'That's about all Lingard is worth,' said one disgruntled United fan.

3

THE BEST OF TIMES

*Being naturally right-footed, he doesn't often
chance his arm with his left foot.*
                              Trevor Brooking

The difference between George Best and the rest was the difference between Luciano Pavarotti and Justin Bieber – authentic genius versus something a little, if not a lot, less.

The late Danny Blanchflower remarked: 'Football is not about winning, it's about glory.' Best's life was a peculiar combination of glory and ignominy. His finest hour was at Wembley the night Manchester United beat Benfica in 1968 to win the European Cup final.

United went into the final at a considerable disadvantage. They were denied the presence of the great Denis Law because of a knee injury. The Best, Law and (Bobby) Charlton era represents a high-water mark of post-war British football. No other team had three different players named as European Footballer of the Year within the space of five seasons. Law was the first of the three to win this accolade.

It was fitting that United's greatest glory up to that juncture should come exactly ten years after the Munich air disaster. On three occasions United had got to the semi-finals of the European Cup only to fail the penultimate test each time.

United's march to the final had taken them first to Malta, second to Sarajevo, and third to Poland – in a match that was played in horrendous conditions with two feet of snow on the pitch and temperatures of minus six degrees Celsius. In contrast, their next fixture in Madrid was played at 90 degrees Fahrenheit. United had won 1–0 in the first leg at Old Trafford, though they found themselves 3–1 down at half-time in the second leg. After Matt Busby's half-time pep talk, United squared the tie at 3–3.

The final, against the Portuguese side Benfica, was played at Wembley the same day as Sir Ivor won the Derby. There were so many fascinating ingredients that, on any other day, this race would have been the big sporting story. Mrs Alice Chandler was a descendant of the American folk hero Daniel Boone. She was also the woman who bred Sir Ivor. After Sir Ivor's first success his owner struck a £500 bet each way at 100 to 1 for the Derby with William Hill.

However, the following morning it was United who were splashed all over the front pages. The result provoked astonishing celebrations – a kind of footballing catharsis, an outpouring of affection built up over ten years for a team which had suffered so much during the Munich disaster and its aftermath.

To escape the hype on the day of the final, the Red Devils went to Surrey where misfortune struck Brian Kidd when he fell into a pond and found himself literally up to his neck in mud.

On a scorching hot night, the United team got a boost when they approached the ground. Although there were thousands of fans outside, what impressed them most were the thirty Egyptians who stood with a banner: *Manchester United Supporters Club Cairo Branch*.

United wore blue on the night because Benfica also wore red.

The half-time score was 0–0, but then Bobby Charlton scored with a header which went in at the foot of the post. United then made a near fatal mistake by trying to hold possession. The Portuguese equalised late in the game. The legendary Eusébio was clean through in the dying moments, but Alex Stepney made a brilliant save. The match went to extra-time.

It was fitting that it was George Best who broke the deadlock when he dribbled around the goalie, having slipped the ball through the centre-half's legs. The team relaxed and a Brian Kidd and a great Bobby Charlton second goal sealed United's victory.

It was Best, though, who stole the show with his unique marriage of the graceful and dramatic. Few players had the power to affect a crowd's response as much as he did. Every time he got the ball something extraordinary was expected of him. The crowd held its breath in expectation. More often than not, they were not disappointed. In fact, 1968 was Best's year. Never one to miss out on the headlines he was voted both English and European Footballer of the Year and topped the First Division scoring charts with twenty-eight goals.

Within a few seasons Best had become a cult figure, a living James Dean, but he was a rebel with a cause. More accurately, two causes: to help Matt Busby achieve his lifetime ambition to make Manchester United the kings of Europe and, more personally, to establish himself as the greatest player of all time. Best was a riddle wrapped in an enigma: the creator of a glamorous new image for football while simultaneously turning back the clock to an almost forgotten era of individuality in an age beholden to the tyranny of convention. A creature of instinct rather than logic, Best's party trick was to drop a penny piece on the toe of his shoe, then flick it up into his top breast pocket. He was the stuff of magic.

Best was the first footballing icon in the global village and one of its greatest ever celebrities; celebrity being perhaps the most potent form of contemporary magic. United's European Cup win was the triumph of magic.

His was an incredible life, one which started out as the supreme Roy of the Rovers story. But then, as the fairy tale turned to soap opera, he became something more, a kind of one-man rainbow coalition of every imaginable trauma from imprisonment to marriage breakdown, from public humiliation to global adulation. People have evoked fictional forms to express this – soap opera, morality play, Greek tragedy and, most often, fairy tale gone sour. The truth is that Best encapsulated all of these and many more. Global communications made his story more vivid than almost any we had ever known. But the essential appeal is ancient. It almost certainly predates written history. It is the appeal of the hero.

In the autumn of his life Sir Matt Busby said:

> George Best was probably the greatest player on the ball I have ever seen. You can remember Matthews, Finney and all the great players of the era, but I cannot think of one who took the ball so close to an opponent to beat him with it as Best did.

This chapter pays homage to the best of the best.

FEVER PITCH

As the newspaper editor in John Ford's *The Man Who Shot Liberty Valance*, observes, 'If the legend is more interesting than the truth tell the legend.' To no sports figure does this adage apply more than to George Best.

He was able to completely deny two apocryphal stories that are told about him. The first is that he once said of an Irish international, 'He couldn't pass wind.' The second is that he spent months chasing a young woman because he overheard two men describing her as having loose morals. In fact, what one – a dentist – said was that she had loose molars!

FOOTBALLERS BEHAVING BADLY

George Best was one of a kind, but he was also a contemporary of players like Charlie George, Rodney Marsh, Stan Bowles, Tony Currie and Frank Worthington – players of genius who were perhaps precluded from fully achieving their talent because of what has been termed 'temperamental deficiencies'.

Best was born on 22 May 1946. In the pre-Troubles era, he grew up on the Cregagh estate in Belfast, where Catholics and Protestants lived side by side. As a boy he supported Wolverhampton Wanderers. He was an intelligent child, the only one in his class from Nettlefield Primary School who passed his 11-plus exam.

Best was football's first real pop star with a consequent prurient obsession about his private life. Like Diana, Princess of Wales he lived his adult life in a goldfish bowl and suffered the same aggressive intrusion into his privacy as she endured imprisoned in her media zoo. Both were subject to the kind of hounding from which very few people would have emerged unscathed.

Like another Belfast superstar, snooker legend Alex 'Hurricane' Higgins, Best had a hard-won reputation as a womaniser – a fact the Hurricane acknowledged: 'I know I've got a reputation like George Best, I've found that it helps being world champion, especially at snooker. I always tell them [women] I'm a great potter. They know what I mean.'

RITES OF PASSAGE

In 1961 two fifteen-year-olds, Eric McMordie and George Best, set sail from Belfast for Liverpool for a two-week trial period with Manchester United. When they got to Manchester, they asked a cab driver to take them to Old Trafford. They had no idea that Old Trafford was also a cricket ground and were stunned when the driver replied: 'Which Old Trafford?' The trip to Manchester was a big culture shock to Best, not least because it was the first time he ever wore long trousers!

SIMPLY THE BEST

Best was not without his disciplinary problems. In 1970 he was suspended for four weeks after an altercation with a referee in which he knocked the ball out of the ref's hand. Characteristically, in his first game back against Northampton in the FA Cup, he announced his return with a fanfare, scoring six goals in an 8–2 victory.

From the earliest days Matt Busby said of him: 'Don't try to change this boy's style. Let him develop naturally. The rest will come in time.'

Best married the spirit of his generation – epitomised by its anthem, 'Hope I d-die before I get old' – with its sense of freedom and optimism. The 1960s generation was one which saw an unprecedented departure from previous ages. It was in the 1960s that life as we know it today was shaped and moulded. This was the decade of the Rolling Stones, pirate radio, monster peace concerts, flower power and Mary Quant. Hope and idealism were the common currency, and sexual fluidity and freedom promised liberation at a time when the threat of AIDS had never been heard of. Now, nostalgically, everything about that decade seems positive, the desire for peace, the socially aware songs of Bob Dylan, Joan Baez and Simon & Garfunkel. Radio Luxembourg ruled the air waves. Their power play, every hour on the hour, made instant hits of songs such as Les Crane's prayer 'Desiderata'. Only the 1960s could have produced a character such as George Best.

Best made his debut for United's reserve team in 1962 against

West Brom. His immediate opponent was Brom's regular full-back – Welsh international, Graham Williams, who was rehabilitating from an injury – a hard man of football with an imposing physical presence. A year later Best made his full debut against West Brom and again his marker was Williams. United won 1–0 and Best earned good reviews for his performance. A few months later Best made his debut for Northern Ireland against Wales and again Best faced Williams. The Irish won 3–2 with Best having two 'assists'. After the game Williams made a dash for Best in the players' lounge. The debutante was petrified as the Welshman grabbed him roughly by the face and looked him deep in the eye before taking the wind out of Best's sails by saying: 'So that's what your face looks like. I've played against you three times now and all I've seen of you so far is your arse!'

TOUGH GUYS

Inevitably, given his skill, Best was a persistent target of the hard men of the game, but such was his speed that he seldom gave them the chance. A recurring feature of United's matches were attempts to psyche out Best as he took the field. An example of this strategy was QPR's Terry Mancini – who had a reputation as a 'robust' tackler. His comment to the United star before their duel began was, 'Don't look so worried, George. I'm in humane mood today. I've put iodine on my studs.'

STORMIN' NORMAN

By the age of ten Norman Whiteside had already made his mark as a footballer in Belfast, scoring a hundred goals in the one season. In 1981 United beat off the scramble of clubs chasing his signature. The following year he made his league debut coming on as a substitute for Mike Duxbury against Brighton and became the youngest Irish player to play for the Red Devils just two weeks short of his seventeenth birthday. His full debut came in the final game of the season when he scored against Stoke in a 2–0 victory.

In January 2020, United were forced to apologise to Whiteside. The club congratulated Marcus Rashford on becoming the third youngest United player to play two hundred games for the club. Norman's wife, Dee, duly drew attention to the fact that her husband had achieved that feat before any of the three. Rashford responded by tweeting due homage to Stormin' Norman.

Who is taken to the cup final every year but never used? The correct answer is the ribbons for the losing team, but in the 1970s one WAG suggested Malcolm Macdonald, following his dismal performances for both Newcastle and Arsenal in that fixture. 'Supermac' was something of a folk hero to Newcastle fans, but his inability to perform on the biggest stage casts serious doubts on his claims to greatness. In contrast, in his prime Whiteside was a fearsome tackler and had an exceptional talent for carrying the ball into the penalty area. He was also a great reader of the game and wonderful opportunist as was evident in his delightful lob over Ipswich goalie Paul Cooper in 1982. His eye for goal and ability to produce the goods on big occasions were his primary attributes.

In 1982 in Spain 'Stormin' Norman' – in the shirt of Northern Ireland – became the youngest player ever to participate in the World Cup finals – taking that distinction from no less a player than Pelé. The following year he became the youngest player to score in a Wembley final with a sweet strike on the turn against Liverpool in the Milk Cup and headed one of United's goals in their 4–0 victory over Brighton in the FA Cup final replay. He is perhaps best remembered, though, for his curling shot which beat Everton's Neville Southall for the only goal in the 1985 FA Cup final. By then Whiteside had dropped back to midfield where his lack of pace was less of a hindrance and where his skill on the ball and aggression found a real outlet.

Following some highly publicised disputes with Alex Ferguson and a series of injuries, Achilles problems and knee damage, Whiteside became unsettled at Old Trafford and he sought a transfer. He missed most of the 1988/89 season with injuries and in the close season it was decided that a move would best serve the mutual interests of club and player. After more than two hundred league games and forty-seven goals he was sold to Everton for £600,000.

It was inevitable that any United player who showed promise of flair was compared to Best. Among those great pretenders was Norman Whiteside who famously said, 'All George Best and I have in common is that we were born in the same area, discovered by the same scout and played for the same club and country.'

A SHARED PASSION

Best was the subject of a bewildering series of lurid storylines. In 1971 there was an affair with Sinéad Cusack, the most famous daughter of the Irish acting dynasty, who is now married to Oscar winner, Jeremy Irons. George had been dropped for missing training but travelled down to London to watch United play Chelsea. To avoid the media scrum waiting for him he detoured to Sinéad's flat in Islington. Ironically, his absence fuelled the circus even further and media and fans alike laid siege to Sinéad's flat for the weekend, forcing the couple to stay inside for three days. Even this incident itself provoked controversy because subsequently Arthur Lewis, the MP for West Ham North, asked why it was necessary to waste public money providing Best with a police escort to take him far from the maddening crowd. In 2018 the 'lost weekend' was reimagined in a new play *Hello Georgie, Goodbye Best*.

Other famous actresses who enjoyed what one Manchester United fan described as 'the full George Best boyfriend experience' are Susan George and Barbara Windsor. Then there was the time when Wilf McGuinness found him in bed with a married woman half an hour before United were due to leave for an FA Cup semi-final against Leeds. Leeds won 1–0 and Best had a stinker.

Perhaps the most infamous episode of all was the Marjorie Wallace affair, which almost coincided with his walkout from Manchester United. Ms Wallace was Miss World at the time and her two-night stand with Best ended acrimoniously. Shortly after he was arrested for allegedly stealing from her flat. After a short time in a prison cell, one of Best's friends mortgaged his house to have the football star released on bail. The case was dismissed, and the judge took the unusual step of informing Best that he was leaving the court without a stain on his character.

The extent of George Best's sexual charisma was brilliantly illustrated – in true *Carry On* style – on a trip to the hospital following an injury during a match. A nurse brought him to a cubicle, where she told him to undress and that she would examine him in a minute. As he turned around, Best asked where he should leave his clothes.

The nurse replied: 'On top of mine.' She had returned totally naked.

THE ROAD NOT TAKEN

The classic Best story tells of how he was in a hotel room, relaxing on the bed with a scantily clad former Miss World alongside thousands of pounds after a day of winning at the races and the casino.

The bellboy enters, turns to Best and asks, 'Where did it all go wrong?'

REGRETS, I'VE HAD A FEW

Best did seek to turn over a new leaf. As he said, 'In 1969 I gave up women and alcohol. It was the worst twenty minutes of my life.'

But he finally resolved to make a real commitment with the words: 'I've stopped drinking . . . when I'm asleep.'

Sadly, of course, he would eventually find that drink was no laughing matter.

MISSING IN ACTION

Best did little to counter any speculation about his fondness for women: 'I used to go missing a lot. Miss Canada, Miss United Kingdom and Miss World.'

And a United fan once said of him, 'If I come back in the next life, I want to come back as George Best's fingertips.'

HEADACHE

Best was dating a former Miss World who often told Best she had a headache when he asked her to spend the night with him. One evening he wined and dined her before they went out to a club.

'Thanks for a beautiful evening,' she said.

'Ah, but the night's not over,' he said, pouring her a glass of champagne. And as she sipped the drink, he pushed two white tablets towards her.

'Aren't these aspirins?' she asked.

'Indeed, they are,' he replied.

'But I haven't got a headache.'

'Good,' he said. 'Then let's go to bed.'

TOM AND BESTIE

Manchester United manager Tommy Docherty had a frosty relationship with George Best, but one day he saw Best down in the dumps and he wondered why, because Best left the club the previous evening with a beautiful blonde on his arm.

'What happened?' asked Docherty.

George replied, 'I took her to dinner, bought her chocolates and champagne and we went back to my place for the night.'

'Then why are you gloomy?'

'I spent a fortune,' said George, 'and the lads have just told me I could have got the same result with a couple of beers and a packet of crisps.'

BEST WIT

Without lapsing into clichés, one of the traits which is often forgotten in assessments of Best is his quick wit. He once took the wind out of a reporter's sails by answering a prying question in the following way: 'If you want the secret of my success with women, then don't smoke, don't take drugs and don't be too particular!'

UGLY COYOTE

Best was able to joke at his capacity for self-destruction, 'If I had been born ugly you would never have heard of Pelé.'

EYE FOR BEAUTY

After all the publicity about his love life, George was walking off the pitch when he heard two women discussing his fondness for variety. The first asked, 'How many wives has that man had?'

The second replied with another question: 'You mean apart from his own?'

LIKE A BIRD ON A WIRE

Best remained impressed by one talent. 'My ex-wife is great at bird imitations,' he once said. 'She watches me like a hawk.'

GOOD RATIO

Best was well able to joke about his life of domestic bliss. 'My wife fed me ten oysters last night to get me in the mood for a night of passion. I think only nine of them worked out.'

BEAUTY IS NOT ALWAYS IN THE EYE OF THE BEHOLDER

While George had few problems attracting women, he had a particular sympathy for Liverpool striker, Peter Beardsley, who was rather less of a ladies' man. Best described him as having a 'face like vinegar' and claimed that when he was young Beardsley used to play hide-and-seek – but no one ever came to look for him.

TRUE CONFESSIONS

Another of Best's stories is of the groom who said to his bride just after they got married, 'I've got a confession to make: I love golf. I sleep, eat and breathe golf. I'm obsessed with golf. You must realise that it completely dominates my life.'

The bride turned to her new husband and said, 'Thank you for being so honest. Now I have something to tell you: I'm a hooker.'

'No problem,' the groom said, taking her wrists. 'You hold your left hand just a little higher than the right, with your thumb down there ...'

THE DEMON DRINK

Drink features prominently in the lore of football the world over. A story tells of how Cork City famously played Bayern Munich in a European tie. Cork's manager Noel O'Mahony was not too perturbed when asked if he was afraid of losing the away leg. He said, 'We'd still be happy if we lose. It's on the same time as the beer festival.'

Best's battle with alcohol addiction was not the stuff of good public relations; the debacle on the Terry Wogan show in 1990, when he was clearly 'out of it', was an excruciating low point. Hence one journalist's claim, 'George Best, a legend in his own stupor.'

On the other hand, his wild friends, Oliver Reed and Alex

Higgins, rang Best up and said, 'We don't know what all the fuss is about, George. You looked fine to us!'

But by 2002, George Best was critically ill and needed major surgery – a liver transplant – which meant he would receive a lot of blood. In a subsequent media interview Best was asked how much blood he had required. George quipped, 'I was on the operation table for ten hours and I needed forty pints. Taking in forty pints in that time was just twenty minutes short of my all-time record!'

ACTING CLASSES

At the height of his fame, Best was unlocking his car when he was prevented from getting in by a policeman who said, 'I'm sorry, sir. I can't let you drive. You're drunk.'

Best replied: 'I'm not drunk.'

'Well, if you're not drunk, you should be on stage because your acting is fantastic.'

BEAUTY SLEEP

Best made a trip to Scotland to play in a celebrity match. He was staying in a plush hotel. The next morning the manager asked him if he had slept well.

Best replied, 'Okay, but the people in the room above me are very annoying. Last night they stomped and banged on the floor until midnight.'

'That's terrible,' said the manager. 'Did they keep you awake long?'

'No. Luckily I was still up, playing my new bagpipes.'

When Best told the story to Sir Matt Busby, his manager asked him, 'How do you know when someone's a gentleman?'

'I don't know.'

'A gentleman never plays his bagpipes.'

SWEET REVENGE

Best once approached an attractive woman sitting alone in a busy bar. 'Excuse me,' he said, 'may I buy you a drink?'

'What, to a motel?' she screamed.

'No, no,' protested George. 'You misunderstood. I just asked if I could buy you a drink.'

'You are asking me to go to a motel?' she screamed, even louder.

Completely bewildered Best retreated to a corner table while everybody glared at him indignantly. After ten minutes the young woman came over to explain. 'I'm sorry to have created such a scene,' she said. 'I'm a psychology student studying human behaviour in unexpected situations.'

Best looked at her and shouted, 'What? A thousand pounds?'

SHARE AND SHARE DISLIKE

Once George was playing in a pro-am with a wealthy banker, who was taking a drink at every tee but never asked Best if he'd like a sip. On the fifth hole it started to rain, and on the ninth hole, as the rain teemed down, the banker looked at Best and said, 'Aren't there any dry spots around here?'

'Well,' George replied, 'you could start with the back of my throat.'

ICE ICE BABY

Once Best was asked, 'What would you like to drink?'

'A large bourbon on the rocks,' he replied, 'without the ice.'

BEING SOCIABLE

Best described himself as 'a social drinker'. Asked to explain this comment he said, 'When someone says they are having a drink, I answer: "So shall I."

MARSH MELLOW

After he played for United, Best went on to play for Fulham where he lined up with one of the most skilful strikers in English football in the early 1970s, Rodney Marsh.

As England struggled to qualify for the 1974 World Cup the manager, Sir Alf Ramsey, was feeling under pressure. In the previous two matches England had missed penalties and so Ramsey was seeking a volunteer to take penalties before the match. Everybody declined his invitation, but his face lit up when he turned to Marsh. 'Ah Rodney surely you'd have the confidence to score a penalty tonight.'

'No problem, boss. It wouldn't cost me a thought. There's just a tiny problem, boss.'

'Oh, what's that Rodney?'

'You haven't picked me on the team.'

SCAPEGOAT

Best was wont to complain to referees. After a series of bad decisions from one ref, George approached him and said, 'If I called you a stupid old goat who didn't know the first thing about football, what would you do?'

'I would report you and you would be in front of the FA authorities,' said the ref.

'What if I didn't say it, and just thought it?'

'Well, nothing could be done about it.'

'Okay,' said Best, 'we'll just leave it at that, then.'

SPEEDY

In his prime George Best was a player so quick that he could catch racing pigeons.

But as the years passed George's drinking slowed him down a little. Once he travelled to a remote small town in Wales to play in a charity game. After he parked his newish car, he was approached by a tourist who asked, 'Scuse me, where's the nearest boozer?'

The United legend calmly replied, 'You're talking to him.'

FIRST IMPRESSIONS

In his later years Best went to the local hospital to visit the sick. He saw a man proudly taping his wife and new baby on a camcorder.

'Is this your first child?' he asked politely.

'No,' replied the father. 'First camcorder.'

SENIOR CITIZENS

One of Best's favourite stories was about the two former United footballers who had been friends for many decades. In their declining years, their activities had been limited to meeting a few times a week to play cards. They were playing one day when one looked at the other and said, 'Now, don't get mad at me ... I know we've been friends for a long time, but I just can't think of your name. I've thought and thought but I just can't remember it. Put me out of my misery and tell me what it is.'

His former midfield colleague glared at him for what seemed like ten minutes before he finally asked, 'How soon do you need to know?'

ANSWERED PRAYERS

The clergy occasionally featured in Best's stories.

A man found a corked bottle on the green while playing golf. Upon opening it, a genie appeared and granted the fellow one wish. After thinking about it for a while, the man said, 'I'd like to shoot par golf regularly.'

'No problem,' said the genie. 'But understand that your sex life will be greatly reduced as a side effect.'

'I can handle that,' the man replied.

Several months later, the genie reappeared on the same golf hole and asked the man how his golf was going.

'Fantastic!' said the man. 'I'm now carrying a scratch handicap.'

'And what effect has it had on your sex life?' the genie inquired.

'I still manage to have relations a couple of times a month.'

'Oh,' said the genie. 'That's not much of a sex life.'

'Well,' the fellow responded, 'it's not bad for a middle-aged priest with a very small parish.'

THE OLD ONES

One night Best and the local parish priest – a sprightly 85-year-old – had an animated conversation about the shortcomings of the Manchester United team. After a few glasses of whiskey, the conversation took a more intimate turn.

Best asked, 'Father, at what age do men no longer find women attractive?'

The priest took a few pensive puffs on his pipe before replying, 'Well, my son, if want to know the answer to that question, I'm afraid you'll have to ask a much older man than me.'

AGEING

When asked about coping with his own old age Best said, 'You know you're getting old when your back goes out more often than you do.'

THE MILKY BAR KID

After he retired from the pitch, Best made a good living as an after-dinner speaker. In his book *The Best of Times* he reflected on the humorous side of his career. Apart from tales of his own life and times, he told stories of other players. In the main they were of characters like himself. In his latter years, the main focus of such stories was Paul Gascoigne.

Once described as 'George Best without brains', Paul Gascoigne became something of a national icon when he cried after being booked in the World Cup semi-final in 1990 against West Germany. Best believed that he should have saved his tears for the Chris Waddle school of penalty-taking. The ball from the penalty he missed in that game is probably still in outer space.

In one of his first games for Newcastle, Gazza was faced with West Ham veteran Billy Bonds. Early in the match Gazza made a robust tackle on the ageing star. Bonds had a reputation for being a hard man and kids like Gazza did not usually mix it with him.

'Are you all right, Billy?' Gazza asked cheekily.

'It's my ankle,' replied Bonds.

'Oh, that's okay then. I thought it might be arthritis!'

But Bonds had the last laugh by not giving Gazza so much as a kick of the ball after that, though he did give him plenty of kicks.

MULTIPURPOSE

In the post-George Best era of the late twentieth century, only Gazza has perhaps inspired the same number of column inches, particularly in the tabloid newspapers – where often it was difficult to delineate what was fact and what was fiction.

Still, one of the many stories Best told about Gazza goes back to when he was a young player trying to break into the Newcastle team managed by Jack Charlton. Gazza was rooming with an apprentice on an away trip to play in a reserves match. That night the apprentice produced a pack of cards and said, 'At least we can pass the time playing poker.'

According to Best, Gazza said he had something better than his mate. 'It says on the advert that you can go riding, swimming, skiing – and play tennis with these,' he declared as he produced a box of Tampax.

A MOUTHFUL

Gazza was selected for the England B team against Iceland in Reykjavik. The Milky Bar Kid asked plaintively, 'How can I play in a place I can't even say?'

CHICKEN KIEV

When he took the England team for a match to Russia, Bobby Robson was disappointed that the team hotel was in such a poor area. The players had few facilities and boredom quickly set in. He walked into a hotel room to see Chris Waddle, John Barnes and Paul Gascoigne hanging out of the window. Their room was twenty floors up.

'What are you doing?' asked Robson.

Gazza replied, 'I'm throwing soap at these chickens.'

Gazza's answer was met with disbelief, 'You're doing what?'

'I'm throwing soap at these chickens.' Gazza repeated.

'Can you really hit them from here?'

'Yeah, of course.'

'Show me.'

Gazza took aim with the soap and scored a direct hit on a chicken.

Robson just walked out of the room shaking his head.

STATING THE OBVIOUS

In his Spurs days Gazza's colleagues were relaxing watching television when Paul walked in. Pointing to the TV, he asked: 'Who's that?'

One of the players replied, 'Mikhail Gorbachev.'

'What does he do?'

'He's the leader of the Soviet Union.'

'What's that on his head?'

'It's a birthmark.'

'How long has he had it?'

A FAIR WAGE

The trouble with political jokes is that sometimes they get elected. At the height of his fame Gazza was asked, 'Is it right that you earn way more money than the Prime Minister?'

'Only fair,' said Gazza. 'I play a lot better than he does.'

THE BEST A MAN CAN GET?

After establishing himself as an England international Gazza was offered a lucrative contract to advertise the aftershave Brut on television. A massive press launch was arranged to bring the good news to the great British public. Unwisely Gazza chose to decline the script that Brut offered him and opted to speak off the cuff. It was a disaster waiting to happen – and it did.

Immediately a journalist asked the obvious question, 'How long have you been using Brut, Paul?'

'I don't.'

'What aftershave do you use?'

'None. They bring me out in a rash.'

BELLY UP

Gazza arrived at a match midway through the second half. 'What's the score?' he asked his friend Johnny Five Bellies.

'Nil–nil,' came the reply.

'And what was the half-time score?' was Gazza's response.

PARISIAN WALKWAYS

Gazza was said to have gone to Paris for his cousin's wedding. The only problem was that he got married in London.

TO SIR WITH LOVE

Another apocryphal story Best told about Gazza went back to his schooldays. The teacher in the mechanics class told him, 'I'm putting this rivet in the correct position. When I nod my head, hit it hard with your hammer.'

Gazza did, and the teacher woke up the next day in hospital.

DON'T KNOW MUCH ABOUT GEOGRAPHY

Sport is always inescapably intertwined with the wider culture. In his prime at Rangers, Gascoigne was more than a footballing icon – before kebabs, cigarettes and nights on the town with Danny Baker and Chris Evans saw his star in rapid decline.

According to Best a Jewish family turned up at a funeral parlour in Glasgow to have one final look at their deceased father laid out. His daughter burst into tears when she noticed her dad had been dressed in a Rangers shirt, white shorts and blue socks. 'What have you done to my father?' she wailed.

'I'm very sorry, madam,' replied the undertaker. 'I was informed that your father's final request was to be buried in the Gazza strip.'

PROPHETIC

It is a little-known fact, but from the perspective of George Best, Gazza has a superpower. He can predict the future: 'I've never made any predictions about anything and I never will.'

BEEFY

Best was a huge fan of two cricket legends in particular – Ian Botham and Viv Richards – perhaps because he saw them as kindred spirits.

To few sportsmen does the old adage that 'he burned the candle at both ends' apply more directly than to Sir Ian Terence Botham. Indeed, it might be suggested that he frequently set fire to it in the middle!

Part of Botham's problems were of his own making – he had a

serious habit of putting his foot in his mouth. He was a thorn in the side of the cricket establishment – with his colourful descriptions of selectors (a curious hybrid of alcoholics and senile geriatrics, apparently); was banned for confessing to having played cricket on grass (the weedy type you smoke); was expelled from the Queensland team following an 'incident' on a plane and was depicted as a man generous with his affections in the romantic stakes. Needless to say, this is a list of qualities that brought him to the attention of George Best.

Botham went to the West Indies where he was met at the airport by his great friend Viv Richards. They went for a few rum punches, but the jet-lagged Botham could only taste the orange juice, so he kept them knocking them back. Assuring Viv that he felt fine, Beefy went back to his hotel and they arranged to meet later. When Ian didn't show up at the appointed time Richards went to his hotel room. Very worried when Botham didn't respond to all his calling, Viv persuaded the chambermaid to let him in. He found Beefy out for the count. Viv and a few of his teammates borrowed some women's makeup and turned him into a poor pastiche of a drag queen. When Beefy finally woke up and looked at himself in the mirror it was said that the glass cracked at the sight of such monstrosity.

WHEN BEEFY MET GAZZA

Beefy was well able to help other sports personalities take a drink. He was also very competitive even when he was captain of one of the teams on the popular BBC series *A Question of Sport* and was always trying to put one over on his opposing captain Bill Beaumont. Paul Gascoigne was scheduled to appear on Bill's team one day during his time as a Spurs player. His manager, Terry Venables, gave strict instructions that the studio should be an alcohol-free zone. Beefy decided to help Gazza beat the ban without him even knowing he was doing it. He convinced Gazza that advocaat was a non-alcoholic beverage and he put a fair few away before he realised what a kick it had. The problem was that just before the programme was recorded Beefy discovered Gazza was in fact on his own team. Needless to say, Beefy's team got hammered in the quiz as well as in the bar.

GROIN STRAIN

Another favourite player in Best's catalogue of stories was Vinnie Jones. In a match against Wimbledon, Gary Lineker – a phenomenal scorer, but not someone known for his eagerness for the physical side of the game – was marked by Vinnie Jones, who shadowed him for the whole match. Vinnie kept saying, 'I'm going to eat you.' Perhaps he was very hungry? Meanwhile, Lineker spent the match in terror thanks to the memory of Vinnie's infamous contact with the most tender parts of England's reigning prince of football, Paul Gascoigne. Lineker barely touched the ball all night because Jones was virtually in his shorts. He spent so much time with his hands cupped over his private parts that his Spurs teammates rechristened him Holden McGroin!

HAPPY NEW YEAR

Another Best story featured the time Vinnie Jones bit a journalist on the ear. The following first day of January, a friend presented him with a colourful card which read, 'Happy New Ear's Day'.

SERGEANT WILKO

In the final Best story about Vinnie Jones he talked about how some players do not react well to being dropped. After signing Gary McAllister, Howard Wilkinson dropped Vinnie from the

Leeds side. One day after training Vinnie burst into the manager's office with a double-barrelled shotgun in his hand. Jones, a keen shot, was off to a shoot directly after training. He 'jokingly' pointed the gun at the shocked Wilkinson and threatened him with both barrels.

MORE THAN WORDS

Best claimed that when he was desperate for material for his speeches he turned to his least favourite subject – Liverpool FC. Bob Shankly was replaced by Bob Paisley in 1974 as Liverpool manager. Like Shankly he was a wonderful manager but not the most articulate of men. Before his first match in charge he gave a passionate speech. Steve Highway, of Liverpool's hugely successful 1970s team, said afterwards, 'I didn't understand a damned word he said but it sounded frightfully impressive.'

SOME MOTHER'S SON

Probably the classic Best story is about the time Liverpool signed Avi Cohen, making him the first Israeli international to play for the Reds. Avi's mother was a devout member of the Jewish faith and was concerned that Avi would lose out on his faith in Liverpool. A few weeks after he arrived in the club, she rang her son and said, 'Do you still wear your skull cap?'

Avi: 'No one wears skull caps in Liverpool.'

Mrs Cohen: 'Do you still go the synagogue on the Sabbath?'

Avi: 'How can I? We have a match every Saturday.'

Mrs Cohen [attributed]: 'Tell me, are you still circumcised?'

MONEY. MONEY. MONEY

George Best knew how to party. Hence his financial analysis: 'I spent a lot of my money on booze, birds and fast cars. The rest I just squandered.'

IN THE MOVIES

Not surprisingly, the story of George Best was turned into a film. Sky Sports' George Gavin seemed to struggle with the concept when he interviewed one of the actors and asked, 'So, this movie you star in, *The Life Story of George Best*, tell us what it's about.'

PRINCE

George Best should have been seventy-five on 22 May 2021. Fame cost him: 'Sometimes,' he said, 'I feel as if I'm a one-man zoo.'

Right to the end of his life, letters continued to arrive at his family home addressed to: 'George Best. Footballer. Belfast.'

The ferry that carried him from Belfast to Old Trafford was called *The Ulster Prince*.

He was footballing royalty.

BITE YOUR LEGS

In April 2020, the football world was saddened by the death from Covid-19 of Leeds United legend Norman Hunter. Norman's nickname was 'bite your legs' because of his ferocious tackling.

On day in the mid-1960s, just before Leeds played Manchester United, their manager Don Revie said to Norman, 'I want you to go in hard on George Best early on and break his leg.'

Norman replied, 'But, Gaffer, if I do that the referee will send me off.'

'That's not a problem, Norman,' Revie responded. 'They'll miss him a lot more than we'll miss you.'

4

THE SPECIAL ONE

*It's slightly alarming the way Manchester United
decapitated against Stuttgart.*
Mark Lawrenson after United presumably
capitulated to the Germans.

A medical professor in Cambridge University had just finished a lecture on the subject of mental health and started to quiz the first years. Speaking specifically about manic depression, the senior doctor asked, 'How would you diagnose a patient who walks back and forth screaming at the top of his lungs one minute, then sits in a chair weeping uncontrollably the next?'

A bright young female student answered: 'A football manager.'

Managers bring great joy to fans – some when they arrive at a club but more often when they leave. Most are paid a small fortune. When it comes to contract negotiations you are not what you are worth, but what you negotiate.

DOOM AND GLOOM
Managers have a unique capacity to see the glass half full when it suits them and half empty when it meets their self-interest.

The latter tendency is to thank for the following . . . my Top Ten managerial whinges:

1. *Even the chef has been out for two weeks with a hernia.*
   West Ham Boss Alan Curbishley bemoans the club's injury crisis in 2008.
2. *I've got more points on my licence – I'm not joking.*
   Paul Jewell's verdict on his Derby team's dismal league results in 2007/08.
3. *I don't mind Lawrie Sanchez spending £25 million of my money on players but in return I expect six points from the next two games. If not, I'm going to send around the biggest bouncer we've got at Harrods to hold him down and shove a pepper suppository up his arse.*
   Mohamed Al Fayed's unique take on the dreaded vote of confidence.
4. *The way Ashley Young is built, he looks like a heavy shower could kill him.*
   Martin O'Neill's weighty thoughts on his Aston Villa winger.
5. *England have to play like England. But maybe a little bit better.*
   Franco Baldini, Fabio Capello's assistant.
6. *Rather than making any comment, I'd like to talk to the player first, but he let us down badly.*
   Bray Wanderers manager Pat Delvin reacts to the dismissal of Wesley Charles against St Patrick's Athletic.
7. *Who wants to be a football manager? Well, people like me who are too old to play, too poor to be a director and too much in love with the game to be an agent.*
   Steve Coppell, who joined Manchester United from Tranmere Rovers in 1975.
8. *The first thing that went wrong was half-time. We could have done without that.*

Graham Taylor explaining England's second half collapse against Sweden in the European championships in 1992.

9. *A lot of hard work went into this defeat.*
   Malcolm 'Big Al' Allison, much loved by Manchester City fans for his part in their surprise win of the 1967/68 First Division.

10. *With our luck one of our players must be bonking a witch.*
    Ken Brown, ex-Norwich manager.

Unlike Heinz, football managers come in more than fifty-seven varieties. It was said of one former Manchester United manager, 'The great thing about him is that his indecision is final.'

Which is a comment that will never be made about José Mourinho.

His reign at Old Trafford ended with a whimper. The former Dunfermline player – and now Scottish Labour Party politician – Jim Leishman once said: 'I was the first professional football player to be forced to retire due to public demand.' For many fans José's departure from the role of Manchester United manager was not a moment too soon. This chapter is devoted to 'the Special One'.

RIVER DEEP. MOUNTAIN HIGH

José is proud of all aspects of his native Portugal: 'Our mountains aren't just funny. They are hill areas.'

ANYTHING YOU CAN DO WE CAN DO BETTER

Business is like a wheelbarrow – you have to push it to make it go. When Peter Ridsdale was made Leeds chairman in the 1990s it seemed to be a marriage made in heaven. However, in 2003 he left his post with the club £70 million in the red. It was a clear case of till debt do us part.

José made his mark in the UK with high-spending Chelsea after they had been taken over by Russian multimillionaire, Roman Abramovich. They were immediately renamed Chelski. Armed with the Russian roubles, Chelski spent money on new players as if it were going out of fashion. Any time a big money player became available, Chelski were in like a flash topping everybody else's bid.

According to reports Abramovich and his wife were being chauffeur-driven to the opening game of the season at Anfield against Liverpool. On the car radio they heard that the American government had offered a reward of $35 million for the capture of Saddam Hussein. As Abramovich's English was not the best, the item lost something in translation. He was said to have immediately got on his phone and told Chelsea's financial director . . . 'That guy the Americans want – let's offer $40 million for him.'

DUFFER

One of the great managerial wits was the man who made Liverpool the force they were in the 1970s, Bill Shankly, who began his managerial career at Carlisle United. In 1951, Third Division Carlisle pulled off a shock goalless draw at mighty Arsenal in the FA Cup. When the aristocrats arrived at Brunton Park for the replay, Bill Shankly – at that time, the Carlisle boss – burst into his side's dressing room to announce with a flourish: 'Boys, I've just seen them getting out of their coach. They should be in hospital; they're in a right state.'

Arsenal won 4–1 but after Shankly told his team: 'Boys you've just lost to the greatest side in England – but it took them two games.' It was a tactic he was to employ throughout his managerial career: make your players feel great, and if you must criticise them, do so in private.

Shankly's dry wit was most evident in his comment to Alan

Ball after he joined Everton, 'Congratulations on your move, son. You'll be playing near a great side.'

Shankly was once asked his opinion on the young Mick Channon – who went on to score over 250 goals in his career. Shanks replied that he was a very good winger. The reporter pushed him further and asked:

'Is he as good a player as Stanley Matthews?'

'Oh, aye, he's as good a player as Stan – but you have to remember Stan is sixty-five now!'

Shanks's waspish wit was also evident in his comment on former Spurs forward Martin Chivers: 'The big boy is deceptive. He's slower than he looks.'

Mourinho follows in that tradition. When he was Chelsea manager José was asked about star winger Damien Duff's legendary capacity for sleep, he replied, 'Damien suffers from adhesive mattress syndrome.'

However, straight talking is not always José's forte: 'Well, to be frank . . . I'd have to change my name.'

THE ITALIAN JOB

In 2009/10 José won an incredible Treble with Inter Milan, culminating in a win over Bayern Munich in the Champions League final. He had itchy feet, though. Hence the report at the time that the message on his answerphone was: 'I am not here at the moment. If you are the president of Real Madrid, I will get back to you.'

PRIDE

When he was appointed United manager José's wife was asked if she was proud of him. 'No,' she replied.

'And what would make you proud of him?'

'If he put out the bins every week.'

HAIR TODAY GONE TOMORROW

The football world was shocked in February 2020 when Mourinho showed up as a 'skinhead'. He explained the disappearance of his hair as follows, 'Sometimes I like to feel the cold weather, but his time was not the case. I fell asleep [in the barber's chair] and when I woke up it was so bad that I said to him, "Bring the [number] one. Hopefully, it will grow back again."'

EGGS-CELLENCE

During the Covid-19 crisis José made the eggs-citing revelation that when it came to cooking, he was a 'specialist in fried eggs'.

One Man United fan ruefully remarked, 'He's gone from being a bad joke to a bad yoke.'

Maybe he'll be comforted to know that José has been banned from the Secret Cook Society. He kept spilling the beans.

SO, THIS IS CHRISTMAS

For the Manchester United Christmas party José tried his hand as a ventriloquist. Paul Pogba was not impressed.

Mourinho accepted his verdict: 'I am terrible ventriloquist if I say so myself.'

Pogba, though, was very impressed by José's great talent for being able to guess Christmas presents before they were unwrapped.

As Pogba said: 'It's a gift.'

NOSE-Y

A woman was celebrating her 104th birthday. The intrepid reporter from the local newspaper came and asked, 'What's the best thing about being a hundred and four?'

The woman paused theatrically before replying in a strong voice, 'No peer pressure!'

In the history of the beautiful game it is doubtful if any player has ever had a higher opinion of himself than Zlatan Ibrahimović.

When Zlatan played for Manchester United José Mourinho had to intervene to stop a brawl between the Swede and his then team-mate Marcos Rojo. Zlatan, annoyed because Rojo had passed the ball to Paul Pogba, had expressed his dissatisfaction in the most emphatic way, telling him what he thought about him in English and – so as to remove any doubt – in Spanish too. But things got out of hand when Rojo give him his response. Ibrahimović flew into rage and attacked his colleague.

So, what were Rojo's offending words? 'What's going on with you, big nose? Shut up!'

CATCH A FALLING STAR

Football management is a fast-moving business. Take the case of Eugenio Corini, who was appointed Brescia manager in September 2018 and sacked in November 2019. Then they reappointed him the following month. In February they gave him the dreaded vote of confidence. Four days later they stated, 'Brescia announce they have relieved Eugenio Corini of his role as coach. The club thanks Mr Corini and for his professionalism, dedication and effort.'

Ruud Gullit was a great proponent of 'sexy football'. And it's true that while José was United manager there was sexy football being played in Manchester, but it was all by the noisy neighbours in sky blue. The following conversation may give a clue as to why.

Reporter: 'Dani Alves has said you were his best-ever coach. To quote him, he said that his experience of your coaching "was better than sex" . . . I'm just wondering what you thought of that?'

Pep Guardiola: 'I prefer the sex. By far.'

During his final days as Manchester United manager Spanish journalist Roberto Palomar described the fading allure of the Special One: 'Mourinho is starting to look like a washed-up rock star, one of those guys that goes around holiday hotels for pensioners playing the old hits on an organ with the bass and the percussion playing on a tape recorder.'

THE WINNER FORSAKES IT ALL

As those four great philosophers Abba famously suggested when they won the Eurovision in 1974, the history book on the shelf is always repeating itself. If you are a manager and the results go against you there is no option but to walk the plank.

Back in 1971 when he was Everton's manager the great Harry Catterick said, 'Every team has a clogger whose job it is to put a clever opponent out of the match.' The problem with football at the moment is that we have too many cloggers – too many players and teams seem too focused on not losing rather than winning.

When he was Chelsea manager Mourinho, in happier times with the club, had announced after losing to Sunderland that he was suspending his attempts to play good football: 'I don't want to do this. I want to play proper football that everyone else can enjoy. But if I have eleven robots playing my system, I can win 1–0 every time. It's one of the easiest things in football. It's not difficult because you don't give players the chance to express themselves. There are few risks.'

Chelsea fans recalled the words of their former chairman Ken Bates referring to Graham Taylor's tactics as England manager in 1993. 'Hump it, bump it, whack it! It might be a recipe for a good sex life, but it won't win the World Cup.'

Some United fans levelled that accusation at the Special One, believing that to win without risk is to triumph without glory.

THE MAN OF FAITH

José followed such legends in the hot seat at Man Utd as Matt Busby. Sir Matt was a man known for his integrity and moral probity. He told Bobby Charlton that he once found £20 in a supermarket car park. 'And what did you do with it?' asked Charlton.

'I asked myself what would Jesus have done?' replied Sir Matt.

'And what was that?'

'He would have turned into wine. So that's what I did?'

For his part José also enjoys a nice glass of wine. He explains it is for health and safety reasons. 'It is not good to keep things bottled up.'

HIGH STANDARDS

Sometimes club officials are not overly supportive of their players. Former Juventus president Giovanni Cobolli Gigli did not exactly give a glowing endorsement of one of his players, Miralem Pjanić: 'The difficulty of the midfield is psychological. Pjanić seems to be as soft as mozzarella.'

José set the bar very high for all his players during his time as manager of Manchester United. I suppose a lot of people would describe him as a perfectionist. A perfectionist is one who takes great pains – and gives them to everyone else!

IF HEINEKEN DID EXCUSES

Sometimes it pays to bluff. John Wayne rode into town, tied up his horse and walked into the saloon.

'Give me a shot of red eye,' said John.

He downed it in one and then walked outside. He noticed that his horse was gone, so he came back inside the saloon. 'If my horse isn't returned after I've had another drink,' said John, 'the same thing will happen here that happened in Dodge City. Now, give me another red eye.'

He downed the red eye in one and walked outside to find his

horse tied up against the rail. He mounted up and was just about to ride off when a cowboy walked up to him.

'Say, John,' said the cowboy. 'What happened in Dodge City?'

'I had to walk home,' John replied.

It is not that José does excuses . . .

But it is striking that when things go wrong at the club he is managing, it always seems to be someone else's fault.

To take one example. Mourinho bemoaned the injury crisis in Spurs in 2020 . . .

'One game we have players A, B and C out of the running, next we are without D, E and F. It's like when you pull a blanket up and your feet are left out and then you cover your feet, but half of your body is out. That's us.'

In June 2020, José's Spurs team played Manchester United in their first game back in 'Project Restart'. United came from behind to draw the game. Mourinho, though, blamed VAR for his side's failure to win.

Whenever I hear of José's word games I am reminded of the old joke:

Why didn't Cleopatra need a psychiatrist?

Because she was Queen of Denial.

WHEN A MAN LOVES A WOMAN

José often says nice things to his wife. However, there was a time when she refused to speak to him for three days.

It started when they were in bed one night and she heard a noise downstairs. She tiptoed down to investigate. She saw a thief eating her beef casserole. When she got back to the bedroom José was still fast asleep. She woke him up and said, 'There is a thief downstairs eating my beef casserole.'

José shook his head sadly and said: 'That will teach him.'

Then he turned over and went back to sleep.

ROOM TO IMPROVE

A journalist asked José what his wife's favourite flower was. He furrowed his brow and thought deeply before answering: 'Self-raising.'

BORN IN THE USA

José was not happy to bring Manchester United to America on a pre-season tour. While it made commercial sense, he was annoyed about all the travel involved. He did not try to conceal his displeasure at his press conferences. He did, though, make one positive comment: 'When the fog lifts in California. UCLA.'

FOOL-ISH

José did win two trophies as United manager but, even in their triumphs, he annoyed the fans by not playing attractive football 'in the Manchester United way'. A correspondent took great pleasure in emailing *The Manchester Evening News* to announce that the most common comment doing the rounds about him in Manchester was, 'José Mourinho can't bear fools. Pity his mother didn't have the same problem.'

THE BOOK OF EVIDENCE

Former Aberdeen manager Ebbe Skovdahl said, 'Statistics are like miniskirts – they give you good ideas but hide the important things.'

Statistics explain why José lost his job as Manchester United manager.

He did not win enough games.

One United fan described Mourinho's time as United manager as 'a sh*t com'. He was keen to stress that the 'h' is not silent.

Another complained that José's methods are outdated. His evidence? He claims that Mourinho still communicates by fax machine.

MIRACLE WORKER

It is a little-known fact, but some football fans think of Mourinho as a lifesaver and a miracle-worker. One United supporter was in a horrific car crash and was on a life-support machine for several weeks. All kinds of prayers were said, and holy medals were placed on his forehead, but to no avail. He was a devoted Manchester United fan and so someone – in a fit of desperation – brought in a DVD player, set it up beside his bed and stuck on a DVD of José's highlights. As soon as the Special One made his first comments the comatose patient got up from his bed and switched off the television. As astonished doctors and nurses looked on, he declared: 'That f**king idiot was wrecking my head.'

GENEROUS GESTURE

Becoming an organ donor can be dis-heart-ening. When he was sacked at United, José revealed he was donating one of his organs to the local hospital.

On hearing the news Juan Mata expressed the hope that Manchester's hospital had proper wheelchair access. When asked why he explained, 'Otherwise they will struggle to get a Yamaha 416 Musical Organ up the stairs.'

VIDEO KILLED THE RADIO STAR

After he left the United job José did some work for Sky Sports. He told Gary Neville that he had taken up meditation. When Neville asked him why, he replied, 'It beats sitting around doing nothing.'

FAIRWAY TO HEAVEN

It was then that Jamie Carragher asked José why he didn't play more golf.

'I have a problem with my drive,' the Special One replied.

'What do you mean?' an intrigued Carragher inquired.

'It's my missus. When I get into my car to head for the golf course she stands in the drive and won't let me leave.'

MUSICAL CHAIRS

Sir Matt Busby, Sir Alex Ferguson and José Mourinho are transported to Heaven where, given their legendary status in the game, they are given an audience with God, who is sitting magisterially on His throne. On His left and on His right are two magnificent chairs.

First, He turned to Sir Matt. 'Tell me, good sir. Why do you deserve to sit on the throne of Heaven?'

Busby replied, 'I turned Manchester United into the most famous and most glamorous club in the world. For that I deserve my place in Heaven.'

God nodded His head thoughtfully. 'My son, you have answered wisely. Come and sit here by my left hand.'

Then He turned to Sir Alex. 'My child, why do you deserve a place in Heaven?'

Fergie cleared his throat and said, 'Well, I brought unprecedented success to United. I led them to a historic treble in 1999. I . . .'

God raised His hand and cut him short. 'My child. Say no more. With your record you more than deserve your place in Heaven. Come and sit on my right hand.'

Then He turned to José. 'Now, Mr Mourinho, tell me why do you deserve your place in Heaven?'

José looked at God with the type of disdain he normally reserves for hostile journalists in press conferences. Then he shrugged his shoulders and said, 'I believe you are sitting on my chair.'

HAMMING IT UP

The book on José's reign at United is available in all good petrol stations now. After his time at Old Trafford ended, José became Spurs manager. And the year 2021 began with the revelation that the Spurs trio of Sergio Reguilón, Erik Lamela and Giovani Lo Celso broke Covid-19 regulations to attend a Christmas party. Mourinho revealed he had gifted Reguilón a suckling pig for Christmas, believing the Spaniard was spending the day alone, and commented that learning of the party was a nasty surprise: 'An amazing gift – a Portuguese piglet which is amazing for Portuguese and Spanish [people],' Mourinho said.

Manchester United fans were very sympathetic to the plight of their former manager. One suggested that he should treat the troublesome trio 'in a very humane way and then send them away in a . . . hambulance'.

Another said, 'It's like something from the Ham-mer House of Horrors.'

I am not sure though about Mark Saggers' verdict on Spurs: 'They need a bit of impotence.'

JURASSIC PARK

Things went from bad to worse for José when Spurs lost a 2–0 first-leg lead against Dinamo Zagreb and got knocked out of the Europa League by a club from a league ranked 19th in Europe.

Oliver Holt's verdict in the *Mail* was the most damning, claiming that the Special One is now 'a dinosaur dressed in a designer coat'.

The defeat came as a shock to Tim Sherwood: 'Let's paint a picture, I think they're favourites to win the Europa League, because of the Mourinho factor.'

In marked contrast Clive Allen saw the warning signs for Spurs under José Mourinho: 'They've played thirteen European games and conceded in fourteen of them.'

A PICTURE PAINTS A THOUSAND WORDS

Things went from bad to worse for José a few weeks later when their brand-new sponsor, Dulux, mocked the club online minutes after the deal was announced. Spurs took to social media to announce the paint company as new commercial partners. The Dulux Twitter account then posted their own tweet, which was less than kind about the club's lack of trophies.

After a fan made a joke about storing paint cans in the club's trophy room because Spurs 'don't seem to put anything else in there', the Dulux account replied, posting a picture of an empty glass cabinet with the Spurs crest, claiming the 'unused trophy cabinet' was 'for sale'.

Dulux continued to respond to fans online. When one suggested they 'paint the dusty trophy cabinet', Dulux replied, 'Don't be silly, surfaces should be dust-free before painting.'

The famous Dulux dog was prominent in the announcement for the deal, leading another fan to ask if the mascot could line out at centre back, with Dulux responding: 'He might do a better job.'

To their credit Spurs responded with grace on Twitter, saying the club would 'gloss over it this time'.

TACTICAL MASTERCLASS

José came up with an idea for a great new tactical formation after a recent visit to IKEA. He now favours a flat pack four.

TIME TO SAY GOODBYE

On the day the football world reeled with the news of the creation of the Super League (described by Gary Neville as 'the attempted murder of English football'), it was announced that Spurs had sacked the Special One.

A 'loyal' United fan was upset: 'On the day he qualifies them into the Super League they sack him!'

Another said: 'José may be Special but he's not Super.'

One United fan claimed that Spurs were setting up a Super League of their own – with Tottenham as the only team. Bookies said they are 7 to 1 on to finish second . . .

THE LIFE OF RYAN

José was replaced as Spurs manager by 29-year-old Ryan Mason. This prompted Alan Hutton to observe: 'Ryan Mason is younger than me at the moment.'

Let's see if that changes any time soon.

DO YOU KNOW THE WAY TO SAN JOSÉ?

Two weeks after he was sacked at Spurs, it was announced that José would become the new manager of Roma.

Irish airline Ryanair responded with a wicked put-down:

'José will be happy to know that we currently fly London to Rome from only £14.99. Due to his lack of trophies at Spurs, we expect a carry-on bag will suffice for this trip.'

5

BECKS

On a global scale David Robert Joseph Beckham OBE is Manchester United's most famous player. The current president of Inter Miami CF was with United from 1992 to 2003, before moving to Real Madrid.

To many David Beckham represents the best of British, as is evident in Hugh Grant's unique and amusing tribute to him in the smash film *Love Actually*.

George Best was less complimentary: 'He cannot kick with his left foot, he cannot head a ball, he cannot tackle, and he cannot score many goals. Apart from that he's all right.'

And it's true that Beckham was never particularly fast. Franz Beckenbauer was once asked how he always seemed to get from A to B faster than his opponent, even though his opponent was invariably quicker. He replied, 'I don't start from A.' Becks was a graduate from the same school.

He was also a darling of the media – not least because of his romance with and later marriage to Victoria Adams, better known as 'Posh Spice' of the Spice Girls, who ruled the pop charts at the time. This chapter is a celebration of all things Becks.

LINGUISTIC SKILLS

Throughout David Beckham's career he has had the occasional moments of 'an interesting relationship' with the English language. Here are my Top Ten:

1. *I'm still trying English.*
   Beckham, when asked if he was learning Japanese for the 2002 World Cup.
2. *It's going to be difficult for me – I've never had to learn a language and now I do.*
   Beckham after his move to Madrid.
3. Gary Newbon: *David, was Wayne Rooney disappointed to lose his youngest goal-scorer record* (at the 2004 European championships) *on Monday to the young Swiss striker?*
   Becks: *No, but I'm sure it'll make him even more determined to get it back against Portugal tonight.*
4. *It was really difficult for us playing in the midday sun with that three o'clock kick-off.*
5. *I definitely want Brooklyn to be christened, but I don't know into what religion yet.*
6. *We've been asked to do* Playboy *together, me and Victoria, as a pair. I don't think I will ever go naked, but I'll never say never.*
7. Interviewer: *Are you a volatile player?*
   Becks: *Well, I can play in the centre, on the right and occasionally on the left side.*
8. *Everything's been so positive and smooth. Apart from, obviously, the season.*
   Becks on his first season in America in 2007.
9. *That was in the past – we're in the future now.*
10. *Alex Ferguson is the best manager I've ever had at this level. Well, he's the only manager I've actually had at this level. But he's the best manager I've ever had.*

GOLDENBALLS

Whatever one might say about his own linguistic deficiencies, Becks has given rise to some wonderful comments. The following magnificent seven are an eclectic mix of Becks-inspired brilliance:

1. *I call him Goldenballs.*
   Posh Spice creates an avalanche of interest in Beckham's private parts.

2. *I bet you two would love to play with him, what with those balls.*
   Ray Wilkins sings the praises of David Beckham's crossing ability, leaving fellow pundits Joe Royle and Alan Shearer speechless.

3. *Without being too harsh on David Beckham, he cost us the match.*
   Ian Wright.

4. *The midfield picks itself – Beckham, Scholes, Gerrard and A.N. Other.*
   Phil Neal.

5. *He's a girl's blouse.*
   German journalist reacts to the news that David Beckham – not content to draw the line at wearing a sarong or Posh's underwear – is spotted wearing nail polish as he leaves Beckingham Palace to attend Elizabeth Hurley's party.

6. *Posh and Becks were so much in love after one year of dating that they're even thinking alike. For their first anniversary, they both gave each other the exact same thing. Earrings.*
   Caller to Five Live.

7. *I would ask anyone to try and understand the world he lives in. We all have to accept that he is married to Spice Girl Victoria Adams – and I think he copes very well with it.*
   Who knew Kevin Keegan had such sense and sensitivity?

MUSICAL INTERLUDE

Chants have always provided football fans with the opportunity to show their wit. At the end of the 2007/08 season when Manchester City fans heard that their Thai owner planned to sack their boss Sven-Göran Eriksson they chanted, to the tune of the Pink Floyd classic 'Another Brick in the Wall':

> We don't want no Phil Scolari,
> We don't need no Mourinho.
> Hey, Thaksin, leave our Sven alone.

Earlier in the season they gave the City fans something else to smile about when they shocked Manchester United to take a 2–0 lead at Old Trafford. As the United players made their weary way down the tunnel to face the fury of Sir Alex's hairdryer treatment the City fans chorused to the tune of 'La donna è mobile':

> Time for your bollicking,
> Time for your bollicking.

'Another Brick in the Wall' is also the tune to which rival fans chant at Swansea:

> Hey, Swansea ... leave our sheep alone!

Chants can sometimes be as tasteful as a bad Manchester United Christmas party, but they do also afford the fans the opportunity to be topical. After Fulham owner Mohamed Al Fayed launched a stinging attack on the Duke of Edinburgh at the inquest into the deaths of his son, Dodi, and Diana, Princess of Wales, the Liverpool supporters sang: 'There's only one Prince Philip.'

Political correctness is seldom a feature of these chants, as can be heard in Liverpool fans' appraisal of Wayne Rooney:

> *He's fat.*
> *He's scouse.*
> *He's going to rob your house.*

Of course, some chants are complimentary – like the Kop's 2006 hit single:

> *He's big, he's red, his feet hang out his bed,*
> *Peter Crouch, Peter Crouch.*

Manchester City fans immortalised an item of clothing in this inventive ditty:

> *Niall Quinn's disco pants are the best,*
> *They go up from his arse to his chest,*
> *They're better than Adam and the Ants,*
> *Niall Quinn's disco pants.*

Often chants can be very triumphalist in tone, as heard here as Chelsea fans flaunt their wealth:

> *Debt-free. Wherever we may be,*
> *We're going to buy everyone we see,*
> *And we don't give a f**k about the transfer fee,*
> *Cos we are the wealthy CFC.*

It is often said that brevity is the soul of wit; in which case, Chelsea fans struck gold with their 'tribute' to their local rivals Fulham:

He's fat, he's round,
He's sold your f**king ground,
Al Fayed, Al Fayed!

Meanwhile, friendly Man United fans greeted Liverpool with a heart-warming song about their Korean star Park Ji-sung, to the tune of 'The Lord of Dance'.

Park, Park, wherever you may be,
You eat dogs in your home country.
But it could be worse,
You could be Scouse,
Eating rats in your council house.

After Victoria Beckham told Johnny Vaughan on *The Big Breakfast* in 2000 that David liked to wear her knickers, and more specifically her thong, opposing fans had a field day. Nobody could miss them chanting – to the tune of 'Jesus Christ Superstar' – when Manchester United played:

David Beckham, Superstar
Wears Posh's knickers,
And a push-up bra.

THE YOUNG ONES

Along with Ryan Giggs, Nicky Butt, Phil Neville, Gary Neville and Paul Scholes, Beckham was part of the 'Class of '92'. They played for the successful Manchester United youth team in 1992 and quickly graduated to the senior team.

They are responsible for one of the most famous moments in football punditry. The BBC's *Match of the Day* is a national institution, which has produced some unintentional moments of comedy. Jimmy Hill once had the job of closing the programme by giving viewers the address where they should send their nomination for the Goal of the Month competition. He had to give them the address twice and, rather than writing the whole sentence out twice, the person who had prepared the cue card had simply added an appropriate instruction. Jimmy obligingly said: 'Goal of the Month, BBC television, Wood Lane, Shepherds Bush, London W12 – read twice.'

TAKE TO THE HILLS

Jimmy Hill added to the gaiety of the nation with some arresting comments. Here are his magnificent seven gaffes:

1. *England have now three fresh men, with three fresh legs.*
2. *He has two feet, which a lot of players don't have nowadays.*
3. *Manchester United are looking to Frank Stapleton to pull some magic out of the fire.*
4. *Despite the rain, it's still raining here at Old Trafford.*
5. *We're not used to weather in June in this country.*
6. *It wasn't a bad performance, but you can't tell whether it was good or bad.*
7. *It's a cup final and the one who wins it goes through.*

TALL AND HANSEN

In the 1990s, former Liverpool great Alan Hansen ruled the world of football punditry from his *Match of the Day* throne. In general, his comments were spot on. But, as in life, timing is everything in football punditry. And there were the odd moments when even he was left eating humble pie.

Hansen did not mince his words. The former Liverpool star called it as it was, irrespective of who it might hurt. He once described Liverpool's defending as 'criminal'. I bet that endeared him to his former teammates. During the 1994 World Cup, hosted by the USA, Hansen commented on the poor positioning of a defender during the Argentina–Nigeria match: 'He wants shooting for being in that position.' Just a few days earlier the Colombian central defender Andrés Escobar – the scorer of an own goal in Colombia's 2–1 defeat by the USA – was shot dead in his hometown of Medellín. It was not Hansen's finest hour.

In 1995 *Match of the Day* was presented by Des Lynam. A bit of humour is great in a presenter or analyst. That is one reason why someone like Des Lynam was so popular. He had some great one-liners like: 'There's Frank Leboeuf and his son – le Spare Rib.' But perhaps his best was: 'Our experts tonight are two guys who between them have won a hundred and six caps for Scotland. Kenny Dalglish who has won a hundred and four and Bob Wilson who has won two.'

SALT AND LINEKER

Gary Lineker and Alan Hansen were Des's two senior analysts in 1995. Long-time star of Walker's crisps ads, Gary Lineker's best-known nickname is 'Big Ears' thanks to his involvement in *They Think it's All Over*. He is also known as 'Junior Des' – because of his admiration for Des Lynam. However, in the early days he struggled as Des's replacement as anchor for BBC's football coverage. His most notable gaffe came in a Montpellier–Manchester United match when he was describing the poor condition of the pitch and came out with the classic line, 'Most of the players will be wearing rubbers tonight.'

It is always good when football pundits have a bit of an edge to their comments. Even those viewers entirely indifferent to BBC football coverage would have enjoyed, Martin O'Neill's comment to Gary Lineker: 'You know what I like about you, Gary? Very little.'

I WISH I HADN'T SAID THAT

When United brought a number of the Class of '92 onto the senior team there were concerns that they had too many young players. Things came to a head in August 1995 on *Match of the Day* when, on the opening day of the season following United's 3–1 loss to Aston Villa, Alan Hansen criticised the then Manchester United manager Alex Ferguson with a comment that has since entered football folklore: 'You can't win anything with kids.' United went on to win the Double that season and had the most successful period in the club's history culminating in the historic treble in 1999.

David Beckham was at the centre of United's success.

POSH BOY

Becks is one of the new English royalty. It is difficult to imagine a football star more interested in fashion – especially if the story from the World Cup in 1998 is true ... apparently the real reason Posh Spice was allowed to visit him for 'morale purposes' was not because he was upset about being dropped for England's opening match but because he'd missed the Armani summer sale in Bond Street!

THE CLOTHES SHOW

One of Ireland's leading writers Joe O'Connor saw Becks more as a stylist off the field rather than on it: 'It is important to remember that a player as talented as Beckham comes with a lot of baggage – most of it Louis Vuitton.'

TRAUMA

During the Covid-19 pandemic, Becks sadly told his suitcase that it would be doing no travel during the crisis. Now he really is left with a lot of emotional baggage.

BIG REGRETS

Becks has achieved so much but he does have one regret. He did not properly clean his bathroom mirror.

It does not reflect well on him.

BOOTS

As a boy, though, Becks's fashion sense was not so well developed. One story told about him goes back to his early school days. As the rest of his class left school at the end of a winter day, Becks remained behind sobbing. 'What's the matter David?' his teacher asked.

'I can't find my boots,' Becks cried.

The teacher looked in the cloakroom and found a pair of boots. 'Are these yours?'

'No,' Becks replied.

The teacher and David searched all over. At last, the teacher asked, 'Are you sure these boots aren't yours?'

'They aren't mine,' the distraught Beckham replied. 'Mine have snow on them.'

MEDIA INTEREST

In 1997 Manchester United beat Liverpool 3–1 at Anfield in a morning match to fit in with the demands of Sky Television's schedule. United went into the cauldron of old brimming with confidence, as befitted a side with thirty-one goals from their previous eight league games. Andy Cole's two goals were verbally replayed and relived with relish especially by the fans who had actually been among the 41,027 in attendance at that game. The first came in the fifty-first minute following a blunder from Bjørn Tore Kvarme and allowed born-again clinical finisher Cole to evade Matteo, before shooting low into David James's right-hand corner. His second of the match, and fifteenth of the season, came from a side-foot from close in after Sheringham had nodded down a Giggs corner.

The superlatives, though, were reserved for David Beckham's goal from a curving 20-yard freekick which rocketed into a space in David James's goal that seemed to be no bigger than a mousehole. Even by the lofty standards expected of Beckham, the consensus was that it was one of the best free kicks in recent memory. There was some bewilderment that the tabloids made little mention of the wonder goal the next day but went to town on the fact that he'd attended the Royal Variety Performance a few days previously with his girlfriend's – Posh Spice – mother.

DO YOU THINK I'M SEXY?

Years later, in a Manchester poll, Becks was voted the sexiest man alive. Are there any dead ones? His mother-in-law was worried that he would develop a roving eye for other women. He tried to reassure her by telling her that his marriage was made in heaven.

'So is thunder and lightning,' she replied.

BOWLED OVER

For years David Beckham, with his upfront devotion to buffness and grooming, was England's uncrowned sporting gay icon – posing on the cover of, among others, *Attitude* magazine. Then cricket produced a challenger in Freddie Flintoff. Freddie took the challenge very seriously, saying, 'I have to watch my skin more and make sure that I look good and have my hair done. I could easily lose my crown back to David Beckham if I'm not careful.'

A DEDICATED FOLLOWER OF FASHION

After he left United for Real Madrid David Beckham was voted the best-dressed man in Britain for the third year running. According to *GQ* editor Dylan Jones, Beckham is a clear-cut example of a 'metrosexual', a new coinage which means 'an urban male who takes pride in his appearance'. *GQ* gave Becks the honour of being 'not only Madrid's favourite metrosexual, probably Madrid's only metrosexual'.

MUSICAL CRIMES AND PUNISHMENT

In 2002 a daring plot – foiled at the last minute – was hatched to kidnap Posh. Cynics, aware of her many shortcomings as a vocalist, remarked that the kidnap was prompted by music fans to ensure no one would never have to listen to her again.

After news of the kidnap attempt broke a police spokesperson stated, 'The Beckhams will now be the subject of intelligence monitoring.' Critics remarked that hell would freeze over before the Beckhams and intelligence would ever be spoken of again in the one sentence.

THE NON-ITALIAN JOB

In April 2003 it was widely reported that Becks was about to sign for Real Madrid. A Manchester City fan claimed that Posh began to prepare for the move by learning Italian!

THE LIFE OF RYAN

One of Becks's challengers to the title of the pretty boy of football was Ryan Giggs.

For his part Giggs affectionately remarked, 'Becks hasn't changed since I've known him. He's always been a flash Cockney git.'

HANDS OFF

Alan Shearer was more troubled by Beckham's hand. When Becks had a hospital visit for an X-ray on his injured hand, Shearer said, 'Fingers crossed there's nothing broken.'

SOME MOTHERS DO HAVE THEM

In 1998, when David Beckham was sent off during England's match against Argentina for a petulant kick at an opponent, the *Daily Mirror*'s headline was 'Ten Heroic Lions, One Stupid Boy.'

One bitter Manchester United fan quipped: 'When Beckham was a boy, his mother prayed that he would grow up and play for England. So far, half of her prayer has been answered.'

ROMEO

After Becks's second son Romeo was born, speculation mounted as to what advice would Dad give his son when Romeo played his first match. One Shakespeare scholar observed that, if he handed him the number four jersey, he could adapt one of the most famous lines in English literature to, 'Wear four out there, Romeo?'

SPELLING BEE

As a boy, one of the songs that Beckham learned at school was 'Old MacDonald had a farm'. Manchester City fans claim that when Romeo started school, he asked his famous dad how to spell 'farm'.

'That's easy,' replied Becks. 'Farm is E-I-E-I-O.'

WITH HELP FROM MY NEW FRIENDS

Becks was feeling hungry as he helped Romeo with his maths homework. He rang his local Chinese restaurant and asked, 'Do you do takeaways?'

'Certainly, sir.'

'Great. What is thirty-two take away nineteen?'

BOOKISH

Liverpool fans claim that the library in Beckham's house was burned down. Sadly, both books were destroyed. They claim that

Becks was inconsolable. He had one of those books almost all coloured in.

LIKE FATHER, LIKE SON

A year after the birth of their first son, Brooklyn, in 2001, Posh and Becks were interviewed by Ali G. He began the interview with a question to Posh: 'Is your little boy starting to put whole sentences together?'

Victoria replied, 'He's saying little bits and pieces, so yeah.'

Ali G: 'And what about Brooklyn?'

He then turned to Becks and said, 'Now, just because it's Comic Relief, doesn't mean you can speak in a silly voice.'

He went on to enquire of Beckham, 'It must be amazing going out with a Spice Girl, but in an ideal world – and with no disrespect – wouldn't you rather be with Baby?'

Then it was back to Victoria, 'Does Brooklyn like your music, or is he getting a bit too old for it now?'

THE FEAR FACTOR

After she left the Spice Girls Victoria released a solo album. Beckham said, 'I've been listening to the new album and it is frightening.'

Most music fans marvelled at his exceptional insight.

CONSTANTLY

Becks always said that Posh was his 'Miss Right'. What he didn't realise until they'd been married for a while was that her middle name is 'Always'.

BETWEEN THE SHEETS

Victoria and David were in bed in LA one night and he was surprised to see she had a book by her bedside. The book was entitled *What 20 Million American Women Want*. He grabbed it and started thumbing through the pages.

A little annoyed, Victoria asked, 'Hey, what do you think you're doing?'

Becks replied, 'I just wanted to see if they spelled my name right.'

FOR BETTER OR WORSE

It is said that Posh wears the trousers in the marriage. Beckham probably got a clue at the marriage ceremony of the way things would unfold. The minister asked him, 'Do you take this woman to be your lawfully wedded wife?'

Before Becks could reply Victoria interjected: 'Yes he does.'

VINO

Last year Becks bought a vineyard for Victoria for her birthday. She announced that she was to make her own wine. In response to the description, 'rather less than full-bodied, somewhat expensive, nice nose but perhaps a little bitter', Graham Norton remarked, 'Fair enough, but what's the wine like?'

THE JURY

Beckham was called up for jury service. The selection process goes on and on, each side hotly contesting and dismissing potential jurors. Becks was called for questioning:

'Property holder?'

'Yes, I am, Your Honour.'

'Married or single?'

'Married for years, Your Honour.'

'Formed or expressed an opinion?'

'Not in many years, Your Honour.'

HOT AND COLD

On a shopping trip to Harrods Beckham noticed a Thermos flask.

'What's that for?' he asked.

'It's to keep hot things hot and cold things cold.' replied the salesman.

Beckham bought one and took it home to show Posh. With wonder in his voice he told her, 'It's to keep hot things hot and cold things cold.'

With a gasp of astonishment, she said, 'You ought to take it to work.'

So, he took it into training the following day. 'What you got there?' inquired Roy Keane.

'It's to keep hot things hot and cold things cold,' said Becks with pride.

'That's a good idea,' said his captain. 'What have you got in it?'

'Coffee,' answered Becks. 'And some ice cream.'

THE GODFATHER

A relative asked Becks to be the godfather of his first child, who was to be called David in tribute. At the baptism, the priest asked Beckham if he understood his responsibilities as a godfather.

Becks replied, 'Oh yes. I've seen the film.'

WHEN SILENCE IS NOT GOLDEN

In 2000 the former FIFA World Player of the Year George Weah – the first African to be awarded the title, and the first former professional footballer to become a head of state (in his case, Libera) – signed for Chelsea. Shortly afterwards, they played Manchester United at Old Trafford. When Weah had an altercation with Jaap Stam Becks ran up to him, put his finger to his lips and said, 'Shhh!' Then he burst out laughing and ran off, leaving Weah confused.

Shortly after that, Weah had a confrontation with Dwight Yorke. Again, Becks rushed up to him said, 'Shhh!' and started wetting himself laughing before running off.

Before the interval, Weah lost his cool with the linesman after a controversial offside was given against him, and Becks repeated his strange act.

At the half-time whistle Roy Keane went over to Beckham and asked, 'What's all this about Weah?'

Becks whispered something into Keano's ear, to which Keane rolled his eyes and replied, 'No you f**king idiot. He's a Liberian.'

MEDIA INTERVENTIONS

Like many sports stars, Becks grew into his role as a media performer. In common with many stars of his age some of his early media performances were memorable for the wrong reasons. However, he was always very modest. His modesty grated with Liverpool fans; one of whom said to him, 'Don't be so modest. You're not that great.'

SHAKIN' ALL OVER

Joe O'Connor once posed the question: 'Is football better than sex?' At first glance this might be considered a highly contentious statement as the two activities are so remarkably different. One involves the complete engagement of the senses, wild abandonment, heart-stopping elation and, above all, orgasmic bliss.

The other is sex.

Few know the sheer toe-curling ecstasy of winning and the adrenalin rush of having the small hairs standing on the back of the neck better than fans at Old Trafford. However, spectating is no sport for the unfit. At best it leaves you shattered; at worst it could kill you.

LOVE ACTUALLY

Sex has been a problem in football clubs.

Gigi Becali, owner of FCSB (formerly known as Steaua Bucharest), said of his own players, 'They are making love with their girlfriends too often, that's why they aren't playing football so well lately.'

He contrasted this with the behaviour of Europa League leaders CFR Cluj, 'Their players have sex only once a week.' (One has to wonder... How does he verify this?)

The next day Julen Lopetegui, coach of Seville, was asked about his side's preparations for playing CFR Cluj in the Europa League, 'Do you control the sexual relations of your players?'

Intriguingly Lopetegui replied, 'I've got enough on my plate controlling mine.'

THERE IS NO SCANDAL LIKE A SEX SCANDAL...

David Beckham found himself scandalously implicated when, in 2004, his former personal assistant Rebecca Loos claimed she'd had a four-month affair with Beckham. He strenuously denied the claims and Posh steadfastly stood by her man.

At the subsequent press conference, Becks was asked what he thought of women in general. This led to a bigger discussion about his views on love and marriage. Becks was asked what advice he would give women looking for Mr Right. He replied, 'Look for a man with ten thousand bees. Then you will know he is a keeper.'

Ironically enough, it has been reported that an older and possibly wiser Beckham has turned to the mindful art of beekeeping during the Covid-19 lockdown.

THE LONG BREAK

After the Rebecca Loos scandal broke, Beckham didn't speak to Posh for six months. He didn't want to interrupt her.

ANIMAL FARM

Becks is clearly comfortable with his sexuality, telling *Marie Claire*, 'I can't dance but I'm an animal in bed.'

ASPECTS OF LOVE

As a child I took my ball to bed with me and she's my one true love. She's honest and has never betrayed me.

Wise words from Chelsea's Adrian Mutu in 2003

Love, sex and everything in between have always been intimately intertwined with the beautiful game: from former Manchester United footballers who have enjoyed visits to a brothel and the company of a 48-year-old grandmother charmingly known as 'Auld Slapper' to those who have graced the pages of *OK* with their glitzy £5-million weddings to equally charmingly monikered 'WAG' of their choice.

We might also mention how, on Valentine's Day in 2008, Sheffield Wednesday's Rob Burch went on live television to ask his beloved to become his lawfully wedded WAG. The then France coach Raymond Domenech proposed to his girlfriend live on TV directly after overseeing his side's inglorious exit from Euro 2008.

In fact, in 1999 *New Scientist* magazine coined a new condition: Sexually Acquired Reactive Arthritis. According to the research, footballers are at greater risk of the condition because they are having too much sex. Evidently, Leonard Cohen was right all along when he sang with the world-weary wisdom of a man who had his heart often broken that there ain't no cure for love.

The course of true love runs problematically in other sports, too. Snooker commentator Ted Lowe famously remarked in a *Carry On Up the Crucible* moment: 'Fred Davis, the doyen of snooker, now sixty-seven years of age and too old to get his leg over, prefers to use his left hand.'

In athletics it might be that romance dies with marriage. David

Coleman observed: 'And there is no "I love you" message because Steve Ovett has married the girl.'

THE LOVE TRIANGLE

Thanks to their marital infidelities, footballers have given a whole new meaning to the phrase 'playing away'. The 'love affairs' of Ashley Cole and Cheryl Tweedy and Posh and Becks have made them tabloid darlings, but few love triangles caught the public imagination to the same degree as the one between former England manager Sven-Göran Eriksson, his girlfriend Nancy Dell'Olio and former weather girl Ulrika Jonsson in 2002. Of course, Sven also earned infamy as part of another 'love triangle' when in 2004 it emerged that he'd had an affair with FA secretary Faria Alam. FA Chief Executive Mark Palios, who was also having an affair with Alam, resigned because of the scandal.

We do have to thank the Sven–Ulrika–Nancy 'romance' for the creation of some true comedy moments.

In the *Sunday Mirror*'s version of events, Sven said to Ulrika: 'Never mind Beckham's toe, let's play footsie.'

As Ireland's most terrifically talented threesome of comedians, *Après Match*'s take on the love triangle was particularly amusing:

Interviewer: *Sven, how do you feel about the World Cup?*

Sven: *I'm feeling very optimistic.*

Interviewer: *How would you feel if you found Ulrika Jonsson naked in your bed?*

Sven: *I'd be very optimistic!*

In Ireland, the media saw the scandal differently and other agendas came into play:

Eamon Dunphy: *We wouldn't have published it* [the Sven–Ulrika story] *here.*

Roy Greenslade: *You would if Mick McCarthy had been having an affair with Andrea Corr.*

Eamon Dunphy: *That would've been regarded as a bloody miracle. Have you seen Mick McCarthy?*

TORN BETWEEN TWO LOVERS

Sven himself said: 'It's no good lying in bed at night, wondering if you've made the right choice.'

No, he's not talking about Ulrika or Nancy – or anyone else – but about his choice of pieces for his classical music CD.

TRUE PASSION

When Nancy and Sven were enjoying happier times, Nancy told *GQ* that Sven recited the names of the English squad during sex – all twenty-two of them.

STANGATE

Sven was not the first football star that Ulrika dipped her toe in, so to speak. Numbered among her ex-boyfriends is Stan Collymore. In 2004, Collymore was revealed to have participated in 'dogging', an activity which entails hanging around car parks and having or watching (or both) sex with strangers. And it wasn't just strangers that Collymore was partial to. He went on to write one of football's most famous kiss-and-tell autobiographies in which he listed women with whom he'd had intimate relations, including fellow celebrities Davina McCall, Sara Cox and Kirsty Gallacher.

When the book was published, Manchester United fans gleefully remarked that it was an awful shame he'd not scored as frequently for Liverpool.

WHAT'S LOVE GOT TO DO WITH IT?

Football is the beautiful game, but it can ruin a marriage. Joanne Bradley from Kent divorced her husband Neil on the grounds that he was obsessed with Norwich City.

Things started to go wrong for the couple when Neil painted their bedroom yellow and green while his wife was out.

Then things deteriorated still further when he took her on a romantic holiday. At first glance this seemed like a good idea. The problem was his idea of a romantic holiday – which was to take her to watch the team training.

The final straw came when he bought her an anniversary present – a pair of Norwich City knickers.

THE LAST WORD

Some men are more fortunate in terms of their understanding spouse.

Before setting off for the Charity Shield one season, Bill Shankly is reputed to have asked his wife, 'Do you have anything to say before the football season starts?'

Many years ago, when Jimmy Hill was the chairman of Fulham, his club were due to face an FA inquiry after some of their players were involved in a post-match brawl against Gillingham. Hill set out to prove that Fulham should not be held responsible with a video presentation of the game's flashpoints. He was very pleased with his efforts and, before the inquiry, boasted to friends that the FA should be selling tickets for his presentation. The only problem was that when he produced his video as evidence, he was shocked to discover that his wife had taped a cookery programme over it!

BOOTGATE

In February 2020, Sky Sports' Jeff Stelling announced, 'Congratulations to Jordan Henderson and his wife Rebecca who have given birth to a baby boy today. The birth comes nine months and one day after Liverpool beat Barcelona by four goals to nil at Anfield. Mo Salah's wife Magi has given birth to a baby today as well – nine months and one day later. You couldn't make it up.'

In response James Milner and Trent Alexander-Arnold gave 'the assist' to the right man with their tweet: 'Origiassist#corner takenquickly'.

At other times, though, footballing personalities do not always get on so well. For the media, a new footballing controversy is an Aladdin's cave, a whole new world, with new horizons and vistas of possibility to pursue. David Beckham's high-profile fallout with Alex Ferguson in 2003 created just that.

Different managers have different styles. Some favour a fire and brimstone approach. In the 1970s Eric Barber was twelfth man for Birmingham City in a league match at a time when no substitutes were allowed during play. The twelfth man was only used if there was an injury or illness. Birmingham were slaughtered in the match, but that indignity was as nothing compared to the humiliation each player was subjected to by their manager. He started off with the goalkeeper and went one by one to the other ten players – pointing out very emphatically and in great detail just how ineffectual each of them was. Eric was fervently thanking God that he had not been selected to play, because that meant he would escape the tongue-lashing. He was wrong. After the manager had finished with the players he turned to Barber and said, 'And as for you. You're not even good enough to play for this shower of useless no-hopers.'

Like that Birmingham City manager, Fergie also believed in the tough love school of management.

David Beckham's relationship with Alex Ferguson became more than strained after Fergie allegedly threw a boot at him – resulting in a media feeding frenzy around photos of Becks with a cut above his left eye and his highlighted locks held back by an Alice band. As Brian Kerr noted: 'I think there's been a lot of pavlova around the whole Beckham thing.'

In fact, Becks was so cheesed off by the whole 'Bootgate' affair that he decided to get away from it all with a holiday in the sun. At one stage, wanting a bit of a break from the beach, he went into an upmarket electrical store to buy a car radio, where the salesman told him, 'This is the very latest model. It's voice activated. You just tell it what you want to listen to, and the station changes automatically. There's no need to take your hands off the wheel.'

Bathed in brightness, Becks returned to Manchester where he had his new gadget installed. That first morning, as he was driving to training, he decided to test it. He said, 'Pop,' and the sound of the Beatles filled the car. He said, 'Country,' and instantly he was listening to Dolly Parton. Then suddenly two pedestrians stepped off the pavement in front of him, causing him to swerve violently.

'F**king idiots!' he shouted at them. The radio changed to a documentary on Sir Alex.

6

FERGIE TIME

To give a penalty for that in a game of such importance, on the linesman's say-so, is absolutely diabolical. Granted the ball hit Carrick's hand.

Alex Ferguson following the penalty
conceded to Chelsea in 2008.

I hate people who quote me, and you can quote me on that.

The noted theologian Arsène Wenger once remarked, 'If God exists, one day I'll go up there and he will ask: "Do you want to come in? What have you done in your life?" And the only answer I will have is, "I tried to win football games." He will say, "Is that all you have done?" And the only answer I will have is: "It's not as easy as it looks."'

Alex Ferguson is, without question, the best manager of all time. Management is a process of replacing one anxiety with another, but Sir Alex is a man who could inspire a donkey to win the Derby. His philosophy can be summed up as: what is complicated is rarely useful and what is useful is rarely complicated.

One test of fame is a person's ability to define an era. The Beatles did just that in the 1960s; Diana, Princess of Wales in the 1980s and –

for Manchester United fans – Fergie defined their lives for years.

Even so, we expect a lot of our heroes. And a lot of the time they disappoint us. Occasionally, as in the case of Sir Alex, they are even better than we could have dared to expect. For Ferguson, the fascination with football arrived, like talking, too early to remember.

It is said that Lester Piggott could identify every horse he had ever ridden even when it was walking away from him in a rainstorm. Fergie had a similar instinct for players.

And when it comes to instinct and drive, nobody ever had a greater will to win than Sir Alex. He is a man who stands head and shoulders above all other managers in our sport of football, which is surely as much a contest of wills as of abilities.

It is indeed right and fitting that this chapter honours Ferguson's inestimable contribution to Manchester United.

ALEX VERSUS ARSÈNE

From throwing pizza to throwing tantrums, the often-fractious relationship between Alex Ferguson and Arsène Wenger brought much colour to the Premier League. Despite the seriousness of their demeanour individually and collectively the two rivals have brought much mirth to football fans. If you are not convinced, consider the following evidence.

UNITED WE STAND

There's no doubt that Alex Ferguson is the manager of his generation. With a fiercely competitive streak, he has always been his own man, which is probably just as well because he's not always received the best advice in the world.

Gary Mabbutt once offered a pearl of wisdom to Sir Alex: 'When I say that he needs to stand up and be counted, I mean that he needs to sit down and have a look at himself in the mirror.'

CHASING CARS

One man who understands the pressure managers are under is the 2007 Open winner Padraig Harrington. No managers would share one of his mantras – 'I want to focus on my focus' – more than Alex Ferguson and Arsène Wenger.

The two men were always looking for any stroke to put their opponent under pressure. One story relates how they were driving up to London together for a promotional event a few days before their teams met in the league. Ferguson, who hates wearing a seat belt, was driving and then went into a panic when he saw a policeman pulling them over. He says to Wenger, 'Quick, take the wheel. I gotta put my seat belt on.'

So he did, just as the cop approached. The cop knocked on the window: 'Say, I noticed you weren't wearing your seat belt.'

Ferguson replies, 'I was, but you don't have to take my word for it – this man here is a good Christian man, ask him; he'll tell you the truth. He doesn't lie about anything.'

'So?' the cop says to Wenger. 'How about it, sir?'

And Wenger says: 'I've known this man for twenty years and one thing I've learned in all that time is – you never argue with him when he's drunk.'

ELEMENTARY

After years of wrangling, a PR executive suggested that Sir Alex and Arsène Wenger should go on a camping trip in the interest of enhancing the image of their respective clubs. And so they did. The two men set up their tent and fell asleep. Some hours later, Ferguson woke up his new friend.

'Wenger, look up at the sky and tell me what you see.'

'I see millions of stars.'

'What does that tell you?'

Wenger pondered for a minute. 'Astronomically speaking, it

tells me that there are millions of galaxies and potentially billions of planets. Astrologically, it tells me that Saturn is in Leo. Time wise, it appears to be approximately a quarter past three in the morning. Theologically, it's evident the Lord is all powerful and we are small and insignificant. Meteorologically, it seems that we will have a beautiful day tomorrow. What does it tell you?'

Ferguson is silent for a moment, then he speaks: 'Wenger, you idiot, someone has stolen our tent.'

BARBED

An Arsenal fan was attending a party when she noticed Sir Alex Ferguson. She walked over to him, and in a quiet voice said, 'If you were my husband, I would poison your drink.'

Fergie smiled, leaned forward, and whispered in her ear, 'If you were my wife, I would drink it.'

THE GOOD JOKE GUIDE

Wenger to Ferguson: 'At least my jokes are proper ones.'

Fergie: 'All your jokes are in the Arsenal squad.'

IT ALL ADDS UP

Arsène Wenger was asked if the team needed to finish above Manchester United to win the Premiership. Wenger coolly responded: 'You've got to finish above every other team if you win the title.'

ACCIDENTAL DISCLOSURE

Alex Ferguson and Arsène Wenger were in a car accident, and it was a bad one. Both cars were totally demolished, but amazingly neither of them was hurt.

After they crawled out of their cars, Ferguson said, 'Wow! Just look at our cars. There's nothing left, but fortunately we are unhurt. This must be a sign from God that we should meet and be friends and live together in peace the rest of our days.'

Wenger replied, 'I agree with you completely; this must be a sign from God!'

Sir Alex added, 'And look at this – here's another miracle. My car is completely demolished, but this bottle of whiskey didn't break. Surely God wants us to drink this and celebrate our good fortune.'

Then he handed the bottle to Wenger. Arsène nodded his head in agreement, opened it and took a few big swigs from the bottle, then handed it back to Ferguson, who immediately put the cap back on.

Arsène asked, 'Aren't you having any?'

Sir Alex Ferguson replied, 'No. I think I will just wait for the police . . .'

WORDS ARE ALL WE HAVE

Wenger and Ferguson have been the source and the subject of some good quotes. The following is my personal Top Ten.

1. *Everyone knows that for us to get a penalty we need a certificate from the Pope and a personal letter from the Queen.*
   Alex Ferguson.
2. *He moves across the pitch like a piece of paper on the wind.*
   Alex Ferguson goes windy about Ryan Giggs.
3. *Everybody thinks he has the prettiest wife at home.*
   Arsène Wenger on Alex Ferguson's claim that Manchester United play the most attractive football in England.
4. *His only weakness is that he doesn't think he has one.*
   Arsène Wenger on Sir Alex.
5. *I have to sit down with him and see where we stand.*
   Arsène Wenger, talking about Patrick Vieira.

6. *As long as no one scored, it was always going to be close.*
   Arsène Wenger.
7. *At some clubs, success is accidental. At Arsenal it is compulsory.*
   Arsène Wenger.
8. *The new manager has given us unbelievable belief.*
   Paul Merson extols the virtues of Arsène Wenger.
9. *He's so greedy for success that when his grandkids beat him at cards, he sends them to bed without any supper.*
   Gary Pallister on Sir Alex, no. 1.
10. *In the early days we used to call the boss the Hairdryer because he would come right up to your face and scream at you.*
    Gary Pallister on Sir Alex, no. 2.

THE LAST JUDGEMENT

There was a terrific lightning strike and tragically Alex Ferguson and Arsène Wegner died, but before they were allowed into Heaven they were sent to Purgatory.

Fergie was walking along arm in arm with a stunning young woman when he met his old foe.

'Well!' said Arsène, 'I see you're getting your reward up here while you purge your sins.'

'She's not my reward,' said Fergie. 'I'm her punishment.'

HAIR TODAY

Alex Ferguson and Arsène Wenger somehow ended up at the same barber shop. As they sat there, each being worked on by a different barber, not a word was spoken. The barbers were both afraid to start a conversation, for fear it would turn to football. As the barbers finished their work, the one who had Fergie in his chair reached for the aftershave.

Sir Alex was quick to stop him with the words, 'No thanks, my wife will smell that and think I've been in a whorehouse.'

The second barber turned to Wenger and said, 'How about you?'

'Go ahead,' he replied. 'My wife doesn't know what the inside of a whorehouse smells like.'

ALL DONATIONS GRATEFULLY RECEIVED

In 2008, a man on his way home from work was stuck in a traffic jam outside the Emirates Stadium, and he thought to himself, Wow, the traffic seems worse than usual. Nothing's moving.

The man noticed a policeman walking back and forth between the lines of cars, so he rolled down his window and asked, 'Excuse me, what's the problem?'

The officer replied, 'Alex Ferguson just found out that the club owners are planning to cut his budget and he's all depressed. He stopped his car in the middle of the road, and he's threating to douse himself in petrol and set himself on fire. He says everybody hates him and he doesn't have any more money since he paid for Ronaldo's new contract. I'm walking around taking up a collection for him.'

'Oh, really. How much have you collected so far?'

'Well, people are still siphoning but right now I'd say about three hundred gallons.'

KING KEV

George Bernard Shaw rather caustically defined a newspaper as a device 'unable to distinguish between a bicycle accident and the collapse of civilisation'. Hence it is no surprise that the media had a field day with the short-lived but intense rivalry between Sir Alex and Kevin Keegan, then at Newcastle United, while both were fighting for the Premier League title in 2006.

Fergie – a master at the dark art of needling his opponents – clearly won the psychological battle as was evident in Keegan's infamous 'I would love it . . . if we beat them' meltdown on live television. It was clearly very personal for Keegan, but as much as he would have love loved to pip Fergie at finish – it was United's title again.

FROM THE HORSE'S MOUTH

Keegan is a national treasure and a national resource. Nobody has produced more natural gas than Kevin as my Top Forty proves.

1. *I am reluctant to tell you all I know, as I really do not know anything.*
    Keegan after Denis Wise was appointed Newcastle's director of football in 2008.
2. *The only way we will get into Europe is by ferry.*
    On his second coming in Newcastle in 2008.
3. *Over a season, you'll get goals disallowed that are good and you'll get goals that are good disallowed.*
4. *Bobby Robson must be thinking of throwing some fresh legs on.*
5. *I'll never play at Wembley again, unless I play at Wembley again.*
6. *It's like a toaster, the ref's shirt pocket. Every time there's a tackle, up pops a yellow card.*
7. *Lineker always weighed up his options, especially when he had no choice.*
8. *Goalkeepers today aren't born until they're in their late twenties or thirties.*
9. *I don't think there is anybody bigger or smaller than Maradona.*
10. *They compare Steve McManaman to Steve Highway and he's nothing like him, but I can see why – it's because he's a bit different.*
11. *Sometimes there are too many generals and not enough, er, people waving to the generals as they, er, walk past.*
12. *That would have been a goal if it wasn't saved.*

13. Unlucky 13: *There's only one team going to win it now, and that's England.*
    In a 1998 World Cup match, just before Dan Petrescu scored Romania's winner.
14. *The ref was vertically fifteen yards away.*
15. *In some ways, cramp is worse than having a broken leg.*
16. *The 33- or 34-year-olds will be 36 or 37 by the time the next World Cup comes around if they're not careful.*
17. *Argentina won't be at Euro 2000 because they're from South Africa.*
18. *Despite his white boots he has real pace.*
19. *They're the second-best team in the world, and there's no higher praise than that.*
    When discussing Argentina.
20. *England have the best fans in the world and Scotland's fans are second-to-none.*
21. *England can end the millennium as it started – as the greatest football nation in the world.*
22. *You can't do better than go away from home and get a draw.*
23. *He's using his strength and that is his strength, his strength.*
24. *The tide is very much in our court now.*
25. *Chile have three options – they could win or lose.*
26. *I came to Nantes two years ago and it's much the same today, except that it's totally different.*
27. *I know what is around the corner – I just don't know where the corner is. But the onus is on us to perform and we must control the bandwagon.*
28. *It's understandable that people are keeping one eye on the pot and another up the chimney.*
29. *I'd love to be a mole on the wall in the Liverpool dressing room at half-time.*
30. *I never talk about Uriah Rennie except to say I don't like him as a ref.*

31. *The substitute is about to come on – he's a player who was left out of the starting line-up today.*
32. *Nicolas Anelka left Arsenal for £23 million and they built a training ground around him.*
33. *I'm not trying to make excuses, but I think the lights may have been a problem.*
    When talking about a David Seaman howler.
34. *Hungary is very similar to Bulgaria. I know they're different countries.*
35. *Life wouldn't be worth living if you could buy confidence, because the rich people would have it all and everybody else would ... would have to make their own arrangements.*
36. *You can't play with a one-armed goalkeeper ... not at this level.*
37. *There'll be no siestas in Madrid tonight.*
38. *You just need one or two players playing well to have a chance in this league. But you need nine or ten players playing well to have a chance to win.*
39. *We don't get any marks for effort like in ice-skating.*
40. *Richard Dunne has always been in the frame for me. When he took himself out of the frame, it was because he took himself out of it for one reason or another.*

SIR BOBBY

In the 2002/03 season, Newcastle were again challenging United for the title but this time it was Sir Bobby Robson who was the manager.

Arsène Wenger said of Robson: 'Can you believe he is still going at about seventy? He must eat a football every day for breakfast.' His comment points to Robson's longevity and his sheer love of the beautiful game.

Sir Bobby's reply was equally instructive: 'Don't you think people are actually saying, "Oh, he's a silly old goat."'

The remark shows the lack of pomposity that characterised Robson's career and is one of the reasons he was the football fan's prince. The following collection is a celebration of one of the greats.

CLUELESS

Journalist David Lacey a little harshly observed of Bobby Robson that: 'His natural expression is that of a man who fears he might have left the gas on.'

However, it cannot be argued that Sir Bobby's comments had a unique power to bewilder and bemuse. Here's my personal Top Twenty-one of Bobbyisms:

1. *Some of the goals were good, some of the goals were sceptical.*
2. *I do not want to play the long ball, and I do want to play the short ball. I think long and short balls is what football is all about.*
3. *We've got nothing to lose, and there's no point losing this game.*
4. *Gary Speed has been absolutely massive for me ... his influence on the team cannot be underestimated.*
5. *I've always enjoyed a night on the town in Newcastle – now you could say I am a knight of the toon.*
   Sir Bobby reflecting on his knighthood.
6. *When we had our recent depressing run and did not win for seven matches, five of them were away from home. And we actually lost the two home games against Middlesbrough and Manchester City. So, while things were bleak, they looked a lot bleaker than they really were.*
7. *The first ninety minutes are the most important.*
8. *We had the game won and then, all of a sudden, we lost it.*
   Robson on Kevin Sheedy's equaliser for Ireland against England in Italia '90.

9. *The last thing I want to do now is win something for the fantastic supporters in Newcastle.*

10. *He's going a bit thin on top and, in this heat, it can happen that he loses his temper a bit quicker than usual.*

    Robson claims that Ray Wilkins was sent off in the 1986 World Cup because of baldness.

11. *With Maradona, even Arsenal would have won it.*

    Speaking here about the 1986 World Cup.

12. *We can't replace Gary Speed. Where do you get an experienced player like him with a left foot and a head?*

13. *Home advantage gives you an advantage.*

14. *Laurent Robert said I was picking the wrong team. At the time I was ... because he was in it.*

15. *He's very fast and if he gets a yard ahead of himself, nobody will catch him.*

16. *Well, we got nine and you can't score more than that.*

17. *I'd say he's the best in Europe, if you put me on the fence.*

18. *Tottenham have impressed me: they haven't thrown in the towel even though they have been under the gun.*

19. *I played cricket for my local village. It was forty overs per side, and the team that had the most runs won. It was that sort of football.*

20. *There will be a game where somebody scores more than Brazil and that might be the game that they lose.*

21. *We don't want our players to be monks, we want them to be football players because a monk doesn't play football at this level.*

SUBS BENCH

However, one Sir Bobby quote stands above all the others. An all-time classic of the genre, it deserves to be savoured:

'We didn't underestimate them. They were just a lot better than we thought.'

TACTICAL CONFUSION

Alex Ferguson would have been in agreement with the former England rugby Jack Rowell, who was once asked what it was like to be a top rugby coach. He replied, 'You have fifteen plyers in a team. Seven hate your guts and the other eight are making up their minds.'

Fergie has always been willing to let players know that their best days are behind them and gone ahead to carry out radical surgery on a successful team. A former United player of some note was speaking to Sir Alex about tactics after giving a less than distinguished performance in a match. The player shrugged his shoulders and said, 'I'm confused, I don't know whether I'm coming or going.'

Ferguson put his arm around the player's shoulder, looked him straight in the eye and whispered softly: 'I'm afraid, Mr X, you're going.'

DON'T JUMP TO CONCLUSIONS

Sir Alex is frequently invited to speak in schools. He likes to tell stories with a moral attached. A case in point is as follows:

> The manager was listening to his clerk on the phone in the department store saying: 'I love you, dear. Only you. Devoted to you. And I love you so. These Miss You Nights are the Longest. I will always love you. You to me are everything.'
>
> The manager became irate and snapped at her icily when she put down the phone: 'Miss Hall, that telephone has been fixed where it is for the purpose of transacting business and not for love-making during business hours. Don't let it occur again.'
>
> Miss Hall: 'I was just ordering some new songs for Department Five, sir.'

FOUR-EVER AND EVER

During his school visits Fergie did have some memorable interactions with his students.

Alex: 'How many wives can a man have?'

Francis: 'Sixteen.'

Alex: 'Where did you hear that?'

Francis: 'The priest at the wedding said: four better, four worse, four richer, four poorer.'

BOOT BOY

Fergie was never known for his sense of humour, but he sometimes showed a waspish streak. He was unhappy with the general level of fitness in the squad but particularly with that of one player. Fergie asked him, 'Have you got a boot sponsor?'

'Yes.'

'Good. I'll get them to send you some lighter ones.'

UNITED WE STAND

Alex Ferguson did not react well to defeat, which explains why it was always somebody else's fault when United lost. His most imaginative excuse was unquestionably when United lost 3–1 to Southampton in 1996. He blamed the kit. The team's new grey strip, he claimed, meant that they were unable to pick out their teammates.

Football's two other contenders for the award of the best excuse are David James and Sir Kenny Dalglish.

In fact, James earned the nickname 'Calamity James' in his Liverpool days for a series of blunders which cost the Merseysiders dearly in 1997. His excuse was that he was fatigued because of the effects of his ten-hour sessions on his PlayStation. A new riddle was born:

'What's the difference between Jesus and David James?'

'Jesus saves.'

The following year, non-league Stevenage held mighty Newcastle to a 1–1 draw. Dalglish's managerial excuse was that, 'Newcastle would have won but the balls were too bouncy.'

THE TRYING GAME

After United won their eighth league title under his management Fergie recognised that some surgery was needed on the team and one or two legends of the greatest team of all time needed to be put out to grass. Ferguson approached one of the players in question with these words:

'You are one of the giants of the game. You have played a huge part in making United the greatest team of all time. A hundred years from now people will still be talking about you.'

The player's chest puffed up with pride but then his expression changed as Sir Alex continued.

'I just don't know how we'd get on without you,' he said. 'But we're going to give it a try.'

PARTING SHOT

In terms of players, Alex once said, 'You know a player is great as he's coming to the end of his career. A great player when he is gone will never be forgotten. A bad player is one who is not yet gone but is already forgotten!'

DON'T FORGET TO REMEMBER ME

Asked how he would like to be remembered, Fergie once joked that he was afraid he would suffer the same fate of Jón Arason and be remembered inappropriately. Arason was the last Catholic bishop of Iceland and was executed at Skálholt in 1550. The Icelanders, rejoicing in their complete religious freedom, felt that a monument should be erected on the site to commemorate his memory. So ... they built a Lutheran church!

RIVALS

Another of Ferguson's favourite stories is the one about the man who went to an auction to buy a valuable parrot he badly wanted. His plan was to bid up to £40. But the bidding went up to £120 before it was knocked down to him. Afterwards he asked the auctioneer who the other man was who kept bidding against him.

'That wasn't another man,' replied the auctioneer. 'That was the parrot you just bought.'

A ROLE IN HISTORY

Sir Alex is also well able to tell stories against himself. One went back to his schooldays. His father asked him, 'Tell me, son, how did your test go today?'

'Well, I did just what Napoleon did.'

'And what's that?'

'I went down in history.'

MEDIA MANAGEMENT

Fergie once met a young journalist on his way into Old Trafford. The journalist was trying to get information from him, but Sir Alex was more enigmatic than the Dead Sea Scrolls. Eventually the journalist lost patience and decided to quit while he still retained a shred of dignity. And so, he asked one final question. 'Can you tell me where to go for the press box?'

'To hell and back,' Fergie replied.

CHEAP SEATS

As a young man Ferguson once attended a match at Old Trafford as a spectator. At the turnstiles it was explained to him that there were seats for £5, £10 and £20, and that programmes were half-a-crown.

'Okay,' said Fergie, 'I'll sit on a programme.'

LET THEM NOT EAT CAKE

In 2012 *Bridesmaids* star and former minor Roscommon goalkeeper Chris O'Dowd said on *The Sunday Game* that his hero was Shane 'Cake' Curran, a man who carved out a career as goalkeeper with Athlone Town. O'Dowd's description of Curran was seen as spot on: 'He's likely to ride a bull into a church.'

Few people get the last word with Alex Ferguson, but legend has it that Shane Curran was a rare exception to this rule. At just sixteen, he had a trial with Manchester United. Uncertain about his future Shane asked Fergie directly, 'What's going on?'

Sir Alex was being evasive and so Shane interrupted in him in full flow and said, 'Alex, it's like this. If you can't handle Paul McGrath you certainly can't handle me.' Curran immediately walked away from his career with United.

THE HORSE WHISPERER

Alex Ferguson is known for his love of racing despite the protracted controversy about his ownership of the champion horse, Rock of Gibraltar.

Once, on a walking holiday, Fergie stopped alongside a field run on a country road to rest for a few minutes. He had just closed his eyes when a horse came to the fence and began to boast about his past.

'Yes sir, I'm a fine horse. I've run in twenty-five races and won over £2 million. I keep my trophies in the barn.'

Fergie computed the value of having a talking horse, found the horse's owner and offered a handsome sum for the animal.

'Aw, you don't want that horse,' said the farmer.

'Yes I do,' said Fergie, 'and I'll give you £100,000 for that horse.'

Recognising a good deal, the farmer said without hesitation, 'He's yours.'

While he wrote out the cheque, Fergie asked, 'By the way, why wouldn't I want your horse?'

'Because,' said the farmer, 'he's a liar – he hasn't won a race in his life.'

SUPERSTITIOUS MINDS

Like Fergie, many footballers are keen on horse racing. During his days with Rangers, Ally McCoist went to the Gold Cup at Cheltenham. Ally had a few too many glasses of Guinness and when he went back to his hotel he walked into the room, into the en suite, went to the toilet then fell asleep. The next morning, he woke up in bed with two strangers. He was in the wrong room.

Fergie has discovered that Cheltenham is the mecca for racing fans, though there are more horses' asses at the festival than there are horses. Hence his whine, 'I backed a horse at ten to one. He came in at ten past two.'

Fergie's biographer, top racing journalist Hugh McIlvanney wrote humorously about a previously unidentified condition known as GOS, 'Groundless Optimism Syndrome'. This affliction is a delusional condition which strikes for the four days of the festival whereby people who have lost the family silver on previous visits to Cheltenham become convinced that they have new mystical powers of prophecy which enables them to bet with certainty. Inevitably when they leave Prestbury Park three days later their wallets are very anaemic.

Another comment was more philosophical, 'The only way to follow a horse at Cheltenham is with a shovel and brush and sell it to the people who grow roses.'

Fergie was to relearn that lesson the hard way at the last Cheltenham Festival. A forlorn punter of high intelligence, mature wisdom and with a sophisticated social sense, was slowly making his way through customs ahead of him at Birmingham airport. The customs officer asked, 'Anything to declare?'

After a dramatic pause, the man replied in a voice as miserable as a flooded meadow, 'Nothing but empty pockets.'

One time, Fergie was luckier and cleaned out a bookie with a huge bet on a horse at 200 to 1. His friends were curious and asked him about the secret of his success. 'I'm superstitious and I watch for omens,' he replied. 'On my way to the races I took a number six bus. It made six stops on the way and it cost me £6 to get into Prestbury Park. It was three sixes telling me something. So, I added them up, three sixes are twenty-one, so I backed number twenty-one and it won by a mile.'

Another day he misread the signals and had to explain a massive loss to his wife. 'As I walked into the racecourse a sudden gust of wind blew my hat off. It was a sure sign,' he said. 'So, I put it all on a horse called Gone with the Wind.'

'And it didn't win?'

'No. Some foreign horse called *Mon Chapeau* won by a mile.'

LICENCE TO THRILL

Punters are notoriously partisan. Fergie once backed a Scottish horse at the Cheltenham Festival which led all the way and was fifteen lengths clear at the end. He declared it the most thrilling finish he had ever witnessed.

NEW KIDD IN TOWN

Brian Kidd was Fergie's Assistant Manager from 1991 to 1998. Alex brought Brian to a race meeting. Kidd bet £1,000 on the winner of the first race at 15 to 1. When he went to collect, the bookie told him he didn't have £15,000 in the bag. Could he drop back a few races later? He did, and the bookie, who was losing all round, still didn't have enough cash. Would he take a cheque?

'No, I bet cash and I want to be paid in cash,' Kidd snapped. 'And if you're going to be running me around like this, I'd just as soon call the bet off!'

SAY LITTLE BUT SAY IT WELL

Sir Alex has a favourite racing story. The late Duke of Norfolk used to tell a story about one of his trainers, Sid Fidell. Whenever the duke had a runner and couldn't be at the meeting, Sid always sent him a detailed telegram with all the facts of the race even though they always met every Friday to discuss the week's racing. The duke got tired of the long telegrams and told Sid to only send him short telegrams in future, and they would discuss the races in more detail on the Friday sessions. Soon afterwards, the duke had a horse running and that evening he received the following telegram. 'S.F.S.F.S.F.S.F.'

On the Friday, the duke asked Sid to explain what it meant. 'Oh, your grace it's quite simple really: "Started, farted, slipped and fell. See you Friday. Sid Fidell."'

THE BARD OF THE BEEB

Fergie enjoys the company of racing people like the BBC's Julian Wilson. The old Etonian with his top hat, unflappable manner and beautifully spoken delivery – the voice of racing on television – was filming a piece for television in the run up to the Epsom Derby near a quiet country road. He was in full flow, 'Three hundred years ago the king of England Charles II would hack up on this very hill and watch in fascination as the horses passed by. Nothing's changed in the last three hundred years ...'

At that point, a motorbike roared by.

Julian's response was out of character, 'Of course what has changed is f**king motorbikes.'

MAKE HASTE SLOWLY

Fergie has also got involved in owning racehorses. It is not without its pitfalls. When one horse he owned trailed in last at a Christmas meeting, Fergie was furious. The jockey was not entertaining any blame for the fiasco and said, 'The horse was so slow, I kept a diary of the trip. If I ever ride him at an evening meeting, I'll be wearing my pyjamas.'

THE PRICE OF PROGRESS

As Fergie got more practice of losing, he could react with a nice, gentle sense of humour. He once ran a not-very-promising horse. Later that day Bobby Charlton asked, 'How did he do Alex?'

'Second.'

'Wow. That's great.'

'Not really. He was second – last!'

THE WINDY CITY

Sir Alex travelled to London to meet Queen Elizabeth. She took him on a tour of the city in a horse drawn carriage. One of the horses let out a thunderous, cataclysmic fart that reverberated through the air and rattled the doors of the coach. Uncomfortable, the reaction of the two powerful figures was to focus their attention elsewhere and behave as if nothing extraordinary had happened. But the Queen was the first to realise that ignoring what had just happened was ridiculous.

She explained, 'Mr Ferguson, please accept my regrets – I'm sure you understand that there are some things that even a queen cannot control.'

Fergie replied, 'Your Majesty, please don't give the matter another thought – you know, if you hadn't said something, I would have thought it was one of the horses.'

BON APPETIT

Sir Alex is known for his 'financial acumen'. Hence the story that every day he goes to a pub for lunch. He always orders the soup of the day which comes with two slices of bread. One day the manager asks him how he liked his meal. Fergie replies, 'It was good, but you could give a little more bread.'

So, the next day the manager tells the waitress to give him four slices of bread. The manager asks him afterwards how he liked his meal. Fergie replies, ''Twas good, but you could give a little more bread.'

The next day the manager tells the waitress to give him eight slices of bread. 'How was your meal today, sir?' the manager asks. Fergie replies, ''Twas good, but you could give a little more bread.'

The following day the manager tells the waitress to give him a whole loaf of bread with his soup. 'How was your meal, sir?' The manager asks when he comes to pay.

Fergie replies, ''Twas good, but you could give a little more bread.'

The manager is now obsessed with hearing his famous customer say that he is satisfied with his meal, so he goes to the bakery, and orders a six-foot-long loaf of bread. When Fergie comes in as usual the next day, the waitress and the manager cut the loaf in half, butters the entire length of each half, and lay it out along the counter, right next to his bowl of soup. Fergie sits down, and devours both his bowl of soup, and both halves of the six-foot-long loaf of bread.

The manager now thinks he will get the answer he is looking for, and when Fergie comes up to pay for his meal, the manager asks in his usual way: 'How was your meal TODAY, sir?'

Fergie replies: 'It was good as usual, but I see you've gone back to giving only two slices of bread.'

THE LEAVING OF MANCHESTER

Anders Lindegaard's verdict on David Moyes's attempt to replace Alex Ferguson as Manchester United's manager was: 'It was like trying to charge an iPhone with a Nokia charger. It just slowly went flat.'

One United fan remarked. 'When Sir Alex was our manager, we were Goliath. Then we got David.'

AGILITY

When the Covid-19 virus broke out Sir Alex decided he needed to boost his fitness. He went to the local Pilates instructor. 'How flexible are you?' asked the instructor.

'Well I can do any day except Sundays,' replied the United legend.

BACK TO THE FUTURE

It was always going to be a tough job to replace Sir Alex as United manager. However, Paul Ince suggests that United's approach to succession planning was unique: 'I'm sure David [Gill, then United's CEO] and Alex will sit down and decide who should be the predecessor to his job.'

7

NICE THINGS MANCHESTER UNITED FANS SAY ABOUT LIVERPOOL FC*

* (This chapter has been left blank to reflect accurately the level of affection United fans have for their great Merseyside rivals.)

8

MATT-ER OF FACT

*The Scots have realistic expectations – they expect to lose –
and dedicate themselves to alcoholic pleasures and exposing
their genitals to foreigners.*
From *Leadership the Sven-Göran Eriksson Way*

Only Sir Matt Busby can attract the type of reverence among
Manchester United fans as Alex Ferguson does. For the sake of
younger readers in particular this chapter begins by explaining
why this is so. It then considers some of the humour that Busby
and his players generated.

PARADISE LOST
In 1958 Manchester United went out to Yugoslavia for the second
leg of their European Cup encounter with Red Star Belgrade. In
another thriller United drew 3–3 and qualified for the semi-finals
of the European Cup on a 5–4 aggregate.

But tragedy swooped like a hawk flying down from the sky;
later people would be struck at the speed at which dreams can be
shattered and how thin the veil between life and death is.

The squad was flying back to Manchester on 6 February, when
their airplane landed at Munich for refuelling. During a third

attempt at a take-off, the aircraft crashed. Twenty-three people on board lost their lives. The crash took the lives of eight United players (five of whom had played in the 3–3 draw the previous day), eight journalists, three United officials, two members of the aircrew (one the co-pilot) and two other passengers – twenty-three from the forty-four who had set out on the flight. The eight United players who died were: Roger Byrne (left back), Geoff Bent (reserve left back), Eddie Colman (right half), Mark Jones (centre half), Duncan Edwards (left half), David Pegg (outside left), Tommy Taylor (centre forward) and Liam Whelan (inside right).

The lucky member of the United squad was Welsh international utility forward Colin Webster. He was due to make the trip to Munich but owing to a severe bout of flu he had to forego the journey.

Before the crash Liam Whelan, a devout Catholic, said, 'Well, if anything happens, I'm ready.' The FAI's *Yearbook* of 1958/59 paid a worthy tribute to their star: 'We shall miss the cheerful smile and cheekily efficient football, but we shall not forget him, nor those other Manchester United players so tragically torn from the field on sport's blackest day.'

Harry Gregg exhibited heroism of an extraordinary kind after escaping significant injury. On a number of occasions, he returned to the wreckage of the plane to rescue the injured. He first rescued a baby and then her mother. Although he thought both Bobby Charlton and Denis Viollet were dead, he grabbed the two of them by their waistbands and trailed them through the snow. After routine treatment in the Rechts der Isar Hospital, Gregg returned home.

Bobby Charlton once said of the great Duncan Edwards: 'If I had to play for my life, and could take one man with me, it would be Duncan Edwards.' He fought bravely clinging on to life for fifteen days before finally succumbing to kidney failure. Apart from severe shock, he had suffered chronic kidney damage, broken ribs, a pneumothorax, a broken pelvis, a smashed right thigh. Six days after the crash his condition deteriorated, and an artificial kidney was rushed from Freiburg. He was dialysed five times, but it was not enough.

Jackie Blanchflower survived, having received the last rites but never played again. He was unable to leave the Rechts der Isar for three months. His pelvis was fractured, and his kidneys were squashed by the seat belt, every rib was broken, both arms and both legs. He tried training again, but he had a bad arm, which had metal gangrene in it. At just twenty-five, his career perished. Likewise, John Berry never played again, and goalkeeper Ray Wood's top-class career was finished in all but name.

The memory of that incident could never be erased, lingering like an unwelcome visitor, leaving an inheritance of quiet despair. H.E. Bates captured the spirit of the city in the *F.A. Yearbook* of 1958/59:

> At six o'clock, out of pure curiosity, I turned on my television set. As the news came on, the screen seemed to go black. The normally urbane voice of the announcer seemed to turn into a sledgehammer. My eyes went deathly cold and I sat listening with a frozen brain to that cruel and shocking list of casualties that was now to give the word Munich an even sadder meaning than it had acquired on a day before the war, after a British Prime Minister had come home to London waving a pitiful piece of paper and most of us knew that new calamities of war were inevitable.

Liverpool's John Aldridge, himself a native of Liverpool, contemplated retirement after the Hillsborough disaster in 1989. Munich induced similar feelings.

There was considerable controversy about the cause of the crash. Two inquiries conducted by the Germans, which found that the decisive cause of the accident lay in wing icing and that runaway slush was a further cause. In June 1969 (eleven years after the tragedy) the final findings of the British Court of Inquiry, *The Fay Report*, into the Munich crash were published. The key witness in the inquiry which cleared Captain James Thain from blame for the collision was a German pilot who was at Munich airport on the day of the disaster. Herr Reinhard Meyer said, 'there was nothing like frost or frozen deposit on the wing of the BEA Elizabethan airliner as it lay at the end of the runway. There was melting snow only.'

PARADISE REGAINED

Having been promoted from coach to assistant manager in 1955, it fell to Jimmy Murphy to steady the ship after Munich. As manager of Wales, he was on international duty which meant that he missed the trip to Belgrade. When he returned to Old Trafford, he had no idea of what had happened. There was only a skeleton staff on duty, and an unnatural, atmosphere seemed to hover in the air. A hysterical secretary greeted him and broke the news. He took a bottle of whiskey from a sideboard and sought sanctuary in his own office and wept.

It was Murphy who signed players and inspired the club with a will to continue – motivated not by a fear of failure but by the desire to partake in a glory-laden adventure. His steely determination and will to win, was combined with a natural modesty and with plenty of good humour.

It was a remarkable achievement in any circumstances. In this case the word remarkable is barely adequate. Loyalty was his creed because he turned down lucrative offers to manage English clubs like Arsenal and overseas sides from Juventus to Brazil. Murphy was responsible for nurturing young talent and generated an assembly line of quality players including Duncan Edwards, Bobby Charlton and George Best.

United's first match after the disaster was on 19 February 1958 when they beat Sheffield Wednesday 3–0 in a fifth round FA Cup fixture before 60,000 highly charged fans. It was the beginning of a wonderful career for a young player. Shay Brennan joined United as a sixteen-year-old in 1953 but did not get opportunity to shine for five seasons. Despite playing at outside-left instead of his customary full-back position the twenty-year-old made a sensational impact in front of the appreciative Old Trafford audience scoring two goals in the 3–0 victory. The fact that Brennan was an attacking full-back with excellent ball control made the transition to the unaccustomed position much easier. In those moments, those breaths of time, when sadness and joy share the narrow path of life hope glowed like a light in darkness.

A further victory over West Brom secured an FA Cup semi-final place against Second Division Fulham. United advanced via a 2–2 draw and a 5–3 victory in the replay. Given the unique circumstances the FA made a concession to United and allowed them to field two cup-tied players, Stan Crowther (signed from Aston Villa) and Ernie Taylor a cup medal winner in 1951 and 1953 with Newcastle and Blackpool respectively. The legendary Hungarian Ferenc Puskás offered to play for United, but the Football League still operated a ban on foreign players.

Both Bobby Charlton and Bill Foulkes, survivors of the Munich crash, lined out for the Reds in the 1958 FA Cup final against Bolton with the backing of unprecedented popular support, just a few months after the tragedy. Bolton's 2–0 win was secured courtesy of a sterling performance by Nat Lofthouse. Despite the defeat it had been an incredible achievement on the part of Murphy to lead United to Wembley in the most difficult of circumstances.

Murphy had an unusual motivational style: 'Now listen boys, I'm not happy with our tackling. We're hurting them but they keep getting up.'

THE ONE THAT GOT AWAY

In 1950, Murphy was impressed by a young player, Roy Sutcliffe, who he saw on trial at United. He wrote to him and invited him back for a second trial. He was surprised and disappointed not to hear back from Sutcliffe and was stunned to hear years later that the promising player had never gone on to play for another club.

In 1994, when he was sixty-three, Sutcliffe's mother opened an old drawer to discover an unopened letter to Roy that she had forgotten to pass on to him. It was Murphy's letter.

It was the ultimate sliding doors story.

THE BOSS

The 1950s saw the darkest hour in Manchester United's long history, but the 1960s would see its finest. One man was responsible for the dramatic upsurge in United's fortunes – the man Ray Wilkins described as 'the figurehead of figureheads', Matt Busby. As he lay in his hospital bed after Munich, he felt both determination and dejection. The nurses had ant-like order conquering chaos, bringing swift ease and massaging his nightmare of torn reality.

Dreams were essential for his emotional survival. They were a theatre of boundless possibilities and lofty visions, disturbing what was and inventing what was not. Past, present and future became one. With stoic courage he fought back from the brink of death to build a third exceptional side that would beat all-comers in a magnificent fashion and claim two more Championships; the FA Cup and the European Cup.

His son Sandy put it well, 'This man came and planted a seed in a bombed-out ground, and he watched the seed grow, he loved it and nurtured it, till the branches started growing outwards and upwards. Then the tree was struck by lightning. He started all over again, loving and nurturing it, and the branches grew and grew to the ends of the world.'

Busby was a man who walked with kings but succeeded in keeping his feet on the ground. The distinguished sociologist Max Weber defined two types of power – traditional and charismatic. The first depends on the trappings of the office. The second rests purely on the aura of the person. As a norm, these two elements are separate but very occasionally and memorably they coincide. They collided in the person of John F. Kennedy, who moulded a new presidency out of a form of celebrity power. Matt Busby too had elements of both as manager of football's most famous club but who also represented a force of change.

He had a kind of aura about him that made players want to earn his favour, and a completely natural, straight-from-the-heart sense of how to inspire players. He was able to bring the best out of his gifted but sometimes difficult stars like George Best. Matt's rule was law, and the more demanding of obedience because it was given in a soft, kind, reasonable way against which it was impossible to argue.

THE LAST LINE OF DEFENCE

United were the team of all the talents and the world was their oyster. In February 1958, the Red Devils were the reigning league champions and had only missed out on the 'double' the previous year when they lost the FA Cup final 1–2 to Aston Villa. They were also riding high on the continent and reached the quarter-final stage of the European Cup competition. The Busby Babes were at their peak.

They went to Highbury on a chilly afternoon seeking two league points. At half-time they looked to be well on the way with a comfortable 3–0 lead thanks to goals from Duncan Edwards, Bobby Charlton and Tommy Taylor. In the sixtieth minute, David Herd pulled one back for Arsenal and incredibly two-and-a-half minutes later they were level with two goals from Jimmy Bloomfield.

This transformation would have shell-shocked most teams, but the Busby Babes were not for turning and gradually took control of the game. United struck back with goals from Dennis Viollet and Tommy Taylor from a difficult angle. Then Derek Tapscott scored Arsenal's fourth. The 5–4 score was an eloquent testimony to the attacking policy of the 1950s and provides, in some respects, the most worthy tribute to the Busby Babes. Those memories are warm and comforting, like a familiar friend.

THE BONNIE BABY

George Best told a story that as he got older Sir Matt could be a little forgetful. Shortly after he became a grandfather some relatives came to visit when he was babysitting.

'May we see the new baby?' one asked.

'Not yet,' said Busy. 'I'll make coffee and we can chat first.'

Thirty minutes had passed, and other relative asked, 'May we see the baby now?'

'No, not yet,' replied Sir Matt.

After another half an hour had elapsed, they asked again, 'May we see the baby now?'

'No, not yet,' replied Busby.

Growing very impatient, they asked, 'Well, when can we see the baby?'

'When it cries.'

'When it cries?! Why do we have to wait until it cries?'

'Because I forgot where I put it.'

THE ABSENT-MINDED PROFESSOR

Another Best story was that, in later years, Busby was approached by a gushing female at a dinner party.

'Don't you remember me, Matt?' she asked.

'I'm afraid not.'

'Well, many years ago you asked me to marry you,' she said.

'Really? And did you?'

PAT ON THE BACK

One of Busby's players, Pat Crerand, said of him, 'Matt always believed Manchester United would be one of the greatest clubs in the world. He was the eternal optimist. In 1968, he still hoped Glenn Miller was just missing.'

MY BROTHER'S KEEPER

No United players are as revered as the 'Busby Babes'. Jackie Blanchflower made his debut at Liverpool in November 1951. He established himself as a regular in the 1953/54 season.

He signed for United in 1950, making his debut in a friendly at Kilmarnock. His first league game did not come until the following year, when he lined out at right-half. He also acted as substitute goalkeeper.

In 1957 United were poised to become the first club to win the Double since Aston Villa in 1897. It was Villa who stood in their way in the FA Cup final. The game was marred by a controversy following a sixth-minute injury to United keeper Ray Wood, who was charged so heavily by Villa's outside-left Peter McParland that he broke his jaw and was forced to leave the pitch. He subsequently returned to play on the wing but was nothing more than a passenger.

Jackie Blanchflower was delegated to be the emergency goalkeeper, with Duncan Edwards deputising for Blanchflower in the centre of defence. Jackie performed heroics in the goal and kept Villa at bay for over an hour. Two goals from McParland midway through the second half effectively sealed the game for Villa despite Tommy Taylor's late consolation goal for United. Despite losing out on the Double, United's young side were apparently on the threshold of greatness. With time on their side it seemed as if further honours were inevitable, particularly as United had reached the semi-finals of the European Cup a few months previously. Although they lost out to Real Madrid, Matt Busby was bullish enough to remark: 'The only difference between us and Real Madrid was in their experience, and we shall soon acquire that.'

Initially it was as a creative inside-forward that Blanchflower established himself. He scored twenty-four goals over two seasons and picked up a league medal in 1955/56. Having the luxury of a number of forwards, Matt Busby then chiefly deployed him as a centre-half, where he battled for selection with Mark Jones. Although he lacked a bit of pace he was known to his teammates as 'Twiggy'. His strengths were his footballing intelligence, his quality in the air and a sure touch with either foot.

He is the brother of the legendary Danny Blanchflower who led Spurs to the double. He played for Northern Ireland in the company of Danny winning twelve caps. Jackie not only shared Danny's bloodline he also shared some of his wit. This Blanchflower trait was most in evidence before the 1961 FA Cup final when Danny introduced the Spurs side to the Duchess of Kent. She said to him: 'The other team [Leicester] have their names on their tracksuits.'

Blanchflower quipped immediately: 'Yes, but we know each other.'

MEDICAL MISTAKE

What is often forgotten is that Denis Law was the first United player to win the European Footballer of the Year Award in 1964. He gave an extra dimension to the side because of his competitive streak. Once after Newcastle goalie Ian McFaul dived full length to hold a long range shot from Charlton, Law bent down to whisper into his ear: 'I'll be here every time.'

Law exuded charisma and enjoyed a laugh with the squad. One evening he approached a sad looking fringe member of the squad and asked, 'Why are you looking so down-hearted?'

'The doctor says I can't play.'

'When did he see you play?'

MINUS ONE

Denis Law attended a reunion of old United stars. All the giants like Bobby Charlton, Bryan Robson, Nobby Stiles, David Beckham, Brian McClair and Phil Neville were there. An old player – who had the reputation of being an utter bore and whose opinion of his own extraordinary abilities was shared only by himself – approached Law. He then looked around the room and said, 'How many United legends do you think there are in this room?'

'One less than you think,' Denis replied.

DENIS THE WISE

In recent years Denis has been celebrating the virtues of old age. His top three gems on the advantages of ageing are:

1. Things you buy now will not wear out.
2. People no longer view you as a hypochondriac.
3. There is nothing left to learn the hard way.

In the interest of balance, he also points out, 'Antiquity is not a voucher for efficiency.'

Denis claims to now spend hours each day studying archaeology. As a result, his life is in ruins.

O'DAIR

In the service of discretion, Denis refuses to name his former United colleague who, on a tour to America, was out for a meal and heard that another guest in the restaurant, Red Adair, would like to have a few words with him. His teammates were surprised when he returned to their table so quickly. They asked him how they got on with Red Adair.

'He wasn't very friendly,' the player told him.

'What did you say to him?' his colleagues asked.

'I simply asked him what it was like to dance with Ginger Rogers for all those years.'

The blood drained from his face when the other United players explained that, whereas Fred Astaire was the famous dancer, Red Adair was the legendary firefighter.

THE LAWMAN

During the 1960s, the United players felt that they deserved a pay increase. They decided to delegate Denis Law to negotiate with the manager on their behalf. Law went to speak to Matt Busby man-to-man while his colleagues waited with bated breath.

They expected a protracted mediation, but Law returned within minutes. To their disappointment he reported that the news was bad, Busby had pleaded poverty and that he was lucky to get five pounds out of him. The only consolation his fellow players could find was that it was better than nothing.

At the end of the week the players found that not alone had their pay not increased it had actually decreased. Mustering all the indignation they could manage the players complained bitterly to their manager.

Busby calmly replied: 'Take it up with Denis. When he came to me looking for money, I let him know how tight we are for money just now and persuaded him to accept a wage cut of five pounds a man to help the club out.'

A TAXING PROBLEM

George Best had some memorable verbal exchanges with Law. One of the most famous came when the 'Lawman' was complaining about the people from inland revenue.

Law: 'I've had a final demand from the tax people. Eight hundred and fifty frigging quid. But I wrote them a letter.'

Best: 'Saying what?'

Law: 'Saying I couldn't remember borrowing it from them!'

THE FAB FIVE

In December 1957, Matt Busby raised more than a few eyebrows when he bought Harry Gregg from Doncaster Rovers for £23,500 – a record at the time for a goalkeeper. Christmas came early for Gregg when he made his debut for United in a 4–0 victory over Leicester City. He succeeded Ray Wood in the United goal and went on to make 247 appearances for the club over the next nine seasons.

Gregg, who sadly died in 2020, was already a Northern Ireland international when he arrived at Old Trafford and went on to win a total of twenty-five caps. The year 1958 saw Gregg not only consolidate his place as number one goalkeeper at Old Trafford but become a major player on the international stage. His performances were one of the main reasons why Northern Ireland secured a place in the quarter finals of the World Cup – their first appearance at the finals – where Gregg was also voted top goalie. He was also embroiled that year in one of the most controversial goals ever scored in an FA Cup final, when in the fifty-fifth minute Nat Lofthouse bundled him over the line for Bolton Wanderers' second goal.

A hero for his role in rescuing people after the Munich crash,

Gregg later showed great bravery in the 1966 European Cup quarter-final when United defeated Benfica 5–1 in the away leg. George Best had one of his finest games ever for United, scoring two goals. After the game, the Portuguese fans started shouting 'El Beatle' at him because his hairstyle was so similar to the Fab Four's. One fan, though, charged at him waving a butcher's knife. Gregg rushed to his teammate's defence and wrestled the knife from him. The police were quickly on hand and, after interrogating the fan, they discovered that all he wanted was a lock of Best's hair.

STRAIGHT TALKING

It is just as hard to stay at the top as it is to get there. Having been a great player in the past does not necessarily make a good football pundit. A good example of this is Sir Bobby Charlton. Given his fame as a player, he was in great demand by broadcasters. The problem was that he was too nice a guy. He was worried about the feelings of others and would never attack anybody. As a result, he was a very bland broadcaster.

In marked contrast his late brother, Jack, was a great pundit because he was honest and always gave forthright answers. A good example of this was when he was assessing the Holland–Germany game on ITV during the 1990 World Cup, when Frank Rijkaard and Rudi Völler had a blowout and Rijkaard spat at his opponent. Jack was asked what he would have done if Rijkaard had done that to him. Without blinking an eye big Jack replied: 'I'd have chinned him.'

HAIR-RAISING

Even in his playing days, Bobby Charlton was follically challenged. He tried to disguise his bald spots with a combover. Long after his retirement, Bobby's wife was out one evening with a group of friends for a meal. One noticed that Mrs Charlton was wearing a beautiful new locket and said, 'It's beautiful. I suppose you carry a memento of some sort in it.'

Mrs Charlton replied, 'Yes, it's a lock of Bobby's hair.'

'But Bobby is still alive.'

'I know, but his hair is gone.'

ALWAYS HAIR FOR YOU

Bobby is reputed to have asked his brother Jack for his help with his hair problem. 'My hair is starting to fall out, can you suggest anything to keep it in.'

Jack was not very sympathetic, 'How about a cardboard box?'

A CUT ABOVE

Bobby never had the closest relationship with George Best. Thus, it is not a major surprise that Best famously poked fun at Bobby's lack of hair. He remarked, 'I sent my son to Bobby Charlton's school of football skills. He came back bald.'

BIG JACK

Bobby's brother Jack was noted for being 'careful' with money. In his Leeds days when Peter Lorimer was a young apprentice, Jack borrowed a fiver off Lorimer. Not only that but he got Lorimer to babysit for him for an evening. When Big Jack and his wife returned from their night out, Lorimer asked Jack if he could have his money back.

Jack replied, 'What do you mean? That fiver was for the rent of my couch for the evening.'

ASK ABOUT GARDENING

Bobby Charlton went to the gardening shop to buy fertiliser. As he was standing in line waiting to pay, a little boy asked him, 'What have you got in your trolley?'

'Fertiliser,' Bobby replied.

'What are you going to do with it?' the little boy asked.

'Put it on strawberries,' Charlton answered.

'You ought to live with us,' the little boy advised him. 'We put sugar and cream on ours.'

WE'RE ALL GOING ON A SUMMER HOLIDAY

Sport is a universal language. In the late 1970s, an English tourist was on holiday in a remote, mountainy part of Spain with his wife and children when his car came to a dead halt. After detailed scrutiny on the part of the owner, it emerged that serious surgery was called for. A garage was needed. Apart from a few mountain goats there was no sign of life anywhere. The man left his family and walked a number of miles in the scorching heat in search of help.

Finally, he came across a rundown farmhouse. The man knocked on the door and an enormous farmer, who had obviously just finished a lavish, garlic-heavy meal, appeared. The farmer expansively gestured for the English man to enter. Hygiene was obviously not the farmer's primary concern. In fact, the house was so untidy that it was the sort of place that you had to wipe your shoes *after* leaving it. The tourist politely and respectfully enquired, 'Do you speak *Inglés*?'

'*Si.*'

Breathing a huge sigh of relief, the English man launched into a full-scale explanation of his predicament. After he had patiently explained all the details, he started to get worried by the continued blank look on the farmer's face. The show of sympathy he was hoping for was not forthcoming. Again, he asked the farmer, 'Do you speak *Inglés*?'

'*Si.* Bobby Charlton.'

The tourist once again told his story but this time with less detail and extensive sign language. Again, there was no flicker of recognition.

'Do you speak *Inglés*?'

'*Si*. Bobby Charlton.'

'Do you speak any other *Inglés*, only Bobby Charlton?'

'*Si*. Jackie Charlton.'

'Help me, please, and I will take you down to the bank and get you some money. *Comprendez* bank?'

'*Si*. Gordon Banks.'

'Please, help me fix my car. *Automóvil*. *Comprendez*?'

'*Si*.'

'*Automóvil*?'

'Ah, *si*, *si*. *Automóvil*. James Hunt.'

NOBBY

Nobby Stiles played on England's World Cup winning side in 1966. Nobby's brother-in-law is John Giles. In Giles's final season with United, both he and Stiles were in and out of the United side. Matt Busby had a habit of asking Nobby how he was playing. Invariably Stiles would say 'okay' and then Busby would inform him he was dropped. Giles advised his brother-in-law that he was handling the manager all wrong. When he was asked how he was playing he should always say he was playing brilliantly and that the team couldn't do without him. Stiles took this advice the next time the manager questioned him in that way. The only problem was that Busby asked an unexpected supplementary question: 'Yes, but can you play better?'

'Yes,' was Nobby's instinctive reply.

'You're dropped for the next match,' was the boss's riposte.

A SORE SPOT

In other company though, Stiles was well able to get in the last word himself. Once, as Peter Hauser was writhing in agony after a tackle from Stiles, Hauser roared: 'The pain is excruciating.'

Stiles replied: 'Excruciating? You can't be that badly hurt if you can think of a word like that!'

NOW AND FOREVER?

Sir Alf Ramsey was giving his team talk before England played Australia. He turned to Nobby Stiles, knowing that Nobby had a reputation for being a hard tackler, and said to him, 'They've only got one good player, and that's Eusebio. So Nobby, I'd like you to take him out of the game.'

Nobby replied, 'What, for this game – or forever?'

FIND AN IRISHMAN

In the 1959/60 season, Shay Brennan made the right full-back position at Manchester United his own. Famous for his tackling and his courage, over the next ten years, he was a constant presence, only missing out through injury. In 1964, FIFA introduced a new law which allowed players to play for a country other than their birth, if they were qualified by ancestry or residence to claim citizenship of their adopted country. Irish football would never be the same again. Shay Brennan was the first player to declare for Ireland in these circumstances. The Manchester born full-back played nineteen times for Ireland, captaining the side five times.

He was the first in a long line of players to do so. One of the most infamous of this motley crew was QPR defender Terry Mancini. According to folklore, on his Irish debut against Poland in 1973 (John Giles's first game as Irish manager) the anthems were played and Mancini turned around to one of his teammates and said: 'God, the Polish anthem doesn't half go on.' He was abruptly told: 'Shut up. That's the Irish anthem.'

The Irish propensity to attract players in this way also led to a rash of jokes: 'The FAI [Football Association of Ireland] stands for Find An Irishman' and 'All you need to qualify to play for Ireland is to drink a pint of Guinness.' The jokes reached a peak when Vinnie Jones, or Vinnie O'Jones as the tabloid press christened him, sought to qualify for Ireland. When he came over to Dublin to check his grandmother's records, the *Daily Star*'s headline was: 'Begorrah! I'm off to pick up my passport now, Jack.'

Vinnie went on to play for Wales. According to one mischievous report he heard of his call-up in the following way:

Mike Smith: Hi Vinnie. I'm the manager of Wales and we'd like you to play for us. You do like Wales, Vinnie?

Jones: Of course I do, I've seen *Moby Dick* twice!

O'SHAY, O'SHAY, O'SHAY

Shay Brennan was at the heart of a memorable exchange with his colleague Bill Foulkes.

Shay: 'How's the mouth?'

Foulkes (with four stitches in his mouth): 'She's at home with the kids.'

A QUESTION OF SPORT

Many a little mug has grown into a big pot. Shay Brennan was also involved in a famous incident with Irish rugby legend, Moss Keane. Moss went to Greystones to play in a match to mark their jubilee season between the club side and the 1982 Triple Crown winning Ireland side. Brennan was a special guest for the game. In Greystones, they are well used to big rugby names visiting but they are not accustomed to famous football personalities like Shay. Moss was with him in the bar, having consumed a few drinks. He was a little cheesed off that Shay was getting all the attention, and everyone was asking Brennan questions, but nobody was passing any remarks on him.

Eventually Moss threw in a question: 'Who played football for Scotland and cricket for England?' There was total silence. Everyone in the bar was a sports fan and were all scratching their heads trying to figure out this riddle. Finally, they all conceded defeat. Moss walked out as soon as he provided the answer: 'Denis Law and Ian Botham!'

9

SKY HIGH

He's done great to get where he got.
Paul Merson

Many footballers' attitude to what Donald Trump calls 'the Lamestream media' is summed up in the story of God and the devil:

On the first day God created the sun, the devil countered and created sunburn. On the second day God created sex, the devil created marriage. On the third day God created a journalist. The devil deliberated throughout the fourth day and on the fifth day the devil created – another journalist. Some people say journalists are compulsive liars and that's the truth!

Broadcasting can be a hazardous experience. During Harold Macmillan's time as Prime Minister, he received a grave message about a diplomatic disaster during a Parliamentary recess. BBC radio reported the event as follows:
'These dismal tidings were delivered to the PM on the golf course where he was playing a round with Lady Dorothy.'

The words read fine in print but when spoken the sentence took on a very different connotation!

The pundit has a long and not entirely honourable tradition in sports broadcasting and journalism. It has been said that when it comes to football punditry, there are three kinds of fools – the pundits themselves, the newspaper editors and TV producers who hire them and, above all, the people who read or listen to them.

Despite all the incredible advances in technology, television is not everything. Most people, given the chance, prefer to 'be there'. From its earliest days, sport was a great spectator attraction. The great Roman architects laid out their stadia not just for the Russell Crowes and Charlton Hestons of their time as gladiators and chariot-racers to showcase their talents but to create 'atmosphere'. Sport is so popular now that only a tiny fraction of fans can get tickets to attend cup finals or internationals. Hence the importance of television, it is now the medium through which the vast majority of people watch their favourite sports. Indeed, some sports like snooker owe their popularity almost entirely to television exposure. New satellite technology brings even more opportunities.

SCREEN TIME

George Bernard Shaw observed that while men will trifle with business and politics, they will never trifle with their games as these are what brings truth home to them.

From the earliest times there were people who reported on sporting events. In *The Iliad*, Homer recorded in considerable detail the games organised at the funeral of Patroclus. The attraction of sport is that it provides drama, tension, excitement, winners and losers, pain, laughter and sometimes even tragedy. It is uncertain, often to the very finish (remember the 1999 Champions League final), and it is intensely human. It makes headlines, it provides a good read, it makes great pictures.

Television creates heroes and, as some former players have discovered, anti-heroes! Muhammad Ali was the first true world star of the TV age. Paul Gascoigne's fame soared after the 1990 World Cup not because of his skills but because he struck an emotional chord in the massive worldwide TV audience for shedding tears on the pitch when it looked as if a yellow card from the referee might rule him out of the World Cup final. Within months he was endorsing a wide range of products, many outside football – board games, deodorants, jewellery, calendars, school lunch boxes, to name just a handful. He also had a hit record even though he doesn't have the best voice. Mind you, that's not a unique achievement!

Even losers can find temporary fame and sometimes fortune through the universal appeal of sport, as the perennial loser British ski jumper Eddie 'the Eagle' Edwards demonstrated. Sports stars have been used to endorse products since 1947, when the English cricketer Denis Compton, a kind of James Bond figure, became the face of Brylcreem. His face and slicked-down hair became one of the best-known pictures in Britain, used in magazines and on billboards all over the country.

Every rose has its thorns. Television has created its own problems for sport. Back in 1983 Sir Dennis Follows, chairman of the British Olympic Association, observed: 'We have now reached a stage where sport at top level has become almost completely show business with everything that one associates with showbiz; the cult of the individual, high salaries, the desire to present a game as a spectacle – with more money, less sportsmanship, more emphasis on winning. All this has come through television.' The following year Jack Nicklaus observed: 'Television controls the game of golf. It's a matter of the tail wagging the dog.'

Sport is vicarious living. It is tense, immediate, glamorous.

Television generally pays large sums of money to bring the drama and entertainment of the major sports events into our homes. Sport is so popular with television companies because they are acutely aware that nothing stops the world in its tracks more effectively. In relative terms, compared with many other forms of entertainment such as film, it is cheap. Sport is important to television companies because it generates a large viewing audience. As such it is a powerful weapon in the ratings war. An example serves to illustrate.

It was not until 1964 that the BBC initiated what was to become the hallmark of British football coverage for an entire generation – recorded highlights on *Match of the Day*. ITV was quick to respond and initiated *The Big Match* on Sunday afternoons, featuring recorded highlights of one of the previous day's top games. For the first time, British viewers were given the benefit of expert analysis to complement the action. The BBC had the advantage of having no commercial breaks. To give them an advantage over the Beeb, ITV invested £60,000 in a slow-motion machine, which was a massive sum in the 1960s.

By the World Cup of 1970, when national interest was high and England's chances of retaining the trophy supposedly even higher, ITV boldly announced it has discovered 'the formula'. A panel of provocative experts would enliven half-times and post-match discussions through a combination of informed comment, passionate debate and full-scale abuse. Malcolm Allison, Bob McNab, Pat Crerand and Derek Dougan, 'the two goodies and the two baddies', sought to establish ITV's credentials as a legitimate alternative to the BBC in bringing football to the television audience. The science, using the term loosely, of football punditry was born.

PARALYSIS BY ANALYSIS
From the outset, television pundits have a history of extending the boundaries of the English language. As a number of them

have struggled to keep their brain and tongue in tune they have also spawned an explosion of 'Colemanballs'. The word 'Colemanballs' comes from David Coleman, a broadcaster whose name is synonymous with sporting howlers. The BBC commentator is remembered for a series of gaffes of which the following are but a tiny sample:

'This man could be a dark horse.'

'The late start is due to the time.'

'He's thirty-one this year; last year he was thirty.'

'The pace of this match is really accelerating. By which I mean it is getting faster all the time.'

'One of the great unknown champions because very little is known about him.'

'Some names to look forward to – perhaps in the future.'

'Her time was four minutes thirteen seconds, which she is capable of.'

'This could be a repeat of what will happen at the European Games, next week.'

'This race is all about racing.'

'David Bedford is the athlete of all-time in the 1970s.'

'It doesn't mean anything, but what it does mean is that Abde Bile is very relaxed.'

And ...

'There is Brendan Foster, by himself, with 20,000 people.'

A NO BRAINER

A Manchester United fan finds out that he has a brain tumour, and it's inoperable – in fact, it's so large, they have to do a brain transplant. His doctor gives him a choice of available brains – there's a jar of rocket scientist brains for £100 an ounce, a jar of dentist's brains for £150 an ounce and a jar of football pundit brains for £100,000 an ounce.

The outraged fan said, 'This is a rip off – how come the football pundits' brains are so damned expensive?'

The doctor replies, 'Do you know how many football pundits it takes to get an ounce of brains?'

OPINIONS WORTH HAVING

In recent years, however, former Manchester United captain Gary Neville has perhaps eclipsed his fame on the playing fields with his brilliance as a pundit on Sky Sports. Of course, his stellar career at United, which saw him winning eight Premier League titles and stack up 602 appearances in his time at the club from 1991 to 2011, gives him great credibility when talking about football. He does not meet Kenneth Tynan's definition, 'A critic is a man who knows the way but can't drive the car.' He does so without fear.

Hence Jürgen Klopp's comment: 'The biggest lesson I learned during the lockdown [for Covid-19] was just how opinionated Gary Neville is.' This chapter marks his outstanding service in his new playing field.

FOOT AND MOUTH

Neville's status as a top pundit is all the more impressive given the demands of the job. One of the hazards of live broadcasting is that on-air blunders cannot been edited out.

Jimmy Hill asserted that Romania's success in the 1998 World Cup group matches could be attributed partly to their players having dyed their hair blond. According to Jimmy it made it easier for them to see their passing options.

In 1996 Anna Kournikova sent men's pulses racing at the French open. Although for two weeks most of the media comment was about her, she didn't make it to the final. The final pairing was Monica Seles and Arantxa Sanchez Vicario. Former English tennis player Chris Bailey was commentating on the match for BBC and at the end the producer asked him to give a snappy soundbite to sum up the tournament. He said, 'A great Vicario win – all the talk may be of the young glamour babes coming through, but just look at the podium, there is life in the old dogs yet.'

Football commentators and pundits have created mirth and mayhem down the years when their brains and mouths were not as well connected as might have been desired. As the following collection indicates, our lives are enriched by the verbal mishaps of these mic-mincers. Here are fifty-four of the finest . . .

1. *The way he darts around the pitch, he's like an empty crisp packet in the park.*
   Tony Cascarino's description of N'Golo Kante.

2. *Messi is a smallpox – but there is no vaccine.*
   Real Valladolid director David Espinar.

3. *My mother would have run round to the shops quicker.*
   Brian Kerr on Ross Barkley.

4. *I can count on a handful of my hands how many close friends I have.*
   Clinton Morrison.

5. *Origi feigning something more serious than it's not.*
   Jim Beglin.

6. *It's one of them days when you just say, 'It's one of them days.'*
   Ian Wright.

7. *The referee was booking everyone. I thought he was filling in his Lottery numbers.*
   Ian Wright, again.

8. *Brighton came from behind against West Ham to take all three points in a 3–3 draw.*
   Georgie Bingham.

9. *It's a worry for Rangers. They've hit the brakes. They went into the winter break like a top of the range sports car and have come out like a spluttering three-wheeler.*

Chris Sutton.

10. *I think he expected the defender to absolutely fly over like an . . . like an emergency defending situation.*
    Trevor Sinclair gets stuck for words.

11. *The Karim rises to the top. Cooler than a polar bear's backside. Cool as a greyhound's nose.*
    Ray Houghton is very taken by Karim Benzema's winner in the Madrid derby.

12. *Pep might be thinking he's took City as far as he can throw them.*
    Darren Gough.

13. *If I didn't want to be under pressure, I would have worked at the Post Office.*
    Maurizio Sarri.

14. *It's like when I met my wife – I saw her and thought, 'Okay, I'll marry her'. And it was like that with the club. It felt right from the first moment.*
    Jürgen Klopp.

15. *Understand your 'tone-alogy' when you say, 'We might finish in the top six.'*
    Stuart Pearce to a caller.

16. *Oreo.*
    Danny Murphy struggles with the name of the Tottenham full-back, Serge Aurier. (Was he taking the biscuit?)

17. *We're giving away a listener.*
    Jim White on Talksport (This must be the most interesting competition ever.)

18. *If you cut Phil Thompson in half, he will bleed red.*
    Caller to Talksport.

19. *The saying is, 'You don't fix something if it isn't broken.'*
    Paul Merson. (Merse fits Sally Nugent's verdict on Lewis Hamilton: 'He's had his ups and downs, but it's been consistent.')

20. *He is the Greta Thunberg of German football.*
    Former Bayern Munich star Mehmet Scholl is not impressed
    by current star Joshua Kimmich's tendency to talk too much.
    (Kimmich's comments include such 'interesting' gems as, 'Hang
    the Greens while there still are trees.' More confusing was his
    observation, 'I'd never put a blind man at an advertising pillar and
    tell him that this is the wall he needs to walk down to get home.')

21. *Julian Dicks is everywhere. It's like they've got eleven Dicks on the field.*
    Metro Radio Sports Commentator.

22. *The Dutch look like a huge jar of marmalade.*
    Barry Davies.

23. *Lukic saved with his foot which is all part of the goalkeeper's arm.*
    Barry Davies, again.

24. *But the ball was going all the way, right away, eventually.*
    Archie McPherson.

25. *Last week's match was a real game of cat and dog.*
    John Aldridge.

26. *Ian Rush unleashed his left foot and it hit the back of the net.*
    Mike England.

27. *To be honest, I can't remember him scoring a goal that wasn't
    memorable.*
    The BBC Five Live school of punditry, no. 1.

28. *Manchester City's Shaun Wright-Phillips, who is of course Ian
    Wright's son. He doesn't look anything like him, though. –*
    The BBC Five Live school of punditry, no. 2. Ian Wright's son is
    adopted.

29. *Sporting Lisbon in their green and white hoops, looking like a team
    of zebras.*
    Peter Jones.

30. *Hodge scored for Forest after only twenty-two seconds, totally
    against the run of play.*
    Peter Lorenzo.

31. *And now for the goals from Carrow Road, where the game ended 0–0.*
Elton Welsby.

32. *Chesterfield 1, Chester 1. Another score draw there in that local derby.*
Desmond Lynam.

33. *With the very last kick of the game, Bobby McDonald scored with a header.*
Alan Parry.

34. *He will probably wake up after having sleepless nights thinking about that one.*
Alan Parry.

35. *If there's a goal now, I'll eat my hat!*
BBC radio commentator Tommy Woodroffe during the 1938 FA Cup final. There was and he did!

36. *It looks like something you'd reject for the kitchen curtains.*
Brian Moore on Arsenal's away strip in 1993.

37. *After a goalless first half, the score at half-time is 0–0.*
Brian Moore.

38. *Wayne Clarke, one of the famous Clarke family, and he's one of them, of course.*
Brian Moore, again.

39. Caller: *Chelsea are building an English side and it wouldn't happen if Frank Lampard wasn't there.* Presenter: *What do you mean an English side? Willian's not English is he?* Caller: *Oh, all right, Great Britain.* (Willian is from Brazil.)

40. *If you had a linesman on each side of the pitch, in both halves you'd have nearly four.*
Robbie Earle.

41. *Obviously for Scunthorpe it would be a nice scalp to put Wimbledon on their bottoms.*
Dave Bassett.

42. *He went down like a sack of potatoes, then made a meal of it.*
Trevor Brooking.

43. *I felt a lump in my mouth as the ball went in.*
Terry Venables.

44. *Here's Brian Flynn. His official height is five feet five and he doesn't look much taller than that.*
Alan Green.

45. *Set pieces are always important, especially corners and free kicks.*
Ian Bright.

46. *The shot brought back memories of Peter Lorimer . . . even though he's not dead yet.*
Sky Sports commentator Chris Kamara.

47. *Burton just couldn't lose tonight. Except that they did.*
Ian Wright, once more.

48. *It was just their presence – they didn't have any.*
Gerry Taggart on Lawrie McMenemy.

49. *The Koreans were quicker in terms of speed.*
Mark Lawrenson.

50. *He [Mark Lawrenson] makes even the most thrilling game sound like a coroner's inquest.*
Fan in *The London Times*.

51. *I always used to put my right boot on first, and then obviously my right sock.*
Barry Venison reveals hidden (very hidden) depths.

52. *Tempo – now there's a big word.*
Barry Venison, ever the linguist.

53. *He hasn't made any saves you wouldn't have expected him not to take.*
Liam Brady goes for a triple negative.

54. Today FM's Matt Cooper: *Is there any chance that Charlton could beat Chelsea?* Tony Cascarino: *In a word, I don't think so.*

BETTER CALL SOL?

Post-match interviews can be hazardous. After his Southend United side had lost 4–0 to Peterborough in League One their manager Sol Campbell was interviewed on Sky Sports.

Campbell was waxing lyrical: I got to say, the young lads – for quite a few of them it was their first game for Southampton – they played really well ...

Presenter: 'Can I stop you? Do you want to do it again?'

Sol: 'Why?'

Presenter: 'Because your team's Southend.'

Sol: 'Oh ...'

BEHIND THE TIMES?

Sometimes pundits can be a little out of step. In January 2020, on the transfer deadline day, Jamie Redknapp was a guest on a Sky Sports marathon programme with Harry Kewell. As they discussed Emre Can's move to Borussia Dortmund, Jamie asked Harry if he played with Can at Liverpool, thus showing himself to be a little out of touch. Kewell left Liverpool in 2008 (when Can, incidentally, was just fourteen years old). Can joined in 2014.

EL TEL

Good preparation, though, can help a football pundit stick away a metaphorical loose ball with the aplomb he once reserved for the real thing.

Witness Terry Venables's gem: 'The 'Ungarians 'ave been goulashed.'

UNDERSTANDING

The late Irish writer Brendan Behan claimed: 'Critics are like eunuchs in a harem: they know how it's done. They've seen it done every day, but they're unable to do it themselves.'

That may be true in the theatre, but not so in sport. Pundits come in all shapes and styles. There's the George Hook school: 'Ireland are a bit like Pamela Anderson: when they're good they're great, when they're bad they're awful.'

There's the unique Jason McAteer. When asked what positives Giovanni Trapattoni would take from Ireland's 1–1 draw with the Czech Republic, the indomitable Trigger replied: 'The major positive is this winning mentality.'

There's the stating-the-bleeding-obvious-tradition, personified by Greg Rusedski: 'In what other sport do you play six hours of tennis.'

Then there's the special case of the late Ray Wilkins: 'Fàbregas literally carries ten yards of space around in his shorts.'

Pundits have to carefully negotiate the landmines along the way; one such landmine is speaking too soon. Just after Niall Quinn, assuming that the 2011/12 league title was on its way to Old Trafford, stated, 'This is probably Alex Ferguson's greatest achievement', Manchester City scored two late, late goals against QPR to claim the title.

Forty-two per cent of people know that all statistics are made up by Homer Simpson. And these statistics are a limited weapon in the pundit's arsenal. David Letterman stated, 'Fifty per cent of the recent winners at Augusta have been left-handed.'

Bubba Watson: 'Yeah, but fifty per cent are right-handed, too.'

Live television is like a trapeze act without a net below. That reminds me of the story of the newsreader who was very laid-back and came in to read the news at a minute to nine each night. One evening he was finishing the news when he came to the weather. He looked at the page and it was blank. The newsreader, being the true professional that he was, said: 'And the weather will continue for the next twenty-four hours.'

Television pundits have to think on their feet. In this competitive television environment, sports personalities are cultivated carefully and selectively by television moguls. Ex-jockeys have not always comfortably made the transition to television personality. In an effort to boost its ratings for the Breeders Cup, NBC, amidst much hype, decided to get Fred Astaire's wife, ex-jockey Robyn Smith to do interviews on horseback. She looked great galloping beside the breathless, mud-splattered winning jockeys. The sound effects were marvellous. The only fly in the ointment was that Robyn had virtually no idea what questions to ask.

I know there is a fine line, though. I certainly don't want us to go down the route of *Vanity Fair* when they interviewed Arsenal's Freddie Ljungberg and asked him first if he 'waxed his bottom' and then, 'Who has the biggest "lunchbox" in the Arsenal dressing room?'

Post-match interviews are fraught with pitfalls. Take Nicolas Colsaerts' response to a request from *Sky Sports* to sum up his Ryder Cup experiences: 'There are no tools you can use out there. You've just got to go with what you have in your pants.'

Then there was Tracy Piggott's infamous interview with horse trainer Peter Casey after Flemenstar won in Leopardstown in January 2012. He was happy: 'I can't believe it, I can't believe it. I'll have f**king sex tonight and everything.'

NEW DIMENSION

Football fans spent years listening to questions and answers on ITV such as:

Dickie Davis: 'What's he going to be telling his team at half-time, Denis?'

Denis Law: 'He'll be telling them that there are forty-five minutes left to play.'

The BBC equivalent is:

John Motson: 'Well, Trevor, what does this substitution mean tactically?'

Trevor Brooking: 'Well, Barnes, has come off and Rocastle has come on.'

THE BOY DONE

It is not surprising that during the 1986 World Cup there was a letter to the *Guardian* on Mike Channon and Emlyn Hughes's performances as World Cup pundits, which made a plea from the heart about the lack of substance in their analysis:

'Conjugate the verb "done great": I done great. He done great. We done great. They done great. The boy Lineker done great.'

It is difficult to believe that some people got well paid to utter banalities like that. The Sky Sports audience, though, will not accept such inanities.

POETRY AND PUNDITRY

Gary Neville is so admired as a pundit because fans want people to analyse and give their honest opinion. Over a period of time, fans have come to accept and trust him. If he says somebody played well or played badly, generally they know he means it. If he continuously pandered to the public, people would soon see through him.

The job of a pundit, to steal shamelessly from Robert Frost, is to provide what is demanded of a good poem, which isn't necessarily something that offers great clarity but rather something that does provide 'a momentary stay against confusion'. Neville is a good analyst because he reacts to the game rather than impose a kind of excitement on it. People watching football on some channels find it dishonest when they have, let's say, Hull City versus Bristol Rovers playing a dull 0–0 draw and some pundits will use language like 'thrilling encounter'. That does not serve the audience – and ultimately an analyst's job is serve the viewer.

The ingredients of a successful pundit are an in-depth

knowledge of the sport, a love for the game that knows no limits and an unfailing ability to convey the flow of a match to both the cognoscenti and those at the opposite end of the spectrum of sporting knowledge. To quote Rudyard Kipling, they must find a very particular balance:

'If you can talk with crowds and keep your virtue,
Or walk with kings – nor lose the common touch ...'

That Mr Kipling writes exceedingly good poems!

Successful pundits also need a calm authority, because on live television when things are not going to plan you can't make a drama out of a crisis.

As an analyst, Gary Neville's job is also to pull no punches when it comes to dealing with the issues of the day. His role affords him the platform to be a thorn in the side of those in authority. He was a player for many years. He sees where the deficiencies are. He sees where the cracks are now. Unless they are faced up to, football will be in big danger. Officials are there to serve the game so that it can be handed on to future generations. If Neville thinks they're not doing their job, he will point it out. That doesn't always make him popular!

One of the giants of Irish rugby, who played in the 1940s golden era of Jackie Kyle, was Noel Henderson. During an international match, Henderson was being slated by the match's radio commentator. Noel's father was so outraged at the stream of insults that he threw his radio out of the window! With the pit of despair that can be social media, pundits are subjected to even more intense criticism today.

Neville is phlegmatic about that, understanding that in the words of Brendan Behan: 'All publicity is good, except an obituary notice.'

PETTY MAN

In his playing days, Neville tended to see things purely through the prism of Manchester United: 'That was extremely disappointing and there can't be any excuses. Chances seemed to go into the goalkeeper's hands. Freak goals went against us and the referee was petty.'

WHEN WILL I BE FAMOUS?

One true test of fame is when the fans chant your name.

Manchester United fans celebrated the Neville brothers in this genius ditty to the tune of David Bowie's 'Rebel Rebel':

> *Neville Neville*
> *They play in defence,*
> *Neville Neville,*
> *Their future's immense,*
> *Neville Neville,*
> *Like Jacko they're bad,*
> *Neville Neville*
> *Is the name of their dad.*

WRONG SAID FRED?

As a pundit, Neville can bring surgical precision to match commentary. Take his verdict on Fred: 'I don't see a goal scorer; I don't see a defensive midfield player. I don't see a runner. I'm not quite sure what I see. Essentially, for £60 million, you'd like to see him fit into one of three categories.'

In response, one United fan came up with an intriguing suggestion to help make Fred a bigger name in football: 'Let's call him Frederick.'

RUBBING SALT INTO IT

Sir Alex Ferguson is often amused at the kind of highbrow analysis his former protégés Gary Neville and Roy Keane sometimes produce in their high-profile role as pundits – hence his love of the story of the two former United players attending a Mensa convention for people with high IQs which, naturally, had its annual convention in Manchester. Keane and Neville were the star guests at the official dinner. While dining, they discovered that their saltshaker contained pepper and their pepper-shaker was full of salt. How could they swap the contents of the bottles without spilling, using only the implements at hand?

The two United immortals debated and finally came up with an ingenious solution involving a napkin, a straw and an empty saucer. They called the waitress over to dazzle her with their brilliant plan.

'Miss,' they said, 'we couldn't help but notice that the pepper-shaker contains salt and the salt-shaker . . .'

'Oh,' the waitress interrupted. 'Sorry about that.' She unscrewed the caps off the bottles and switched them.

TESTING TIMES

On television, Neville has formed an acclaimed partnership with former Liverpool great Jamie Carragher. Manchester United fans love Neville but have little love for Carragher, as is evident in the following story.

Sky Sports decided that it should have a test for all its sport pundits. After the exam, the supervisor Haley McQueen pulled Jamie Carragher over to her desk and said, 'Jamie, I have a feeling that you have been cheating on your tests.'

'What makes you think that?' Carragher asked her.

'Well,' said the supervisor, 'I was looking over your test and the first question was, "Who is the leader of the Conservative Party?" Gary Neville, who sat next to you, put Boris Johnson and so did you.'

'Everyone knows that he is the leader of the Tories,' Carragher defended himself.

'Well, the next question was: "Who was Conservative leader

before Boris Johnson?" Neville put, "I don't know," and you put, "Me neither."'

One United fan was less subtle, 'When Carra is on the telly mice throw themselves willingly on the mouse traps.'

BAD ENGLISH

Neville and Carragher can have a testy relationship. Neville describes how he once walked out of the Sky Sports studios and he saw that Carragher and one of his friends were being assaulted by a group of Everton fans. Carragher had made an incendiary attack on the Toffees. Carragher yelled out: 'Gary, could you give me and my friend some help?'

Neville coolly replied: 'I'm always glad to help. You don't say: "Me and my friend." You say: "My friend and I."'

Then he got into his car and drove off.

A GRAVE MATTER

A bus load of football pundits, including Jamie Carragher, were driving down a country road when, all of a sudden, the bus ran off the road and crashed into a tree in an old farmer's field.

The old farmer, after seeing what happened, went over to investigate. He then proceeded to dig a hole and bury the pundits.

A few days later, the local sergeant saw the crashed bus and asked the farmer where all the pundits had gone. The old farmer, a Manchester United fan, said he had buried them. The officer then asked the old farmer, 'Were they all dead?'

The old farmer replied, 'Well, Jamie Carragher said they weren't, but you know how them pundits lie.'

CHANGES

A Manchester United supporter watching *Monday Night Football*: 'That was some programme. I'd only have changed one thing.'

His wife: 'What's that?'

'The channel.'

TWIN PROBLEMS

Another United fan on social media where 'the usual suspects' can sometimes morph into 'the usual cesspits' identified a twofold issue: 'We have the problem of spam on the internet and the problem of Carragher on TV.'

WHAT'S ON THE MENU?

When you appear on a high-profile television programme you are not nearly as pampered as people expect. On his first day in the job with Sky Sports, Gary Neville went to the Sky Sports canteen for lunch and asked, 'What are my choices?'

The man behind the counter replied, 'Yes or no.'

THE LAST WORD

Neville is philosophical about his role: 'How do I sum up my life as analyst? I can only quote the wise words of David Brent, star of *The Office*: "Accept that some days you are the pigeon, and some days you are the statue."'

SPEED OF THOUGHT

Some players resort to unorthodox methods to put off an opponent. In the 1974 FA Cup final, Liverpool's Phil Thompson did not give Newcastle star forward Malcolm MacDonald a kick of the ball. Afterwards MacDonald discovered that Thompson could not stand the smell of garlic. Subsequently MacDonald would eat cloves of garlic before every match against Liverpool, and breathe on Thompson the moment he got near.

Sky Sports pundits allegedly bring such tactics on to the fairways. Jamie Carragher and Gary Neville were out playing golf, and they decided to put some competition into the game by putting some serious money on the round – one pound.

With such a sum at stake, both of them were concentrating fiercely and were perfectly matched for the first nine holes. On the tenth, though, Neville drove into the rough and couldn't find his ball. He called Jamie over to help and the pair of them searched around. Finally, desperate to avoid the four-stroke penalty for a lost ball, Neville popped a new ball out of his pocket when Jamie wasn't looking.

'Jamie, I've found the ball,' Neville said.

'You filthy, cheating swine!' exploded Jamie. 'I never thought that any friend of mine would stoop so low as to cheat in a game that had money on it.'

'I'm not cheating!' Gary protested, 'I've found my ball, and I'll play it where it lies.'

'That's not your ball,' snarled Jamie. 'I've been standing on your ball for the last five minutes.'

AWOL

Carragher extracted some retribution in 2020 after Liverpool ended a thirty-year drought to win the Premier League. The football world was quick off the blocks to pay tribute to Liverpool's triumph with one noticeable exception ... Gary Neville. Carragher launched a 'Where's Gary?' campaign on social media.

For his part, Ole Gunnar Solskjaer did extend his congratulations to Liverpool. Every rose has its thorns. But he had a sting in the tale when he expressed the wish that United would not have to wait as many years again to win their next title.

EXTRA TIME

Sport has the capacity to shock. A new bride took her husband by surprise on their wedding night when she said, 'I have a confession to make. I used to be a hooker.'

'I see,' replied her husband. 'And what was that like?'

'Great. My name was Tom and I was a hooker for Manchester Rugby Club. We won loads of games.'

GOOD HOUSEKEEPING

Jamie Carragher was happy. After years losing verbal battles on Sky Sports to Gary Neville, he finally won an argument. It was with his wife about the way the new furniture was to be arranged in the family home.

But then, disaster.

When he got back home late one night after *Monday Night Football,* he could not believe his eyes.

The tables were turned.

MR BRIGHTSIDE

To give due credit to Carragher he has produced one memorable line: 'Manchester United have given us some of the biggest pin-ups in football . . . and . . . Steve Bruce.'

THE NUMBERS GAME

While Gary Neville has got many plaudits there have been some stinging comments. A case in point was that of RTÉ commentator Darragh Maloney: 'Paul Scholes with four players in front of him – five if you count Gary Neville.'

I, KEANO

As a player with Manchester United and as manager of Sunderland, Roy Keane was never known to mince his words. Keane showed his acid tongue when he mused on Sunderland's efforts to get Kenwyne Jones back from the Caribbean: 'We have to help with the travel arrangements. If we let them [the Trinidad and Tobago Football Association], I think he'd be on a ferry.'

A TALL STORY

Keane's ability to tell it as it is was also shown when he signed Andy Reid for Sunderland: 'He's not six foot four; I don't think he ever will be.'

THE WORKING LIFE

Reporter: 'Have you ever thought of a career in the media?'

Roy Keane: 'No, no. I want a proper job.'

SHARPENING THE TONGUE

Keane also has a talent for damning with faint praise. Keane's former teammates at Manchester United are all too aware of his sharp tongue from biting observations like: 'It was an excellent cross by Gary [Neville], I was surprised by the quality of it.'

Another time Gary Neville sent around a text message to his friends which said, 'This is Gary Neville's new mobile number.'

A few minutes later, his phone beeped with a reply from Keane stating, 'So what.'

Neville confirmed: 'That was Roy's sense of humour.'

O BROTHER, WHERE ART THOU?

Relatively speaking, Roy Keane was kinder to Gary than to his brother: 'Do I stay in touch with Phil? I wasn't that friendly with him. I went to his wedding. That was enough.'

SAINTS ALIVE

Neville will always have great respect for Alex Ferguson, but Geoff Shreeves once lifted Nev onto Fergie's high horse: 'What was he like in the sanctimony of the dressing room?'

POSH BOY

Some United fans feel that Nev has become more posh since he became a TV star. When his 'frenemy' Jamie Carragher was asked for his opinion on Nev's poshness he answered, 'You'd have to ask his new butler.'

POWERS OF PERCEPTION

In the pre-Christmas Manchester Derby in 2019 Gary was thrilled at half-time as United led 2–0: 'Rampant! Relentless! Absolutely scintillating!' For once Neville was speechless, though, at the level of insight of his fellow pundit Micah Richards. 'If it stays the way it is, United will win the game.'

Mind you, Nev has had some gaffes of his own, as the following selection shows:

'We've only seen three of these goals in twenty years – that's what makes it unique.'

'No way that's handball. His body's connected to his midriff.'

'It's the greatest moment of your life. People will mention kids, but everyone has kids. Not everyone has a Premier League title.'

NO SEXUAL HEALING

Jamie Carragher gloated over Liverpool's Premier League title in 2020 and chose to damn Gary Neville while praising Liverpool's Trent Alexander-Arnold's brilliance as a right full-back. 'He has made it sexy again,' he declared, 'shall we say, after Gary Neville made it very unsexy.'

HAIR-IFFIC

Jamie Carragher was deeply troubled by the news of another lockdown: 'When Boris said we were in isolation, my first fear was for Gary Neville's wife. How is she gonna cope with him?'

Meanwhile Peter Crouch was more concerned about the fact that he would not have access to a barber: 'In a couple of months I expect to emerge looking like Michael Bolton.'

SO THIS IS CHRISTMAS

Sky Sports' special treat for their viewers on Christmas Day 2020 was a montage of Roy Keane's greatest moments of the year as a pundit. Among the many was a debate he had with Gary Neville.

Keano: 'When I played for United I had no interest in squad rotation. I wanted to play in every game because I thought I could influence the match. I thought squad rotation was for just players like Gary.'

Neville: 'I'll have you know I was a stalwart of the club.'

A pregnant pause ensued.

Keane looked at his former teammate with a stare that would frighten children. Then he said, 'That's because you were the only right-back at the club, Gary.'

DON'T LOOK BACK IN ANGER

It was disrespect at a level that had not been seen since Noel Gallagher signed Neville's guitar with the message:

How many England caps did you deserve? Fu**kin' none!
Lotsa love, Noel.

SOME MIGHT SAY

Nev, though, should not feel aggrieved by Keane's lack of respect. Keane has long had a turbulent relationship with Mick McCarthy. It began in 1992.

Back then Keano was a young midfielder who had quickly established himself at Nottingham Forest. Jack Charlton called him into the Ireland squad. Mick McCarthy was the squad's leader and captain. Ireland went to play in a tournament and went drinking for a day and a half afterwards. Some of them were late getting back to the bus, and Jack had already gone to the airport, leaving Mick in charge. Big Mick took his duties seriously. Seeing that

Keano was late for the bus, Mick shook his head and reprimanded him: 'First trip. Disgrace.'

But Keano immediately responded with a killer comeback: 'First touch. Disgrace.'

A STORM IN A TEACUP?

In March 2021 Gary Neville was getting greedy as United prepared to face Milan in the Europa League: 'United need to try and win a trophy and one of the cups as well.'

BAD NEIGHBOURS

Rivalry is at the heart of sport. Manchester United's rivalry with Liverpool is among the most high profile of the species. Gary Neville retains a deep antipathy for Liverpool, as was evident when he couldn't help but poke fun in his Sky role at Jamie Carragher after he moaned in disappointment at an Alisson mistake during their clash in 2021.

Liverpool were very much in the match with Manchester City at Anfield and drawing 1–1 before a series of howlers from the Liverpool shot-stopper handed the away side the points. Alisson misplaced a pass to Phil Foden, who quickly set-up İlkay Gündoğan to score before moments later misplacing another pass to Foden, who assisted Raheem Sterling to net. Liverpool lost 4–1.

After Alisson's initial mistake, Carragher let out a loud sigh in disappointment. Neville picked up on the noise and said to Carragher: 'I'll make that my ring tone!'

We can all agree with Steve Harmison that United's rivalry with Liverpool 'enhances the Premier League rather than dehances it'.

HARD TIMES

After the horror show of 2020 – not the pandemic but Liverpool winning the Premier League for the first time in thirty years – 2021 was a much better year for Neville. There is no English language equivalent to 'schadenfreude', the glee taken in the misfortune of others. But, still, Neville understands the concept well. There were three things to be enjoyed:

1. The unravelling of Liverpool's title season – their *Kloppitulation*.
2. Their unexpected run of poor home form – their *Kopitulation*.
3. After a series of howlers their goalkeeper Alisson Becker's transformation from the best keeper in the world to *Alisson Blunderland* or *Comical Ali*.

LOSING ITS MARKLE
The Oprah Winfrey interview with Meghan Markle and Harry caused huge media fanfare. Gary Neville, though, saw the ensuing controversy from a different angle. He asked:

Q: What's the difference between Harry and Jürgen Klopp?

A: Harry is much more likely to get his title back.

LOST IN TRANSLATION
However, the classic Neville putdown came when he was interviewed on Sky Sports after Thiago Silva was transferred to the Merseysiders from Bayern Munich.

Martin Tyler: 'His dad won the World Cup with Brazil, Thiago was born in Italy but represents Spain because he grew up there, and he speaks and understands English perfectly.'

Gary Neville: 'That will be no use to him where he's going.'

10

THE END OF DAYS

I've always said there's a place for the press
but they haven't dug it yet.

Tommy Docherty

The role of the media is variously to inform, educate, enlighten and entertain.

Sometimes the football journalists manage all four at once, notably *The Sunday Times'* headline announcing the replay date after Arsenal and Sheffield Wednesday drew in the 1993 FA Cup final:

Arsenal, Wednesday, Thursday.

1. LET ME ENTERTAIN YOU

Often the media are at their most entertaining when they are putting the boot in, such as *The Sun's* malicious verdict on the Intertoto Cup:

The InterTwobob Cup.

2. EVERY DAY IS A SCHOOL DAY

From time to time the print media betray their ignorance of their beautiful game:

Commodore already sponsors Tessa Sanderson, Chelsea FC and a football team, Bayern Munich.

3. THE ENLIGHTENED ONE

While the media may aim for enlightenment, they sometimes create confusion.

John Inverdale: 'What do you think the score will be?'

Caller to Five Live: 'Nil–all draw.'

'So, who'll score for Everton then?'

SEAMAN LOGIC

Interviewer: 'What did you do after the Romanian defeat?'

David Seaman: 'We discussed everything, the things that went wrong and those that went right. Then we studied the videos very carefully.'

Interviewer: 'Why do you think you lost, then?'

Seaman: 'Well, it were just one of those things.'

THE STAR OF DAVID

England's goalkeeper David James was interviewed by *FHM* magazine. The most revealing part of the interview unfolded as follows.

Interviewer: 'French author Albert Camus, a fellow goalkeeper, once wrote, "One sentence will suffice for the modern man: he fornicated and read the papers."'

'Doesn't that describe modern football? Shagging birds and then reading about it?'

James: 'No.'

Interviewer: 'No? Can't you elaborate a bit? I spent ages on that question.'

James: 'I don't read the papers.'

BUMPER STICKERS
Football pundits are cleverly disguised as responsible adults.
FOOTBALL PUNDITS & DIAPERS BOTH NEED TO BE
CHANGED OFTEN AND FOR THE SAME REASON.

EYESORE
The world of the football commentator is a very fast moving one, as is evident in Peter Jones's comment: 'It really needed the blink of an eyelid, otherwise you would have missed it.'

APOCALYPSE
It may depress you to imagine what will happen when the world ends. You may be interested to know that the media has already contingency plans in place for that eventuality and in fact most top print outlets have their headlines ready:

- *USA Today*: We're Dead.
- *The Wall Street Journal*: Dow Jones Plummets as World Ends.
- *National Enquirer*: OJ and Nicole, Together Again.
- *Microsoft Systems Journal*: Apple Loses Market Share.
- *Victoria's Secret Catalogue*: Our Final Sale.
- *Wired*: The Last New Thing.
- *Rolling Stone*: The Grateful Dead Reunion Tour.
- *Readers Digest*: BYE.
- *Discover Magazine*: How will the extinction of all life as we know it affect the way we view the cosmos?
- *Lady's Home Journal*: Lose 10 lbs by Judgement Day with our new 'Armageddon' diet!
- *America Online*: System temporarily down. Try calling back in fifteen minutes.

- *Inc. magazine*: Ten ways you can profit from the apocalypse.
- *TIME magazine*: Renew your subscription for eternity.
- *Sports Illustrated*: Game Over.
- *Financial Times*: Manchester United the most successful club in history.
- *The Sunday Times*: Wenger claims Arsenal can still win the League.

11

PLAYING FOR FUN AND LOADS OF MONEY

Glenn Hoddle hasn't been the Hoddle we know.
Neither has Bryan Robson.

Gary Newbon

It is a fact universally acknowledged that there are two kinds of players: those who play for Manchester United and those who want to play for Manchester United. Mind you, it may be that this view is not shared widely beyond the confines of Old Trafford.

Sometimes players have great expectations. Harry Redknapp recalled the acquisition of Jermaine Defoe: 'I signed a player once, a fantastic player. We did the deal and he wanted a goal bonus. I said what do you think we are paying you £50,000 a week for? To miss them?'

Other players, such as former Arsenal midfielder David Bentley, try to keep abreast of things: 'Look at the way people look up to Jodie Marsh and Jordan. But what are they actually famous for? Well, apart from the obvious.'

Some former players have a keen sense of nuance, like the former Newcastle player Warren Barton: 'Man United's defensive record is second to none. Apart from Liverpool's that is.'

Clubs do not invest small – or big – fortunes on players for the sharpness of their intellect or their verbal dexterity. It is probably just as well, as this chapter illustrates. Often it seems that players are not really tuned in to their environment. Think of Chelsea's Wayne Bridge after the 2007 Carling Cup final win over Arsenal: *The important thing was that we got the three points.*

Other times, a footballer can be the master of the obvious. Consider Dave Beasant's comment that: *If you make the right decision, it's normally going to be the correct one.*

DEDICATION

Paul Scholes was renowned for his dedication to, as much as his achievements in, the game. The story goes that when Bill Clinton was president and wanted to promote the game in the United States, his first choice to spearhead the campaign was Scholes. Clinton flew over to Manchester and brought him back across the Atlantic on Air Force One. It was shortly after the Monica Lewinsky scandal broke. After they took off from Manchester an air hostess came over to Scholesie and Bill, and asked them if they would like a drink.

Bill replied, 'I'll have a scotch on the rocks.'

She immediately got him his drink. Then she turned to Scholes and asked him if he would like a drink.

Scholes replied, 'I'd sooner be ravaged by a loose woman than have a drink pass my lips.'

Straight away Bill handed back his drink and said, 'I didn't know there was a choice.'

BITCHERY

Some sports personalities have a high opinion of themselves and have a fatal attraction for the spotlight. A case in point is Sol Campbell talking about the arrival of . . . himself, 'Macclesfield fans will probably say, "What's going on here?" You've got an international footballer who has been one of the best footballers in the world coming to your club.'

Paul Pogba's agent Mino Raiola hit back at Paul Scholes after he criticised Pogba – again, 'Some people need to talk for fear of being forgotten. Paul Scholes wouldn't recognise a leader if he was in front of Sir Winston Churchill.'

TRY NOT A LITTLE TENDERNESS

Love for Steven Gerrard continues unabated among Liverpool fans, despite the fact that he is the Rangers manager. Such is the love for the legend of the Kop that a campaign began in February 2020 to get him to sign 'a five-day contract' so that he could finally win that league medal that had eluded him during his distinguished playing career. As the campaign gathered momentum, the feasibility of the idea was floated with Peter Moore, the club's chief executive. He chose to deal with the question in a roundabout away.

'Look, we all love Stevie G, but I keep seeing "bring him in on a five-day contract so he can win a medal". The question I ask you is: which player do you want to cut from the squad to make that happen?

'And if you haven't noticed, he's the employee of a different football club at the same time as well. Thirdly, you can't add a player to a squad once it's locked. Other than that, it's really possible.'

However, putdowns are also part of the culture of sport. Peter Ustinov remarked once of Pavarotti, 'Luciano is difficult to pass at the net in tennis – even when he is not playing.'

A TOWN CALLED MALICE

Tony Mowbray brought a no-nonsense style to management. He told his former Celtic teammate John Hartson: 'You are the only striker I know who puts on weight during a game.'

Early in 2020 the world was getting carried away with the rising star Erling Haaland son of Alf-Inge Haaland and former heptathlete Gry Marita. Graeme Souness, however, put the boot into his father: 'His mother must have been a good player because his dad was a plodder.'

Against this background, it is nice when we hear players compliment each other. A case in point was Martin Braithwaite who was as excited by getting a hug from Lionel Messi as he was about making his Barcelona debut: 'I will not wash my clothes after receiving his hugs.'

In 2018, at the end of Martin O'Neill's time as Irish football manager, a fan remarked with real feeling: 'Warning: if you receive an email with the subject line "Two free tickets for the next Republic of Ireland home game" DON'T OPEN IT. It contains two free tickets for the next Republic of Ireland home game.'

One of the sports stories of 2019 was the news that the Leeds United manager Marcelo Bielsa sent people to spy on upcoming opponents. 'Spygate' provoked some noteworthy responses. First there was a bizarre interview on Sky Sports News.

Peter Shilton: 'He's Italian.'

Jim White: 'No, he's Argentinian.'

Shilton: 'Oh, is he?'

White: 'Yes.'

Shilton: 'Oh, it makes it even worse then, doesn't it?'

However, for a slice of cutting humour it was hard to top the exchange between Leeds' official account and Pizza Hut.

Pizza Hut: 'Hi, @LUFC, we've just seen a suspicious-looking man peering through our chef's window. Can you let us know if you're planning to put pizza on the menu in the club canteen?'

Leeds: 'Prefer @Dominos thanks! They don't take a week to deliver a tweet.'

Pizza Hut: 'Bit rich for a club that hasn't delivered since 1992.'

DAISY AND DOLLY

Steve Bruce is a Manchester United legend. In his nine years at the club (from 1987 to 1996), his central defensive partnership with Gary Pallister (affectionately known as 'Daisy and Dolly') was central to the club winning three Championships in 1993, '94 and '96. He made 414 appearances for the club, scoring fifty-one goals. In July 2019 when Steve Bruce was appointed manager of Newcastle United one fan observed, 'I would be happier if we got Fiona [the BBC presenter] Bruce.'

COMPLIMENT OR INSULT?

Other putdowns are more accidental. In February 2020 Newcastle manager Steve Bruce was asked why his £40million striker Joelinton had only scored a solitary goal. Bruce replied, 'The great strikers, the goal scorers, all they're interested in is scoring a goal – Joelinton is not like that. He is more of a team player.'

ON THE VOLLEY

Some players are injury prone. Steve Bruce has discovered that Andy Carroll takes things to a whole new level: 'There was a time just before Christmas when Andy had made a few assists and started a few games but unfortunately he volleyed a ball and hasn't been the same since.'

INTERESTING OBSERVATION

Steve Bruce has an interesting take on the beautiful game: 'Professional football is easy; you just stick in the back of the net. You can do it with your eyes folded.'

TRUE LOVE WAYS

In the immediate build-up to the 2008 European Championships, the football media gave virtually no coverage on the tournament itself as it was so preoccupied by the soap opera of whether Real Madrid could prise away Cristiano Ronaldo from Manchester United. A major factor in the equation was said to be Ronaldo's Spanish model girlfriend, Nereida Gallardo, who was lying in wait in Madrid. *The News of the World* breathlessly described her as 'a wild animal in bed'.

George Best was big admirer of Ronaldo and when asked about comparisons between them he replied: 'There have been a few players described as the "new George Best" down the years but this is the first time that it is a compliment to me.'

Although Cristiano Ronaldo smashed the world transfer record when he moved from Manchester United to Real Madrid in the summer of 2009, he also made the headlines that week because he was spotted being affectionate with famous-for-being-famous heiress Paris Hilton. Inevitably this led to jokes like 'Ronaldo in Paris' and 'Ronaldo Spends Night in Hilton'. Commenting on the relationship in the *Sunday Times*, Rod Liddle went so far as to compare it with Susan Boyle and Gordon Brown getting together. I imagine he meant that it did not really bear thinking about?

People are divided on Ronaldo's sex appeal. Modesty personified, Ronaldo said: 'It would be hypocritical of me to say I think I'm ugly.'

Former Derby manager Paul Jewell is less of a fan: 'If he was good looking, you'd say he has everything.'

The good news for prospective WAGs who might want to flutter their eyes in his direction (Ronaldo's not Paul Jewell's) is that he is nowhere near as shallow as most footballers: 'For me, it is what is inside a beautiful woman that is important.'

Splendid. This is a man who surely has taken on board

Shakespeare's insight in *The Merchant of Venice* that 'all that glitters is not gold'?

Maybe not because Ronaldo added a caveat that sets the bar very high in the physical beauty stakes: 'Although she must also be beautiful, like Angelina Jolie.'

ME TOO?

Tempora mutantur nos et mutamur in illis: Times change and we change with them.

The Me Too movement has had a huge impact on society at large but has had more difficulty penetrating all corners of the footballing world. Alan Brazil played for Ron Atkinson's Manchester United from 1984 to 1986. Since he retired, he has carved out a successful career as a pundit.

On Talksport, Laura Woods was heading to the 2019 Sportswoman of the Year Awards, buoyed by an enormous sense of pride: 'It's a massive celebration of what has been a pretty incredible year for women in sport, so many different landmarks have been reached, and so much more coverage, more...'

Alan Brazil's interjection suggested that he had not really got Laura's essential point: 'So what are you wearing tonight?'

THE LONG LIFE OF RYAN

Many players have great service to Manchester United over many years. Nobody more so than Ryan Giggs, who was with the club for twenty-three years.

Two elderly Americans were finally discovered and, against all odds, found to be alive in a disused Japanese POW camp after being captured during the Second World War.

They first asked, 'How is President Roosevelt?'

'Oh, he died a long time ago.'

'And how is Stalin?'

'Oh, he died a long time ago?'

'Please tell us that Winston Churchill is still alive and well.'

'Alas, I'm afraid he died as well.'

'Tell us, is Ryan Giggs still playing for Manchester United?'

SWEAT STUFFY

One of the reasons for the longevity of Giggs's career was his dedication. Not all players were so dedicated. Stan Collymore tells the story of Neil Ruddock while they both were playing for Liverpool. The club was managed by Roy Evans at the time and Collymore contends that discipline was lax. One day the players who were rehabilitating from injuries were told by the physio to work on the treadmill for thirty minutes. The physio left the room then and Ruddock immediately got off the treadmill. Ruddock was looking out the window and saw the physio returning almost half an hour later. He splashed his face, hair and clothes with water so that it looked like he was sweating like a pig. When he came in the physio complimented Ruddock for being a model professional!

CELEBRITY FRIDGE-OFF

United fans love drawing attention to the foibles of former Liverpool greats. Hence one comment about Neil Ruddock: 'I don't want to say he is eating too much, but he is getting a tan from opening the fridge so often.'

TRAGEDY

'It was the most impressive thing I have ever seen.' This was one Manchester United fan's verdict after perhaps the most famous goal in the club's history – Ryan Giggs's goal against Arsenal in the 1999 FA Cup semi-final. He was not talking about the goal though, but about the sight of Giggs's hairy chest after he took off his jersey in celebration.

Giggs's importance to the United side is revealed in the story of a staff member at Old Trafford who was informed by colleague: 'I have terrible news for you.'

'What?'

'I'm afraid your wife is having an affair.'

'Is that all? I thought you were going to tell me that Ryan Giggs was injured.'

TAXING

Bruno Fernandes's girlfriend was training to be an accountant. He asked her to help him with his tax returns. She declined, singing in full Meatloaf mode: 'I would do anything for love, but I won't do VAT.'

JEEPERS KEEPERS

David de Gea was considered for a number of years to be the best goalkeeper in the world. However, in recent seasons he has made a series of blunders which have proved costly for United. Inevitably this has spawned a number of jokes.

Q: Why is David de Gea like an old computer?

A: He can't save anything.

Q: What's the difference between a botanist with the flu and the Manchester United goalkeeper?

A: Only one can catch a cold.

A variation of this is the story that de Gea is thinking about setting up his own range of condoms. It has two unique selling points: extra slippery and guaranteed not to catch anything.

MARTIAL LAW

During the Covid-19 lockdown, Manchester City fans claimed Anthony Martial got into a fight with another customer in Tesco for the last toilet roll. He sustained soft tissue injuries.

OWEN-LY KIND

Although best known for his time with Liverpool, Michael Owen also lined out for Manchester United. After retiring, Owen carved out a career as a pundit. He uses implications when making criticisms: 'I'm not saying Benteke is lazy – but he could work harder.'

HANGING ON THE TELEPHONE

In 2004 the FA eventually handed down a lengthy ban to Rio Ferdinand for missing a drugs test. To digress for a moment, I heard that Vodafone are bringing out a new Rio Ferdinand phone: it has very short memory and takes four months to charge.

CAPTAIN FANTASTIC

Rio Ferdinand had an interesting take on the Manchester United captaincy: 'Gary Neville is the club captain but has been injured for the best part of a year now, so Giggsy's taken on the mantlepiece.'

THE GLOBAL GAME

I'm not a betting man – but I bet you Italy will win. Graham Taylor

Such has been the influx of foreign players into the Premiership that when none of the home countries qualified for Euro 2008 it was waspishly observed that watching the tournament would be the same as watching the Premiership. Of course, there has also been traffic in the other direction, though am I the only one to find Steve McManaman's comment in 2003 a bit odd? 'Coming to Manchester City, if anything, is more exciting than being at Real Madrid.'

In 2009 Manchester United sold Ronaldo, described by the *Daily Mail* as the 'Lily Savage' of football for his devotion to fashion, to Real Madrid for £80 million. Former English international Chris Waddle was a big fan: 'The one thing Cristiano Ronaldo has is pace, quick feet and great eye for goal.' One fan wondered if he could turn water into wine. Though, perhaps given some of his petulance, Manchester City fans claimed it would be more accurate to wonder if he could turn water into whine.

THE FRENCH CONNECTION

Some signings are transformative. Think of the immediate impact of Bruno Fernandes on Manchester United in 2020. Sir Alex Ferguson's most transformative signing was Eric Cantona in 1992.

When Cantona first came to England he struggled with the culture change. It took him a few years to figure out the English class system. You are part of the upper class when your drive to work and your name is written in the reserved car park spot; part of the middle class when your name is written on the desk and part of the working class when your name is written on a badge on your shirt.

THE ARTIST KNOWN AS PRINCE

Eric's seemingly biggest problem was to understand why Lady Diana Spencer married Prince Charles. He couldn't figure out why she married a bloke with big ears and who talks to plants. Somebody told him she thought she was getting married to Prince the singer!

DRIVEN TO SUCCESS

Cantona's most infamous moment was when he assaulted a Crystal Palace fan on 25 January 1995. In April 2020 it was voted the Premier League's 'most bonkers moment' by *Match of the Day*. When the furore was at its height United were said to have provided Cantona with a driver to insulate him from the pressure of the media. At one stage Cantona asked, 'Tell me, Fred, does your wife give you a hard time now that you are driving for me?'

'Difficult to say, Mr Cantona. Since I started driving for you, she's stopped talking to me altogether.'

DRACULA THE SEQUEL

There is no such thing as bad publicity. A few mornings after assaulting the fan, Cantona was woken up at an ungodly hour by a call from his agent. He was so excited that Eric found it difficult at first to understand what he was saying. Cantona had been offered a role in the forthcoming Hollywood blockbuster – a remake of Dracula. Eric decided to decline the offer. It was only a bit part.

EVERY FACE TELLS A STORY

Cantona was a lot more cerebral than most footballers. When he met Gazza, he talked about philosophy. Eric had no difficulty proving to Gazza that he did not exist. Asked what he thought about Gazza, Cantona is reputed to have said, 'There's nothing I'd change about him – apart from his face and body. He has the sort of face that once seen is never forgotten.'

WIZARDRY

One night, Cantona and his wife went to the local school to see a production of *The Wizard of Oz*. During the show, he heard people whispering that it had started to snow heavily, and so decided to leave before the driving became hazardous. As he dashed out of the school, the headmaster looked at him quizzically.

'We're off to flee the blizzard!' he called to him.

HAIR TODAY

Cantona was sometimes a little catty about other player's hair-styles. He was particularly scornful of a United player who turned a hairdo into a hair-don't. In fact, he had so much hair under his arms he had to wear it in a ponytail.

RUBBING PEOPLE UP THE WRONG WAY

Eric was never short of self-confidence. This did not always endear him to his managers. One of them was heard to say, 'He's down there now, letting people know how good he is playing.'

Eric wasn't always complimentary to his teammates. After a club game, a disconsolate new recruit to the team said, 'I've never played so badly before.'

Eric appeared surprised, 'You mean you've played before?'

After a game one of his colleagues said proudly, 'That was the best game I ever played.'

Eric replied, 'Well you mustn't let that discourage you.'

LANGUAGE BARRIERS

Cantona had a few memorable interviews.

Elton Welsby: '*Magnifique*, Eric.'

Cantona: 'Oh, do you speak French?'

Welsby. '*Non*.'

CATS

In the 1980s, there was no player more loved in Old Trafford than Bryan Robson. Footballers are like tea bags – you have to put them in hot water before you know how strong they were. Some players have the attitude of never going for a 50–50 ball unless they are 80–20 sure of winning it. Robson was the very opposite. He played as if his philosophy was that the lion and the lamb shall lie down together, but the lamb won't get much sleep.

To this day he is a revered guest when he attends home United games. One time he was alarmed to hear a Tannoy call saying that there had been a telephone call for him, and would he report to reception as soon as possible. He made his way anxiously there, only to be told that his neighbour had rung to say he was going away, and would he mind looking after his cat?

LEGACY

Bryan Robson liked a drink with teammates like Norman Whiteside and Paul McGrath. From time to time they chatted with the fans.

Fan: 'Is the glass half-empty or half-full?'

Bryan Robson: 'It depends on whether you're drinking or pouring.'

MODERATION

Norman Whiteside was asked if he enjoyed a quiet drink. Norman nodded his head vigorously in the assent. 'Yes. We're just off for a quiet pint. Then about twenty loud ones.'

MR BIG

A story told about the experiences of the United team on tour illustrates a more generous side of their nature. Peter Schmeichel had many admirers, including one young lady from Australia, who engaged him in idle conversation.

''Scuse me, are you the goalkeeper?' asked the attractive, blonde Aussie. The great Dane nodded his assent. She responded with an obvious comment, 'You know you are one hell of a big man.'

Again Schmeichel nodded his head.

As she barely reached his bellybutton, she gazed wistfully over his manly charms and asked, 'Are you all in proportion?'

He was forced to admit he was not.

The light died in her eyes, only to be rekindled when he replied, 'If I was in proportion, I'd be six foot ten.'

LITERARY CENTRE CIRCLES

Some sports stars are known for their clever comments. A case in point is Irish rugby legend Brian O'Driscoll who said: 'Knowledge is knowing that a tomato is a fruit. Wisdom is knowing not to put in a fruit salad.'

Canadian-born Jimmy Nicholl moved with his family to Belfast in 1957. He joined Manchester United as an apprentice straight from school in 1972 and turned professional two years later. Nicholl was capped seventy-three times for Northern Ireland, culminating in appearances at the World Cup finals in 1982 and 1986.

George Best tells a wonderful story about Jimmy Nicholl's involvement with the Irish team. In 1978 the Northern Ireland squad were making their way from their hotel to Windsor Park for a fixture against Iceland. Their manager was Billy Bingham, a very erudite man. Throughout the bus journey, Bingham was enthralled by the book he was reading and oblivious to everything that was going on around him. Eventually some officials summoned him to the top of the bus. Nicoll rushed up to see what he was reading and asked him the title of this book.

'*The Diaries of James Joyce 1930 to 1935,*' Bingham replied.

A few minutes later Nicholl tapped Bingham on the shoulder and said: 'This Joyce must have been some kid. He kept a diary up to when he was a five-year-old child!'

UNDER THE HILL

Gordon Hill's arrival from Millwall in November 1975 led to a restructuring of the United midfield. At Millwall, Hill had earned the nickname 'Merlin' for his sorcery on the wing and went on to win six caps for England. He was less assured though of his defensive duties. At United, Martin Buchan once boxed his ears during a match for his recklessness at the back.

FRENCH FLAIR

Martin Buchan caught George Best on the hop when he complimented him on his new coat: 'From its style, it looks French.'

Best's reply was: 'It is from France. It's Toulon and Toulouse!'

SHEER PLEASURE

Alan Shearer came close to signing for Alex Ferguson and Manchester United. However, Kevin Keegan went on a charm offensive and took him to Newcastle instead. Shearer was not a womaniser, unlike many football stars. In fact, two directors of Newcastle were quoted in *The News of the World* calling their star player 'Mary Poppins' and 'boring'. The Newcastle players kindly bought Shearer the video of *Mary Poppins* to mark the moment.

Shearer had an unusual approach to self-assessment, famously saying: 'One accusation you can't throw at me is that I've always done my best.'

THE DUBLIN-ER

After failing to sign Alan Shearer, Alex Ferguson instead signed Dion Dublin for £1 million. Despite playing for United and winning four caps for England, Dion did not always attract the recognition he might have expected. After Liverpool's Djibril Cissé broke his leg he said, 'A lot of people phoned to wish me a speedy recovery. I have spoken to Cantona, Thuram, Henry, Vieira. Even some people who I have not heard of before, people like Dion Dublin.'

PANCHO

Stuart 'Pancho' Pearson won fifteen caps for England as a striker and played in the 1976 and '77 FA Cup finals for Manchester United. He was honest in every sense: 'Bobby Gould thinks I'm trying to stab him in the back. In fact, I'm right behind him.'

WAYNE'S WORLD

Wayne Rooney is Manchester United's all-time leading goal scorer with 253 goals. He missed the odd chance, too. Former Arsenal manager George Graham gave his verdict on one of them: 'There's only one person who knows how he missed that and that's Wayne Rooney, and even he doesn't know.'

One of United's greatest legends Bobby Charlton tried to encourage Rooney when he joined United: 'The first time I met Wayne was as at an awards ceremony. Everyone was talking about him being a really good player but not able to communicate. So, I said to Wayne, "You probably find speaking a little bit difficult, but the more you do the better you'll get."'

Bobby's prophecy did not come true exactly as he would have wished. When Rooney was arrested for 'public intoxication and swearing' at Dulles Airport in 2019 the official report stated that he spoke in 'broken English'.

PENSION PLAN

There are many heart-breaking stories of former players who go through very hard financial times after they retire from football. One club, though, has been particularly generous to its players who are injury prone. As a result, they got involved in the pensions business. The following is the text of the latest advertisement for Manchester United Life Plan:

Need a pension? Are you worried about the future? You are not getting any younger and you have to think about your lavish lifestyle, after your career is over. Are you well past your best?

Are you looking for an easy life? Yes? Then you are eligible for the Manchester United Life Plan. Man United pay you at least £90,000 a week, there's a pointless medical. CALL NOW. There's a FREE house, luxury car and limitless golf at some of England's finest courses.

I know this sounds like something Hans Christian Andersen would write. If you think this is too good to be true just read these recommendations by some of our satisfied clients:

'When I'm no longer playing, I know my family will be financially secure.' Phil Jones.

'The generosity of the Manchester United plan is unmatched in the world of pension finance.' Luke Shaw.

'It is the best move I ever made.' Marcos Rojo.

'Despite being permanently injured, I was still eligible for the Life Plan – year after after year to play basketball in America.' Paul Pogba.

WHAT'S IN A NAME?

Nicknames are an important part of football culture. Witness Arsenal fans' description of Ray Parlour as 'the Romford Pelé'. Those same fans had more malice when they rechristened Ashley Cole as 'Cashley Cole', when he was not happy with the money he was offered at Highbury.

In fairness he is not the only player interested in money. Gareth Bale's agent Jonathan Barnett was explaining the rationale behind Bale's apparent willingness to sign for Jiangsu Suning in China in the summer of 2019: 'He wanted to create a legacy. He had a vision that he could make Chinese football great. It was to create a legacy, to be the first great player to go to China. But it wasn't to be.'

So, was that the only reason, Jonathan?

'The money was special too – it would have made him the highest paid player on Earth!'

THE BROTHER GRIM

Ashley Grimes joined United from Bohemians in March 1977 for a fee of £35,000. As a schoolboy he had an unsuccessful trial at Old Trafford. In fact, just before signing for United, he had agreed terms with Dave Sexton and QPR but Tommy Docherty stepped in at the last moment. In an unexpected twist of fate, it was Sexton who quickly had responsibility for nurturing Ashley's career at United.

In his six years at Old Trafford, Grimes clocked up over one hundred first team appearances in a variety of positions: midfield, both flanks and full-back. In certain quarters his career at United is remembered for the wrong reasons. He hit the headlines when he was sent off for allegedly striking a referee in a match against West Ham. The press had a field day with such puns as: 'Grim Day for Ashley'. As a consequence, he was charged with bringing the game into disrepute and fined £750. Most United fans remember him more affectionately though as 'Spiderman', courtesy of his long-striding style. His pace, intelligence and, in particular, his 'cultivated left-foot' won him many admirers.

ROAD RUNNING AND BEDTIME DRINKS

Like Liverpool's David Fairclough, David McCreery earned the nickname 'Supersub' in his United career. He made fifty-seven full appearances for the Reds and fifty-one as substitute. He was also known as 'Roadrunner' because of his incredible work rate. The high point of his time with United came in 1977 when he replaced Gordon Hill in the Red Devils 2–1 FA Cup final victory over Liverpool. The previous year he had also replaced Hill in United's cup final defeat at the hands of Southampton.

Gary Megson, who managed West Brom to a place in the premiership in 2002 was known as 'Suitcase' during his playing days because he was never at one club for long.

During his brief stay at Sheffield Wednesday, Megson played alongside Paul Hart. Paul was said by some fans to have two nicknames, 'Fossil' and 'Horlicks'. He was known as 'Fossil' because of his lived-in looks and 'Horlicks' because most of his conversation had the same effect on people as the bedtime drink.

DEAD CERT

The one player I cannot name is the former Manchester United star who became an undertaker. His first client was a woman who lost her husband at a young age. She was very distressed that the new undertaker had laid him out in grey as she hated the colour on him.

The second client was a woman who had lost her thirty-year-old son. She was very distressed that the former player had laid him out in red as she hated the colour on him.

The great footballer appeased both of them, and said he would just do a swap around. A few weeks later he met up with Bobby Charlton and was explaining the adjustment to his new life. He told the story of his first two clients. Bobby nodded his head solemnly: 'Ah, I see. You swapped the suits. That was very resourceful of you.'

'Not at all,' replied the former player. 'It was much easier to swap their heads.'

WHO DO YOU THINK YOU ARE?

Discretion also prevents me from naming the first ever United star I ever approached, seeking an interview as young writer. He was less than encouraging. He asked me my name and when I replied he said: 'That name means nothing to me. But give it time... It will mean even less.'

BOYZONE

Some United players took a while to learn the pitfalls of social media. A case in point was Cristiano Ronaldo on Twitter: 'Thank you all for participation in the CR7 Boys Underwear Competition – it's been a real pleasure to see all of your photos.'

12

THE BIG ISSUE

And now we have the formalities over,
we'll have the National Anthems.

Brian Moore

After captaining America to a tense victory at the Belfry in the 1993 Ryder Cup, Tom Watson quoted Teddy Roosevelt, choosing words that managers and players would readily agree with:

> It's not the critic that counts, not the one who points out how the strong man stumbled or how the doer of deeds might have done them better. The credit belongs to the man who is actually in the arena; whose face is marred with sweat and dust and blood; who strives valiantly; who errs and comes short again and again; who knows the great enthusiasms, the great devotions and spends himself in a worthy cause and who, if he fails, at least fails while bearing greatly so that his place shall never be with those cold and timid souls who know neither victory nor defeat.

Every year football managers and players of the past and present get together for an annual conference to discuss one of the major issues of the game. Few people are more regularly accused of being of dubious parentage than referees, and players and managers have never been shy of letting them know their feelings towards them. However, they also consider more cerebral topics. This year the big issue was the perennial question: Why did the chicken cross the road? For the first time we publish extracts from the conference.

Arsène Wenger: From my position in the dug-out I did not see the incident clearly so I cannot really comment. However, I do think that he gets picked on by Manchester United players who are clearly chicken-phobic.

Alex Ferguson: As far as I'm concerned, he crossed the road at least a minute early according to my watch.

Peter Reid: Just cross the f**king r**d, you chicken f**k.

Glenn Hoddle: The chicken was hit by the lorry when crossing the road because in a previous life it had been a bad chicken.

Sven-Göran Eriksson: I don't know any chickens. I have never known any chickens.

Ruud Gullit: I am hoping to see some sexy poultry.

Ole Gunnar Solskjaer: In my day, we didn't ask why the chicken crossed the road. Someone told us that the chicken crossed the road, and that was good enough for us.

Ron Atkinson: Clive, for me, Chicko's popped up at the back stick, little eyebrows, and gone bang. And I'll tell you what – I've got a sneaking feeling that this road's there to be crossed.

Ashley Cole: I did not cross the road with THAT chicken.

Gary Lineker: To boldly go where no chicken has gone before.

Roy Keane: The point is that the chicken crossed the road. Who cares why?

Bill Gates (special guest at the conference): I have just released 'Chicken Coop 2021', which will not only cross roads, but will lay eggs, file your important documents, and balance your cheque-book and Explorer is an inextricable part of the operating system.

Ian Wright: Did the chicken really cross the road or did the road move beneath the chicken?

Niall Quinn: I envision a world where all chickens will be free to cross roads without having their motives called into question.

Mike Phelan: Crossing the road justifies whatever motive there was.

Kevin Keegan: Okay, so the chicken's dead, but I still feel, hey he can go all the way to the other side of the road.

Alex Ferguson (again): This was an unprovoked act of aggression against Manchester United.

13

DO DO RON RON

The keeper was unsighted – he still didn't see it.
Big Ron

Some sports personalities are renowned for their modesty. Ron Atkinson is not one of them.

He famously said, 'I met Mick Jagger when I was playing for Oxford United and the Rolling Stones played a concert there. Little did I know that one day he'd be almost as famous as me.'

This chapter celebrates a one-off.

OFF THE WALL

Ron Atkinson became the Manchester United manager for five years in 1981, having made his name with WBA. In the late 1970s West Bromwich Albion were a high-flying team in the old First Division. Ron brought the squad on an end-of-season tour to China. At one stage, the players were offered the opportunity to visit the Great Wall of China. One player, who would have preferred to have stayed in his own hotel playing cards, was asked his opinion on one of the wonders of the world.

'See one wall,' he replied, 'and you've seen them all.'

THE LAW OF UNINTENDED CONSEQUENCES

Football autobiographies are not always riveting. A revealing story in this respect is that of Robbie Fowler. He tells the story of the conversation that unfolded between former Liverpool stars Rob Jones and Jason McAteer.

Jones: 'I'm writing my autobiography.'

McAteer: 'What's it about?'

Jones: 'It's about my story, isn't it?'

McAteer: 'Is it any good.'

Jones: 'I don't know. I haven't read it.'

Former Arsenal goalkeeper Pat Jennings' book was memorable for one exchange.

Interviewer: 'You've devoted a whole chapter of your book to Jimmy Greaves.'

Pat Jennings: 'That's right. Well, what can you say about Jimmy Greaves?'

In his book *United to Win*, though, Ron Atkinson gives an amusing insight into how personality clashes between a player and a manager can end a player's career at a club. In his pre-United days, Atkinson had succeeded John Giles as manager of West Brom. One of the players he inherited was Paddy Mulligan who had given great service to the club but who was then in the autumn of his career. Big Ron took an instant dislike to Mulligan's verbosity and Mulligan found himself in the reserves. Atkinson's assistant, Colin Addison, suggested the manager should meet Mulligan in an effort to lift his spirits. When Mulligan arrived in the office, he took the initiative and said: 'Boss, I don't think you like me.'

True to form Atkinson did not mince his words and replied: 'Paddy, I can't stand you!'

Mulligan responded, 'Can I take it, then, that I'll be going at the end of the season?'

'You can bet money on it!' Atkinson countered.

After Atkinson left the office Colin Addison commented, 'Thanks, Ron. I only brought him in so that you could give him a bit of a confidence booster.'

A DISCERNING EYE

Taking advantage of a balmy day in Manchester, Big Ron donned his polos and khakis for a game of golf. Before he teed off, he watched four men produce some really horrible shots. After twenty minutes watching the foursome Atkinson asked, 'You guys wouldn't be priests by any chance?'

'Actually, yes, we are,' one cleric replied, 'How did you know?'

'Easy. I've never seen such bad golf and such clean language.'

DEATH BECOMES HER

Big Ron tells the story of one of his friends who was a keen golfer. On one particular afternoon, when he was joined by his wife, he was having a disastrous time. Teeing off on the fourteenth, he pulled his shot so badly it spun off towards a groundsman's hut. Unfortunately, the hut was obstructing the line. However, his wife, noticed that the hut had two doors, and it was possible that if both doors were opened, he would be able to play through. He asked his wife to go around the back and open the far door. When she did, sure enough, there was a clear path through to the green, although the ball needed to keep flat. He pulled out a wood, lined up and took the shot. As the ball cracked off, his wife, curious, looked around the doorway. Tragically, the ball hit her in the centre of the forehead, killing her stone dead.

A few weeks later the new widower was playing the same course with a friend. Again, he pulled his shot at the fourteenth, and ended up in front of the hut. 'Hey, you might be able to play through if we opened both doors,' observed the friend.

The man shuddered and went pale. 'No way. Very bad memories. Last time I did that, I ended up with a seven.'

MOORE TO THE POINT

Sometime after he became Manchester United manager, Big Ron took his wife out to a restaurant for Sunday lunch. As they sat waiting to order, their eyes were caught by a young couple at a nearby table. They had both chosen soup, but there seemed something wrong with the woman's helping as she seemed to be toying with it. After examining the offending dish, her partner called the waiter over who looked into the bowl and then rushed off. A moment later he reappeared with a straw and the woman started drinking her soup with the assistance of the straw.

Shortly after when the same waiter came to take their order, Ron asked, 'Please excuse my vulgar curiosity but why is that young lady drinking soup with a straw?'

'Well, sir. It's the best option when you've dropped your contact lens in there.'

A few minutes later a different waiter arrived with Atkinson's soup. His wife noticed he had his thumb in one of the bowls and pointed this out to him.

'Don't worry, madam,' he replied calmly, 'the soup is not hot.'

LOVE AND MARRIAGE

Big Ron attended a wedding of friend who was also a Manchester United official. Atkinson's task was to escort worshippers to their seats before the service. At one stage, as he returned to the sanctuary entrance to show the next party to their pews, he greeted two players and asked them where they would like to sit. Looking confused, the United captain Bryan Robson smiled and answered, 'Non-smoking, please.'

All through the ceremony the groom was very nervous. When

he went with his blushing bride into the vestry to sign the register, the vicar, wanting to change for the reception, said, 'Sign your names here and wait.'

Ron was delegated to oversee proceedings. He burst out laughing when he saw what his friend had written.

'Michael Finn, 174 lbs.'

The groom had turned up in the church obviously under the influence of drink. In fact, Ron had to hold him up. When the vicar saw this, he told the best man to take him outside and bring him back when he was sober.

'Sure, I had to make him drunk to get him here in the first place,' groaned Ron.

MEAT IN A RELIGIOUS SANDWICH

Atkinson was once invited to a big, public dinner and found himself seated between a famous bishop and a respected rabbi. He was determined to be witty, though everyone was so engrossed in serious conversation. He interrupted the rabbi, 'I feel as if I were a leaf between the Old and the New Testaments,' he said.

The rabbi turned to him and answered, 'That page, Mr Atkinson, is usually a blank.'

THE PLEASURE PRINCIPLE

After his retirement, Big Ron was in great demand as an after-dinner speaker. One of his favourite things was to quote George Bernard Shaw, who was once asked at a dinner to give his observations on sex. He rose and said, 'Ladies and Gentlemen, it gives me great pleasure,' and resumed his seat.

A CAPTIVE AUDIENCE

Ron was a great raconteur.

He did initially have a few prejudices to overcome. A club in

Manchester was considering him for their function. The chairman asked, 'Why don't we have Ron Atkinson as our after-dinner speaker.'

The treasurer replied, 'Don't be silly. He couldn't wait that long.'

The secretary butted in, 'He'd be no good at it. I bet he'd even stuff up the minute's silence.'

After one of his longer speeches at a club function, Ron asked the chairman, 'Did I put enough fire into my speech?'

The chairman replied, 'I don't think you put enough of your speech into the fire.'

UPLIFTING

Atkinson also featured in a number of commercials. One of them involved the phrase 'Keep it up'. The phrase, though, has taken on a new connotation in the world of celebrity-endorsement after Pelé became the spokesman for Viagra.

WISHFUL THINKING

A friend of Ron's was being driven crazy by his mother-in-law and sought the great sage's advice as to what he should do about it. His friend was very sceptical when Ron suggested that he should send his mother-in-law to the local wishing well. Eventually he did. She fell in and was never seen again in. The next time they met the man reported the sequence of events to Ron who looked at him and said, 'Imagine. You didn't believe in wishes.'

A GOOD WALK SPOILED

Former Liverpool manager, Bill Shankly, said of his full-back, Tommy Smith, that he would raise an argument in a graveyard. The same comment could be made about Big Ron.

One of his most redeeming qualities is his capacity to tell stories against himself.

'Bryan Robson, Norman Whiteside and myself assembled for a round of golf on Mother's Day. All three of us were quite surprised at having been able to escape from the family for the day, and so we compared notes on how we managed it.

'Robbo said, "I bought my wife a dozen red roses, and she was so surprised and touched that she let me go."

'Norman said, "I bought my wife a diamond ring, and she was so thrilled that she let me go."

'I said, "Last night I had a big feed of garlic. When I woke up this morning I rolled on top of my wife, breathed with gusto onto her face and asked, 'Golf course or intercourse?' She blinked and replied, 'I'll put your clubs in the car.""'

MR BOJANGLES

It is fair to say that Ron's sense of style is truly ... unique!

Hence his nickname Mr Bojangles!

Tommy Docherty produced the best joke about his sense of fashion during Big Ron's time as Manchester United manager, 'Ron Atkinson couldn't make it. His hairdresser died ... in 1946.'

HELLO DOLLY

Given that Big Ron's sartorial style is so ... distinctive he has attracted many 'admiring' remarks. Some have even applied Dolly Parton's famous comment to Atkinson: 'It costs a lot of money to look this cheap.'

WAR CRIMINAL

In the 1980s it was widely reported that Big Ron would have to take time off from football to travel to the Hague to face charges as a war criminal. His many crimes were against fashion.

In a fashion sense he is confirmation of Quentin Crisp's assertion: 'If at first you don't succeed, failure may be your style.' It has been said that even the North Korean army could not force Ron Atkinson to dress properly.

One of the 'Brat Pack' was Sammy Davis Jr. Like Ron Atkinson, he had a penchant for wearing jewellery. He was a big golf fan. Whenever he hit the ball eighty yards, his jewellery flew one hundred.

Big Ron enjoyed jokes about Sammy's golfing buddies. The galleries always flocked to see Bob Hope play, especially when he brought his showbiz pals. At one pro-am, Dean Martin was five up on Bing Crosby and that was before they left the bar.

Kojak star Telly Savalas was another regular but because he had played a cop so long when he struck a wild shot instead of shouting 'Fore' he screamed 'Freeze!'

During his Dirty Harry phase Clint Eastwood was easy to spot on the course. He was the only one who carried his putter in a holster.

After a terrible round of golf, Sammy Davis Jr. was asked how it went. He replied, 'I missed a spectacular hole in one – by only five strokes. At least I hit two good balls today. I stepped on a rake.'

One day Davis was having a very bad round. He was thirty over par after four holes, had lost fourteen balls in the same piece of water and had practically ploughed the rough trying to get a ball out. Then, on the green of the fifth, his caddy coughed just as he took a ten-inch putt, and he sliced it. Davis went wild.

'You've got to be the worst damn caddie in the whole wide world.'

The caddie looked at him sourly, and replied, 'I doubt it. That would be too much of a coincidence.'

PAIN IN THE BUM

Big Ron once asked Bryan Robson if he had any good butt jokes. When Robbo said no Atkinson replied, 'Well I have piles.'

RIDDLE ME THIS

Atkinson enjoys riddles. His favourite is: What do you get when you cross a football club with a florist?

Answer: Nottingham Florist.

QUIP

Big Ron has produced many great quips down the years. The constraints of good taste prevent me from naming the Manchester City striker of whom he said: 'He couldn't score in a brothel.'

For that reason, some Manchester United fans compare Big Ron to Tony Soprano because they would say his mouth is a weapon of mass destruction!

FAT CHANCE

One of the United reserve goalkeepers was putting on a bit of weight. Big Ron was not impressed when he missed a cross in training and roared, 'I bet you would have caught it if it was a hamburger.'

MARITAL DISCORD

Given his celebrity status Ron's local priest considered inviting the footballing legend to speak at an event he was organising for engaged couples to help them prepare properly for the sacrament of marriage. The priest decided to first give the footballer a little test to see if he would strike the right tone. 'Tell me Ron what advice would you give a newly married couple?'

The Manchester United legend paused deeply before saying, 'Never go to bed at night after a row.'

The priest nodded vigorously and was about to issue the invitation to be the guest speaker when Ron added, 'Stay up all night and fight like cats and dogs.'

WE NEED TO TALK ABOUT KEVIN

Big Ron's predecessor was Dave Sexton. His reign at Manchester United was celebrated in the song 'Onward Sexton Soldiers'. To no United player did the metaphor of a soldier apply more appropriately than Kevin Moran. Initially Dave Sexton deployed him in midfield in United's reserves but when Ron Atkinson arrived on the scene, he immediately moved him to centre-half and in October 1981 he made his debut against Wolves. Injuries to Gordon McQueen and Martin Buchan opened the door for Moran to win a place in the heart of United's defence.

Having won an FA Cup medal in 1983 in 1985 Moran became the first player to be sent off in an FA Cup final by Peter Willis for a clumsy, rather than malicious, tackle on Peter Reid. A major controversy developed when Moran's medal was initially withheld.

A regular feature of United's matches throughout the '80s was Moran, wearing a blood-stained jersey or head bandage, making scything tackles and diving headers, immune to the threat to his own safety. He collected over one hundred stiches, mostly facial, in his United career and gave enough blood to keep Dracula going for months. The message to his opponents was loud and clear: 'Thou shalt not pass.'

Inevitably given Moran's bravery, throwing his head and body where no sane person would go, injuries came his way. Ron Atkinson once joked that he was going to give him a part-time contract because he never finished a match!

KEEN KEVIN

Kevin Moran was always willing to put his body on the line and played on despite injuries. This created one memorable post-match interview on live television.

Broadcaster: 'How's the leg Kevin?'
Kevin Moran: 'It's very fuc … It's very sore.'

TESTING TIMES

In 1993, the Irish government introduced a new £10 note which featured the image of James Joyce. There were a lot of forgeries in circulation and one evening on a visit to Dublin Big Ron demonstrated to every single customer in the pub what they had to do to ensure theirs was legal tender. He got everyone to take out a £10 note; then they had to fold it in half, then they folded in half a second time; then (to bemused looks all round) they had to take off one of their shoes; then they had to hit their tenner with the shoe. Everyone paused expectantly to see the solution to the conundrum. Ron posed theatrically before informing them, 'Now lads if James Joyce's glasses are broken when you look at your note again ye'll know 'twas a forgery.'

BLIND DATE

When Ron was a young man, he set up his friend Joe on a blind date with a young lady-friend of his. But Joe was a little worried about going out with someone he had never seen before. 'What do I do if she's really unattractive? I'll be stuck with her all night.'

'Don't worry,' Ron said, 'just go up to her and meet her first. If you like what you see, then everything goes as planned. If you don't just shout "Aaaaaauuuuuugggghhhh!" and fake an asthma attack.'

So that night, Joe knocked at the girl's door and when she came out, he was awe-struck at how attractive and sexy she was. He was about to speak when the girl suddenly shouts, 'Aaaaaaauuuuuuggggghhh!'

CHOOSE YOUR WORDS CAREFULLY

Ron's ability to tell it as it is doesn't always have the results he anticipated. He was in a hotel one evening when the venue was descended upon by a party of women. Anxious to find out the nature of the occasion, he asked one if it was a hen party.

'No,' she answered, 'it's a Weight Watcher's convention.'

'Oh, not been going long?' he inquired casually. That was the moment she floored him with a cracking right hook.

SOLICITOUS

One evening in Los Angeles Big Ron was propositioned by a 'lady of the night'. She said, 'Would you like to sleep with me for twenty dollars?'

Atkinson is said to have replied thoughtfully, 'I'm not very tired but the money will come in handy.'

BORN TO RUN

Back in his playing days Ron met an attractive young woman in a pub in Manchester. It was just after he had become something of a local celebrity. The woman was very impressed by his athletic abilities. He was very excited when she asked if he would like her to show him a good time. He gulped before he said he would.

She took him outside.

First, she took off her jacket.

Then she took off her jersey.

Then she ran the 100 metres in ten seconds.

DILEMMAS

Big Ron was asked, 'If you had to give up wine or women, which would you choose?'

Atkinson thought for a moment, 'That would rather depend on the vintage of each.'

ERECTIONS

Ron didn't always have the best of relations with his neighbours.

One of them was a DIY enthusiast and was putting up a monument. Big Ron commented, 'The person next door has a large erection in his back garden which is unsightly and dangerous.'

RONGLISH

'As we know, there are known knowns; there are things we know we know. We also know there are unknown unknowns; that is to say we know there are some things we do not know. But there are also unknown unknowns – the ones we don't know we don't know.' Thus spoke Donald Rumsfield, former United States Secretary of Defence.

Such a comment would not seem out of place among football pundits given their unique use of the English language.

Outstanding in his own field was Ron Atkinson, before he lost his jobs as a pundit, or in 'pundit parlance' took an early bath, following racist remarks about Chelsea's Marcel Desailly live on TV when he thought his microphone was off on 20 April 2004 in Monaco. Nobody was laughing when viewers heard his words.

However, the perpetually tanned and bejewelled Mr Bojangles himself has devoted his life to entertainment and football, sometimes it seems in that order. Generally, nobody does it better. Baby, despite occasional lapses of taste – in fashion as well as in punditry – Ron is the best. Like David Coleman he has given us a new word 'Ron-glish' because of Do-Ron-Ron-Ron's unique use of the language of Shakespeare.

MIGHTY MOUTH

When Big Ron took refuge in punditry and immediately made his mark with comments like: 'They only thought the shirts had to go out to get a win.'

As the following Top Twenty indicates, Atkinson had no peers for a breath-taking ability to transform mere words and give them new meanings and his classics will endure forever whenever the history of punditry is written.

1. *I never comment on referees and I'm not going to break the habit of a lifetime for that prat.*
2. *The action replay showed it to be worse than it actually was.*
3. *If Glenn Hoddle said one word to his team at half-time, it was concentration and focus.*
4. *Liverpool are outnumbered numerically in midfield.*
5. *I know where he [the referee] should have put this flag up, and he'd have got plenty of help.*
6. *Well, either side could win it, or it could be a draw.*
7. *Giving the ball away doesn't seem to work in international football.*
8. *I'm not going to make a prediction – it could go either way.*
9. *Now Manchester United are 2–1 down on aggregate, they are in a better position than when they started the game at 1–1.*
10. *Sometimes you just can't do nothing about anything.*
11. *They must go for it now as they have nothing to lose but the match.*
12. *He dribbles a lot and the opposition don't like it: you can see it all over their faces.*
    Here Big Ron is presumably speaking about dribbling with the ball.
13. *Giggs is running long up the backside.*
14. *I wouldn't say Ginola is the best left-winger in the Premiership, but there are none better.*
15. *Zidane is not very happy, because he's suffering from the wind.*
16. *The lad throws it further than I go on holiday.*
17. *The keeper was unsighted – he still didn't see it.*

18. Clive Tyldesley (as the camera focused on a stunning female percussionist wearing a Brazil shirt.): *Ron, I didn't know your wife was Brazilian.*
    Ron Atkinson: *I didn't know she played the drums.*
19. *You can see the ball go past them, or the man, but you'll never see both man and ball go past at the same time. So, if the ball goes past, the man won't or if the man goes past they'll take the ball.*
20. *He's not only a good player, but he's spiteful in the nicest sense of the world.*

HISTORY MAKER?

We will probably never see someone like Big Ron manage United again, but as he said: 'If history repeats itself, I think we should expect the same thing again.'

14

FAN ZONE

*Manchester United have a very experienced bench which
they may want to play to turn the tide of the match.*

Bryon Butler

Neville Cardus observed that 'a great game is part of the nation's
life and environment; it is indeed an organism in an environment... as our great game is inevitably an expression in part of
our spiritual and material condition as a nation and a people, it
must go through metamorphoses; it must shed skins and grow
new ones...'. Though Cardus was writing about his beloved
cricket, he could have been writing about football in the latter
years of the nineteenth century.

The times they were a-changing.

In 1895 the superb all-round athlete, cricketer and footballer C.B.
Fry donned the mantle of social commentator when he remarked:
'The great and widespread interest in football is a manifest fact.
So much so that nowadays it is frequently urged that cricket can
no longer be regarded as our "national game" in the true sense
of the word. Football, it is claimed, has now the first place in the
popular heart.'

To modern eyes, Fry's comments might appear curious.

However, for much of the 1800s football was alien to the lives of industrial workers. Time off work was minimal apart from Sundays and holidays or leisure activities were considered inappropriate for the Lord's day. The only formal holidays were at Easter and Christmas. If sport was to emerge as a significant feature in the lives of working-class people significant economic changes were essential. Campaigns to improve life for workers began to reap their harvest in the 1840s. An important milestone came in 1850 with the Factory Act which introduced a sixty-hour week for women.

However, the most crucial development was the so-called *la semaine anglaise* which provided workers with a free Saturday afternoon. The textile industry was the first to introduce this concession but by the 1860s it had become commonplace. This allowed the industrial labour force to spend their free afternoons in the pursuit of structured recreation. Moreover, working men now found that they had more to spend as in real terms their wages rose appreciably from the 1850s onwards.

This development was not to everyone's taste. In 1863 the *Illustrated London News* complained that: 'There is, perhaps, no social problem more difficult of solution than that which involves the affording of more holidays to the working classes without at the same time diminishing their means of subsistence.' In a flurry of moral indignation in 1871 *The Times* bemoaned, 'an increasing tendency of late years among all classes to find excuse for Holydays'. That same year the first ever Bank Holiday was introduced. The Bank Holiday Act boldly went where no legislation had gone before transforming old religious holidays into secular days of recreation sanctioned by the state. This was much to the chagrin of *The Times* which stubbornly continued to call such days 'holydays'. The first such bank holiday witnessed unprecedented chaos at the railway stations and steamboat piers.

By the end of the nineteenth century football had become the sport of the industrial working class; a major social change. This was reflected in the remarks of a Manchester industrialist in 1881, reminiscing on life in the city in the 1830s: 'As for a Saturday afternoon holiday, it was not even dreamt of. Hence people had fewer opportunities of indulging their inclinations in this direction.'

While workers saw football as a leisure activity, others saw it as an opportunity to pursue another agenda. Clergymen viewed it as an ideal antidote to urban degeneracy. Vigorous physical activity would benefit the young on every level including the spiritual which led to a proliferation of football teams associated with working-class churches. By 1880, eighty-three of the 344 clubs in Birmingham and, by 1885, twenty-five of the 112 football clubs in Liverpool had religious affiliations. Some of the top teams of today began life as church teams including: Aston Villa, Birmingham City, Bolton Wanderers, Blackpool FC, Everton, Fulham, Liverpool, Southampton, Swindon and Wolves. Schools too got in on the act and Blackburn Rovers, Chester, Leicester City, Queen's Park Rangers and Sunderland owe their origins to particular institutions.

The local authority in Manchester was one of the first to introduce new municipal parks in an effort to introduce a shaft of light into the greyness of their industrial city which enabled the masses to play football. The game's new popularity was reflected in the growth of working-class kit. In 1880, Lewis's of Manchester sold knickerbockers at 6s 9d, jerseys for 3s 11d – and hand-sewn footballs for 10s 6d.

The factory floor itself spawned a number of football teams. In a northern suburb of Manchester, employees at the carriage and wagon department of the Lancashire and Yorkshire railway Company established the Newton Heath team in 1878 at their depot. Initially their name was Newton Neath (LYR), but they dropped the initials LYR as the club gained more popularity and expanded its activities, recruiting players from outside the local railway yard. Twenty-four years later, following the club's bankruptcy, they took the name Manchester United. The club first joined the league (as members of the First Division) in 1892 and have never dropped out of the top two divisions. Crucial to the club's success from its foundations to the present day has been its links with its fans. This chapter explores some manifestations of that close relationship.

MORE THAN A GAME

In his prologue to *The Go-Between* L.P. Hartley wrote: 'The past is a foreign country: they do things differently here.'

Interviewer: 'Was there much TB then?'

Manchester United fan of the 1920s: 'No, but we had radio.'

THE EMPTY SEAT

Old Trafford is a place for nostalgia. The memory of great matches and star players lingers for life in the minds of these United fans who grew up with them, leaving a warm after-glow to light up numerous conversations years later.

Older fans draw on the memories of decades past. They remember their first acquaintance with the Busby babes and knew intuitively that something special had arrived on the sporting scene, or recall the times they saw Ronaldo glide through bedraggled defenders, making a feast from a famine of poor possession. The United stars appeal to the finer side of the imagination, with memory cherishing not only what they did, but how they did it, with panache and elegance. For Manchester United fans not every day is good but there is some good in every day.

A man had a ticket for the Manchester Derby but was seated right at the top of the stand, in the corner of Old Trafford, with the worst possible view of the pitch. As the match started, he noticed one empty seat, beautifully positioned, exactly in front of the half-way line. Taking a chance, he raced down from the top of the stand, to where the spare seat was.

'Excuse me, sir,' he said to the man sitting next to the empty seat. 'Is anybody sitting there?'

'No,' replied the man. 'That seat is empty.'

'That's incredible, who in their right mind would have a seat like this for the Manchester Derby, and not use it?'

'Well, actually the seat belongs to me,' replied the United fan. 'I was supposed to be here with my wife, but she passed away.'

'Oh, I'm sorry to hear that. That's terrible, but couldn't you find someone else – a friend or even a neighbour to take the seat?'

The United fan shook his head. 'They've all gone to the funeral.'

A NAME CHANGER

Manchester United fans are a very judgemental lot. I know just by looking at them.

To take just one example, there's the Conservative Party supporter who calls Tony Blair 'Tony Bliar'.

A TICKET FOR ALL SEASONS

It took a while for some United fans to figure out to get the most of their season ticket seats. I saw that at first hand myself the first year when I noticed that the two seats next to mine had been empty for every match during the year. Puzzled why anyone would spend all that money on these tickets and never use them, my confusion deepened when at the first match the second year and a middle-aged man and his teenage son occupied the seats. Unable to contain my curiosity any longer, at half-time I turned to the man and asked why he hadn't used the season ticket until then.

'They were a Christmas present from the wife,' replied the man with a weary expression, 'and she didn't actually tell us about them until Christmas Day.'

SPARKY

A rather timid kind of man was in Glasgow on a visit and got an opportunity to attend a Rangers v. Celtic match. Mindful of the potential for violence on such occasions, rooted in the Catholic–Protestant antagonism, he decided that discretion was the better part of valour and resolved to play it safe and keep his head down and display no emotion whatsoever. Rangers scored and the man on his right went into a frenzy of cheering, shouting and singing. The man remained stoically passive.

A short time later Celtic scored and the supporter on his left went completely wild with joy. But still the man remained indifferent. At which point he was hit by a bottle from behind as someone roared at him, 'You bloody atheist.'

DIETARY STAPLES

One of the great sagas in Irish sport came during 2018/19. For what seemed like an eternity, the football world got itself into a tizzy about whether West Ham's rising star Declan Rice would declare for Ireland or England. Finally, after a journey that lasted longer than a transatlantic ocean liner, Rice declared for England in February 2019. An indication of the rivalry between the two countries came in the comment of one Irish fan: 'The f**king English. They took all our potatoes away from us during the Great Famine. Now they have taken our bloody Rice as well.'

TERRITORIAL, MUCH?

After these two amusing examples of the place of rivalries in football ... We all know how fans like to put over on their sworn enemy.

One Sheffield United fan took this to a whole new level when he visited Hillsborough, home of Sheffield Wednesday. He pooed on the centre spot and got his friend to film it. For reasons best known to anthropologists, the video went viral.

MAKING A MARK

When he played for Wales with Ian Rush, Mark Hughes was the subject of an unusual error. A print journalist was reading his column down the line to the paper's office. He said: 'There are those who would say Rush and Hughes are the most dangerous strikers in Europe.' He was shocked to read the next morning: 'There are those who would say Russian Jews are the most dangerous strikers in Europe.'

BIRDS OF A FEATHER

Right to the very end, Hughes played to a high standard. Hence Gianluca Vialli's comment: 'He's playing better than ever, even if he is going grey and looking like a pigeon.'

TURNCOAT

However, the Manchester United fans attitude to Mark Hughes changed significantly when he did the unthinkable and went to manage Manchester City. It is fair to say that his eighteen months in the job (2008/09) were less than a resounding success. In the Emmy Award-winning series, *The Office*, David Brent called a staff meeting to announce job cuts.

'There's good news and bad news. The bad news is that some of you will lose your jobs. I know: gutting. On a more positive note, the good note, the good news is: I've been promoted! So, every cloud has a silver lining.'

Manchester United fans were enjoying Sparky's frustrations. Hence this story from the time.

Father: 'Son, what'll I buy you for your birthday?'

Son: 'A bicycle.'

Father: 'What'll I buy you for your first communion?'

Son: 'A PlayStation?'

Father: 'What'll I buy you for Christmas?'

Son: 'A Mickey Mouse outfit.'

Father, with a twinkle in his eye: 'No problem son. I'll just buy you the Manchester City football team!'

ASSISTED CONCEPTION

Mind you, some United fans were less forgiving. They had had their own revenge. They told a story that involved Mark Hughes walking into a sperm donor bank and saying to the receptionist, 'I'd like to donate some sperm.'

She asked him: 'Have you ever donated before?'

He replied: 'Yes. You should have my details on your computer.'

The receptionist said: 'Oh, yes. But I see you're going to need help. Shall I get a lap dancer for you?'

'Why do I need help?' he asked.

The receptionist replied: 'Well, it says on your record that you're a useless wanker.'

GAME OF CONES

Legend has it that Hughes was getting so desperate by his failure to live up to the owner's expectations that he rang Alex Ferguson and asked: 'What's the recipe for winning the Premier League?'

Fergie told him you get the following drill: get loads of cones, placing them carefully around the field, loads of balls, have the players dribbling around the cones, doing one-twos, side-steps, swerves, and kicking the ball into the net.

After a few weeks Fergie was surprised that Hughes had not

rang him to thank him for his brilliant advice, so he rang him and asked him how well they had got on.

Hughes replied: 'Not great. The cones beat us by six goals.'

HIS CUP FLOWS UNDER

It is sacrilege to some, but Manchester City are good for the game, if for no reason other than their rivalry with United. When Mark Hughes was their manager City had been waiting for a long time to win the Premier League. United fans told the story that in the middle of the night Sparky was woken up by a call from his local police station:

'I'm afraid the trophy room has been broken into, sir.'

Horrified, Hughes asked, 'Did they get the cups?'

'No, sir,' replied the policewoman, 'they didn't go into the kitchen.'

Rumour had it that City were sued by the burglars for wasting their time.

A BIT FISHY

When City were spiralling down the league, Manchester United fans claimed that Mark Hughes's wife bought two fish claiming they would relax the players. One disgruntled fan said, 'They will link up perfectly with the rest of the squad. They're carp.'

A TALE OF WOE

Part of the problem for Mark Hughes was that he did not have enough prolific scoring forwards. One Manchester United fan observed, 'If Lee Harvey Oswald was a Manchester City player JFK would still be alive.'

MATHS PROBLEM

As City found it so hard to win that season a new riddle was born.

What's the difference between Manchester City FC and a triangle? A triangle's got three points.

PREMATURE DEATH

The United–City rivalry has added so much to football.

A referee died and went to Heaven. Stopped by St Peter at the gates, he was told that only brave people who had performed heroic deeds and had the courage of their convictions could enter. If the ref could describe a situation in his life where he had shown all these characteristics, he would be allowed in.

'Well,' said the ref, 'I was refereeing a game between United and City at Old Trafford. United were a goal ahead, with seconds left in injury time. Gabriel Jesus made a break and weaved through the United defence and scored a goal. However, he had handled the ball first, but as City were clearly the better side, I ruled that he scored a legitimate goal.'

'My word, that was indeed brave of you, but I will have to check the facts in the celestial book,' said St Peter, and departed to look it up. He returned with a puzzled look and said, 'Sorry, but there is no record of this. Can you help me to trace it? When did it happen?'

The ref looked at his watch and replied, 'About forty-five seconds ago!'

JUNGLE WORSHIP

Even the clergy react to the Manchester rivalry. A famous example of their holy wit is a story set in an African country, where there was a river infested with crocodiles. On the other side there was a group of people who various missionaries wanted to convert. However, nobody was willing to take the risk of crossing the river.

In 2021 along came a group of priests who waded across the river without coming to any harm.

They were going to see the jungle's football classic of the year, the annual grudge match between animals and the insects, and by half-time the elephants, zebras and cheetahs had proved too much for the grasshoppers, beetles and ants with an emphatic score of sixty-three goals to nil. However, when the match resumed, the animals noted a substitute player run onto the field with the insects. It was a shiny black centipede. From then on, the centipede became the star of the game peppering the goals from all angles. Indeed, the animals failed to score another goal and the insects ran out winners, with the score standing at 64–63.

At the bar afterwards, the animals' captain, a teak-tough elephant, said to the insects' skipper, a gentle grasshopper, 'Great game, but you were damned lucky that centipede arrived at half time.'

'You're so wrong,' said the grasshopper. 'He was here from the start of the game, but it took him until half time to put his boots on!'

Shortly after, the priests revealed their secret for the safe passage over the crocodiles: 'We wore T-shirts bearing the words *Manchester City – Champions League Winners 2021*. And sure, not even a crocodile was willing to swallow that!'

ON GUARD

Mind you, as City in recent years have had access to unrivalled funds, were able to buy expensive players like confetti at a wedding and to emerge as a serious threat to United's long supremacy it has not been to everybody's taste. Hence one United fan's withering comment: 'We win trophies. They buy them.'

THE FALLING STAR OF DAVID

To be manager of Manchester United requires exceptional gifts for a job punctuated by all the mundane functions of existence, but whose responsibilities dwarf those of others. A strong personality and an intelligent analyst of the game is called for.

The Emperor Napoleon used to ask his aspiring generals whether they were lucky. Sporting champions need their fair share of luck. The weather and the toss of a coin can make a huge difference, dictating surfaces, ends and directions. The wind is arbitrary, the sun has no favourites, the rain like the tide waits for no one. The best prepared manager cannot prevent his star player pulling his hamstring or breaking his leg and hopes of glory can vanish in an instant. David Moyes was not lucky when he managed Manchester United.

'How can a loser ever win?' mused the Bee Gees. Moyes must have had a similar question.

That explains why United fans tell the story of a plane with five passengers: a grandfather and his grandson, Bryan Robson, Eric Cantona, and Moyes. The plane is about to crash but there are only four parachutes. A crisis meeting is held to decide who is going to get the four parachutes.

Eric Cantona is first to speak: 'I'm the greatest footballer Manchester United has ever seen. Given my service to the club I have to be saved.' He takes the first parachute and jumps out of the plane.

Next up is Bryan Robson. He says, 'I'm the finest captain United has ever produced. I made more tackles than any other player. For all that I deserve to live.' He takes the second parachute and jumps out the plane.

Then Moyes get up and says: 'I am a great manager. I'm one of the biggest names in football. I must be let live.' So, he takes the third parachute and jumps out of the plane.

At this point the grandfather turns to his grandson and with tears toppling in steady streams down his cheeks he says: 'Listen, Tiny Tim, you take the last parachute. I've had a long life. You've got your whole life ahead of you.'

Tiny Tim says: 'Don't worry, Grandpa, there are still two parachutes left. I gave that useless idiot, Moyes, my schoolbag and that's what he jumped out the plane with on his back!'

Manchester United fans believe in equal opportunities. They dislike Liverpool and Manchester City with equal vehemence. Hence their dismissive comment: 'An intelligent Liverpool player is one whose I.Q. is higher than his shirt number.'

THEM AND US

Who has the most loyal supporters? There has always been a great rivalry between Manchester United and Liverpool fans. A Liverpool supporter goes up to Heaven and he is very surprised to see that St Peter is wearing a Manchester United jersey.

'Why should I let you in here?' asked St Peter.

The Liverpool fan replied: 'Well last month I gave £100 to Unicef. Last week I gave £60 to Amnesty International. Yesterday I gave £40 to Christian Aid.'

St Peter replied, 'I'm not sure if we want a Liverpool fan in Heaven, but seeing as you gave generously to charity, wait here and I'll check out with God what he thinks of your situation.'

St Peter came back a few minutes later and said: 'God agrees with me. Here's your £200. Now f**k off out of here.'

DON'T CRY FOR ME ARGENTINA

It is fair to say that Manchester United fans had a love–hate relationship with Carlos Tevez. They loved him when he played for them in 2007 to 2009.

But then he did the unforgivable.

He signed for Manchester City.

Immediately he was the butt of comments at Old Trafford like: 'What is the biggest joke I know? Carlos Tevez.'

BEAUTY AND THE BEAST

The definitive Tevez story from 2009 among United fans, though, is:

Quasimodo is in his study and once again is feeling depressed about how ugly he is. Looking for some reassurance, he goes in search of Esmerelda. When he finds her, he asks her once again if he really is the ugliest man alive.

Esmerelda sighs and she says, 'Look why don't you go upstairs and ask the magic mirror who is the ugliest man alive? The mirror will answer your question once and for all.'

About five minutes later a very pleased-looking Quasimodo bounced back down the stairs and gave Esmerelda a great big hug.

'Well it worked,' Quasimodo beamed. 'But who on earth is Carlos Tevez?'

BLESS ME, FATHER

Thierry Henry scored nine goals for Arsenal against Manchester United. Needless to say, this did not endear him to United fans. A United fan was driving his lorry down the road when he saw a priest. Feeling it was his duty, he stopped to give the priest a lift. A short time later, he saw Thierry Henry on the side of the road and aimed his lorry at him. At the last second, he thought of the priest with him and realised he couldn't run over the Arsenal star, so he swerved, but he heard a thump anyway. Looking back as he drove on, he didn't see anything. He began to apologise for his behaviour to the priest.

'I'm sorry, Father. I barely missed that f**k ... that man at the side of the road.'

But the priest said, 'Don't worry, son. I got him with my door.'

THE KING OF HUMANITY

In 1990 Nelson Mandela was freed from his years in captivity. A visit to his cell on Robben Island has since become one of the tourist destinations when people tour to Cape Town. Inside the sterile, cinder block cell was a toilet, a thin mattress with pillows and a brown blanket. The single window looking into the courtyard has thick, white bars, matching the ones on the door to the cellblock's hallway. Yet while he was a prisoner there, Nelson Mandela could see a better future – one worthy of sacrifice. Standing outside that same tiny spot – which is now a monument to Mandela – where he was incarcerated for eighteen years during his long campaign to end the policies of racial apartheid and oppression in his country, is an intense experience.

The emotional impact is accentuated by a small courtyard where Mandela and other prisoners were forced to work, and where they occasionally played sports – some of the guides leading the tour were these prisoners on Robben Island with Mandela for years. Along one wall stood lattices for grapevines behind which Mandela, while a prisoner, stored his pages of a manuscript that eventually were smuggled out of prison and became his acclaimed book, *Long Walk to Freedom*.

A black and white photograph of prisoners at work in the courtyard doesn't tell the whole story: guards would take away the prisoners' hammers and take pictures to show the world that the inmates were only doing light work. Once the pictures were taken, the hammers were soon given back.

According to United fans an additional feature of the tour is the handwritten note which Mandela left under the bed in his prison cell, 'Have Manchester City won a match since I was thrown into this bloody place?'

ARRESTED DEVELOPMENT

Man United fans relish casting aspersions on the intellectual abilities of Manchester City players. They claim that Pep Guardiola asked Sergio Aguero why he spent so much time staring at his glass of orange juice.

'Because it said, "concentrate" on the cartoon,' the City player replied.

RELEGATION

Given that he had such skill you would imagine that Manchester United would say nice things about David Silva. Not a bit of it. A publication written by a Man United fan made jokes about Silva's shortcomings in the brains department. To illustrate his deficiencies in this area they published the tale of an incident involving himself, Einstein and Shakespeare going to Heaven. When they get to the gate St Peter is introducing an identity check. He begins with Einstein who proves his identity by demonstrating the theory of relativity. He is then welcomed into Heaven. Next is Shakespeare who proves himself by composing an incredible poem about the Gates of Heaven. The great Bard is warmly welcomed into Heaven.

Then St Peter turns to David Silva and says: 'Einstein and Shakespeare have demonstrated their identity very decisively. How are we to know that you are who you say you are?'

A blank look came over my face and after a few minutes of thought he asked: 'Who are Einstein and Shakespeare?'

St Peter beamed a beatific smile and said: 'Well answered. You really are David Silva. Make yourself at home here in Heaven. You'll be glad to hear we have a dunce's corner prepared especially for you.'

HUMILIATION

A man was driving home from a night in the pub. He was pulled over by a policewoman. The officer said: 'I'm going to have to get you to blow into the bag.'

The driver pulled out a card from his pocket which read: 'Asthmatic. Don't take breath samples.'

The policewoman said, 'I'm going to have to take a sample of your blood.'

He took out a card from his pocket, 'Haemophiliac. Don't take blood samples.'

The policewoman said: 'I'm going to have to take a urine sample.'

The motorist took out another card from his pocket. This one read, 'Member of Manchester City supporters club. Don't take the p**s.'

CONFIDENCE

In the Sir Alex era, Manchester United's cup was full, but Manchester City's plate was empty. In the Pep Guardiola era to a certain extent the position has been reversed. Now it is City fans who are the cocky ones. Take one City fan's prediction before the 2019 Manchester Derby: 'I predict three each. Sterling will score three, Aguero will score three and Silva will score three.'

FANDOM

Kevin Baldwin's entertaining manual for fans *This Supporting Life: How to Be A Real Football Fan* (which suggests that the way to get into Old Trafford for free is to join a parachute team) has an amusing spin on the crass commercialism that clubs subject fans to in their frequent changes of jerseys for merchandising purposes. He suggests that the word 'UMBRO' that appeared on the kit stands for 'United's Massively Big Rip-Off'. He went on to point to the fact that sponsors whose names are initials are usually tailor made for a club, witness:

- JVC (Arsenal): Just Very Cautious
- LBC (Wimbledon): Long Ball Creed
- NEC (Everton): Not Even Close

NO LAUGHING MATTER

Manchester United fans are known for their ability to dish out wicked little barbs to opponents. In autumn 2002 as the Hammers seemed rooted to the bottom of the Premier League they asked: what is the world's best joke? West Ham.

It is United fans themselves who often dish out the harshest criticism of the team – witness the caption in Manchester United's fanzine *Red Attitude* under a photograph showing a plump, elderly nun kicking a football which read: 'David May Models New Team Strip.'

HARRY'S GAME

Former Liverpool striker Luis Suárez attracted the antipathy of Manchester United fans because he made racist comments to Patrice Evra.

Shortly after Suárez's bite on Branislav Ivanović in 2013 the quip of the year came when Cooles under tens played the Burren in Galway. A very quick-witted Harry Minogue, after spotting a hole in his jersey remarked, 'Look lads Suárez must be in town.'

AH, REF

It may have been the knowledge of the hostility referees attract that inspired Henry Winter to observe: 'Modern referees need the wisdom of Solomon, the patience of Job, the probity of Caesar's wife, the stamina of Mo Farah and the acceleration of Usain Bolt. Oh, and the thick skin of a rhino.'

EYESORE

A referee's lot in such an environment is not a happy one. They are the only occupation where a man has to be perfect on the first day on the job and then improve over the years. One spectator at a club match at Old Trafford was complaining bitterly all through the game about the referee's poor eyesight. At one stage, though, the fan was responsible for a Coleman-ball when he shouted, 'Ah, ref, where are your testicles?'

CONVERSATIONS

Attending Old Trafford on match days is a sensory pleasure on many levels. The conversations one overhears always adds to it. One fan has a nice line in self-deprecation, 'I have a massive admiration for skilled people. I would give my right arm to be ambidextrous.'

He added, 'My wife signed me up for the Royal Sceptic Society. Like they exist. I think her problem is she goes to psychics that are either too angry or too sad. I think she just needs to find a Happy Medium.

'She also bought me a new puppy. I called him 1999 Treble Winners. Despite the bad breath, hairy nose and barking voice he really seems to like me.'

I always maintain that a high level of skill is necessary to decipher comments about footballers in Old Trafford. Some fans are very subtle:

'He always makes the ball do the work', which means in code 'he is lazy'.

'He could get more out of the ball', i.e. he is stupid.

'He has to train a little bit harder', i.e. he is completely unfit.

'In fairness he has a powerful shot', i.e. he never hits the target.

'He is a grafter', i.e. a carthorse, a player with no skill, to be brought on as a sub, usually when the team is four goals down and playing against the wind and has no chance of winning.

The gravest allegation is that he was 'a great prospect', i.e. he had not played a good game since he was sixteen.

YOU'RE IN THE ARMY NOW

The BBC World Service was featuring Manchester United's home tie with West Ham. The soldiers had a recreational break and the 81st Infantry Battalion were riveted. A poster on the wall stated, 'Improve Morale. Increase Flogging.'

WORDY MATTERS

A young Manchester United fan was decorating his room, so he wrote to Old Trafford and asked for 'stickers, brochures, and *pennance*'. A few days later he received a package with this letter, 'We are sending you the brochure and stickers but would suggest that for *pennance* you spend an hour a day with the Oxford Dictionary.'

THE HOUSE OF NO FUN

Two bricklayers, Man City fans, were chatting at work. 'Are you going to the match on Sunday?' said one. 'City are playing United.'

'No,' said the other. 'My wife won't let me.'

'What? said the first. 'It's easy to get out of that. About an hour before the game, what you do is pick her up, take her to the bedroom, rip off her clothes and make mad passionate love to her. Then she'll let you do anything you want.'

'I'll try that,' said the other man.

The following Monday the two men met on the building site. 'How come you didn't make it to the game?' asked the first man.

'Well, I'll tell you what happened?' said the second man. 'About an hour before I was planning to leave, I did as you said. I picked her up, took her to the bedroom and ripped off her clothes, and then I thought, City haven't been playing that well for ages.'

DOCTOR KNOWS BEST

A doctor with a serious heart condition encouraged his patient to start watching Manchester City. The doctor said he should avoid any excitement.

PERFECTION

Man City took a hammering in a match and afterwards a Man United fan was asked, 'Are City good losers?'

'Good? They're perfect!'

CRUEL TO BE KIND

Another story is of the Manchester City fan who got so depressed that he dressed up in his full City kit and threw himself in the river. When the police retrieved his body, they removed the strip and replaced it with stockings and suspenders. They told the coroner that they did this 'in order to avoid embarrassing the family.'

FAIRY TALE REVISIONISM

Man United fans have also rewritten the Snow White story. In their version Snow White arrived home one evening to find her house destroyed by fire. She was doubly worried because she'd left all seven dwarfs asleep inside. As she scrambled among the wreckage, frantically calling their names, suddenly she heard the cry: 'Man City to win the Champions League.'

'Thank goodness,' sobbed Snow White. 'At least Dopey's still alive.'

City fans retaliate with barbs of their own. When the bald Jaap Stam bestrode the United defence like a Colossus, City fans chanted: 'Keep your hair on.'

ALL HE NEEDS IS LOVE

In fairness to Man City fans, they enjoy a good laugh.

A year after his tenure ended as England manager in 2007, Manchester City appointed Sven-Göran Eriksson as their manager. His season in charge was less than an unqualified success culminating in a terrible 8–1 defeat to Middlesbrough in the last game of the season.

Nonetheless, fans were behind their man as their chant that season to the tune of 'Lord of the Dance':

> *Sven, Sven, wherever you may be*
> *You are the pride of Man City*
> *You can shag my wife on your settee*
> *If we win the cup at Wemb-er-ley.*

Sven's reputation as a ladies' man followed him everywhere. When it was announced that he was to take up the position as director of football with Second Division Notts County, the *Daily Mirror* featured a cartoon that had Sven asking; 'So is it true that there are five women for every man in Nottingham?'

Fans asked, in the spirit of Mrs Merton, 'Tell me, Sven, what was it that attracted you to the billionaire bankers of Notts County?'

OLD TRAFFORD'S MOST FAMOUS RESIDENT

It is not that Manchester United fans have a superiority complex. They just think they are better than everybody else. Hence the story that when England went into lockdown during the Covid-19 crisis, God was spotted walking around Old Trafford. When someone asked him what he was doing he replied, 'I'm just walking from home.'

KNOCK, KNOCKING ON HEAVEN'S DOORS

Two Manchester United fans, sitting at a bar counter, were reliving the latest game they had seen. After a brief lull in the conversation, one said to the other: 'I wonder if there is football in Heaven?' His friend said that nobody knew for sure but suggested that they should make a pact there and then that whichever of them died first would come back and tell the other. They both agreed and the pact was soon sealed with another round of drinks. In due course one of the men died and the day after being buried he turned up at the foot of his friend's bed as arranged. The man in the bed almost died with fright, but soon remembered the purpose of the visit. He sat up immediately, eager to hear the news.

'Tell me quick,' he said, 'is there football in Heaven?'

The dead man replied: 'Well, I have good news and I have bad news. The good news is that, yes, there's football in Heaven all right. But the bad news is that there's a game next Saturday and you're playing full-back.'

HAPPY DAYS ARE NOT HERE AGAIN

Manchester City are pining for their first Champions League trophy. How realistic is that? A story serves to illustrate.

Yaya Touré was walking slowly by Old Trafford with his three-legged poodle when he came across a bottle. When he unscrewed the top of the bottle, a genie appeared and said, 'I'm so grateful to get out of that bottle that I will grant you one wish.' Touré thought for a moment and said, 'I have always dreamed that my poodle would win the major prize at Crufts but that's not possible as he only has three legs. Could you give him a fourth leg, please?'

The genie thought for a moment and then said, 'I'm sorry, I can't do that. Just think of all the operations that would be involved in putting the leg together. I'm sorry, but could you ask for an easier wish?'

Touré said, 'Well there is one other thing. I'd like to win the Champions League with Manchester City.'

The genie thought about it for a few minutes and then said, 'So, what kind of paw do you want on that new leg for your poodle?'

FOREVER AND EVER?

The transfer saga for four months over the summer of 2020 was whether Jadon Sancho would join Manchester United from Borussia Dortmund. One United fan was so keen for the transfer to happen that he spent his every waking moment watching Sky Sports' breathless coverage of the saga. His girlfriend was so disillusioned by his obsession with the transfer window that she tearfully told him she was leaving him.

Without taking his eye off the screen he replied: 'Is that a permanent deal?'

THE BITTER WORD

In October 2020, the football world went into shock after Liverpool sensationally lost 7–2 to Aston Villa. Manchester United fans claimed that the entire Liverpool squad went to Spain on holiday to escape the shame and rented a huge house. Apparently, you can't beat A Villa at this time of the year.

15

SCOTLAND THE BRAVE

Scotland are a good team with strong English character.
Ruud Gullit

Scotland has given Manchester United some of its biggest names: Sir Matt Busby; Sir Alex Ferguson; Denis Law; Joe Jordan; Gordon Strachan; Martin Buchan; Willie Morgan; Brian McClair; Jim Leighton; Lou Macari; Alan Brazil; Darren Fletcher; David Moyes; Arthur Albiston; Pat Crerand; Stewart Houston, Ryan Fraser; Jim Holton and Scott McTominay to name but a handful.

It is also fair to say that Scottish football has produced more than its fair share of 'characters' who have left an indelible imprint on the sporting landscape, not always in the way they might have liked. This chapter celebrates some of the country's more memorable individuals who played for United.

BIG JIM

Nostalgia can be a dangerous pastime when it clouds the memory and impedes our ability to recall accurately the strands of the past. I am reminded of the day Lester Piggott went into a shop to buy an ice cream. The excited girl at the counter asked, 'Are you Wilson Pickett?'

However, my most vivid memories of Manchester United players are those of my childhood. A case in point is that of the late Jim Holton who went to play for Scotland in the 1974 World Cup. It was Mae West who famously said, 'A hard man is good to find.' Manchester United found one in Big Jim. He was loved by the fans and they celebrated him with the chant:

> *Six foot two, eyes of blue.*
> *Big Jim Holton is watching you.*
> *There isn't a single forward*
> *He doesn't put the fright into.*

Mind you there are many who doubt if Jim was in fact six foot two!

> *Psycho*
> *Mary had a little lamb.*
> *Her father shot the shepherd.*

Jim Holton took no prisoners on the field. Hence the suggestion that his nickname should have been 'Psycho'. In his case it was not the winning but the taking someone apart that counted.

Jim did not believe in keeping up with the Joneses. He always dragged them down to his level.

THE IRON MAN

The story goes that when he made his debut for United, Jim's mother was concerned about the physical nature of the exchanges. She turned to her husband and said, 'Poor Jim will break a leg.'

According to folklore her husband looked at her reproachfully and said, 'He might but it won't be his own.'

EXTRA LEG

Another story told about Jim goes back to the time he had a terrible leg on him, returning to the dressing room, after a bruising encounter in a league match. It was covered in cuts and bruises and had a massive gash from the top of the thigh to the knee. He had no idea whose it was.

SEXY FOOTBALL

Sexy football is not synonymous with Scotland in the same way as it is with Brazil. In August 2003, Airdrie United chairman Jim Ballantyne announced that his second division football team would soon be sponsored by Glasgow's Seventh Heaven strip club after he had enjoyed its sights with some friends. His idea was that when players were running on to the pitch, they would be greeted by billboards depicting scantily clad strippers.

'I rank it as one of my greatest achievements since I took over at Airdrie United,' he explained, 'that one way or another. I will be the only chairman in Scottish football who'll still be in seventh heaven, even if we get gubbed 4–0.'

THE DOC

One of Manchester United's most colourful managers was the late Tommy 'The Doc' Docherty. He managed United from 1972 to 1977. His term as United manager ended in a media fanfare when it emerged he was having an affair with the wife of the club's physio. Hence his oft-repeated line, 'I'm the only manager ever to be sacked for falling in love.' The Doc was full of good humour, often at his own expense. He readily admitted to making many mistakes. However, there was one thing he never regretted: the relationship that cost him the job he always said he was made for, manager of Manchester United. Forty-three years after he was fired because of his love for her, Mary was beside him when he died.

When he left United, The Doc was also starring in a national TV advertisement for razors. This led to a rash of bad puns about 'close shaves'. In 2019, a year before his death, when he was ninety-one years young, Docherty joked he was still available to take a manager's job.

Among his other clubs was Villa. Of the Aston Villa team of 1968, he said: 'Brains? Listen there's a lot of players who think manual labour is the Spanish president.'

Tommy took the United job having just guided Scotland through the qualifying rounds for the 1974 World Cup finals. In fairness, it was a major achievement as was evident from the old joke, 'What do you call a Scotsman at the knockout stages of a major football tournament?'

'A referee.'

In typical Doc style, he boasted that United was the 'best job in football'. Moreover, he was prepared 'to walk from Scotland to Old Trafford for the job'. One WAG was heard to matter that was probably because the Scottish FA was too mean to give him the expenses. The Doc's salary was £15,000 a year, twice as much as he earned for the Scottish job.

He endeared himself with United fans by describing Manchester City's light blue strip: 'There are three types of Oxo cubes. Light brown for chicken stock, dark brown for beef stock, and light blue for laughing-stock.'

A LITTLE PATIENCE

Docherty was once told he was too impatient. His response was quicker than a bullet from a chamber, 'That's not true. I have patience. I just don't like to use it.'

LOQUACIOUS

Few managers prove more conclusively than Docherty that for wit, originality and generally great laughs, it really is 'a funny old game'.

The dazzling dozen 'Docisms' are:

1. [Aston Villa chairman] *Doug Ellis said he was right behind me, so I told him I'd rather have him in front where I could see him.*
2. *The ideal board of directors should be made up of three men – two dead and one dying.*
3. *Ray Wilkins can't run, he can't tackle and he can't head the ball. The only time he goes forward is to toss the coin.*
4. *He's* [a fellow coach] *not so much a coach as a hearse.*
5. *Robert Maxwell has just bought Brighton and Hove Albion, and he's furious to find it is only one club.*
6. *They serve a drink in Glasgow called the Souness – one half and you're off.*
7. *Preston? They're one of my old clubs. But then most of them are. I've had more clubs than Jack Nicklaus.*
8. *Some teams are so negative they should be sponsored by Kodak.*
9. *After the match an official asked for two of my players to take a dope test. I offered him a referee.*
10. *Football wasn't meant to be run by linesmen and air traffic control.*
    (The Doc dismissed the 'long ball' game in 1988.)
11. *Stan Collymore has got all the ability in the world but there's something missing. He must be a brain donor. Brian* [Little] *wanted a Colly but all he got was a cabbage.*
12. *Mark Wright would get an injury if he went on Question of Sport.*

However, the most bizarre quotation that ever came from Docherty's lips was surely his response to the signing of George Graham: 'George is the Gunther Nezter of British football.'

One United fan was not a big fan of Docherty's intelligence and told the following story:

'Tommy Docherty was walking out of Old Trafford one day with Denis Law and has a paper bag in his hand. He says: "Denis, if you can guess how many bars of chocolate I have in this bag you can have both of them."'

The Doc often left clubs he managed after a short time. 'They offered me £10,000 to settle amicably,' he said on one occasion when he faced the sack. 'I told them they'd have to be a lot more amicable than that.'

BARRY'S GAME
Scottish goalkeepers have often been ridiculed in the media. The BBC's Barry Davies though was a big fan of one Scottish goalkeeper who played for Manchester United: 'Jim Leighton is looking as sharp as a tank.'

FRANKLY SPEAKING
Frank Stapleton made his league debut for Arsenal in March 1975 in a 1–1 draw with Stoke City. By the end of the 1980/81 season he had notched up seventy-five league goals for the club and had earned himself the reputation of being one of the best centre-forwards in England. His tally of cup goals was equally impressive, scoring fourteen goals in twenty-seven matches between 1977 and 1980 was an important factor in Arsenal's three-year cup run in that period when they reached FA Cup finals in consecutive seasons: losing 1–0 to Ipswich in 1978; beating Manchester United 3–2 in 1979 and losing 1–0 to Eastenders

West Ham (courtesy of a rare Trevor Brooking headed goal) in 1980. He also played in the European Cup Winners' final against Valencia (which starred Argentina's hero of the 1978 World Cup winning side, Mario Kempes) in 1980 when Arsenal lost on a penalty shootout which saw Kempes, Liam Brady and Graham Rix missing from the spot.

Stapleton was voted Arsenal's 'Player of the Year' in both 1977 and in 1980, so that when he left Arsenal in the summer of 1981 the Highbury faithful were bitterly disappointed – particularly as it followed so closely on the departure of the fans' beloved Liam 'Chippy' Brady. Brady joined Italian giants Juventus for £600,000 despite the fact that Manchester United were prepared to shatter the British transfer fee record with a £1.5 million offer. The Arsenal fans' agitation was compounded by their belief that the club did not do all in their power to keep their two star players. However, their contracts were up, and they felt it was the opportune time to seek new challenges.

When the news of Stapleton's desire to leave Arsenal broke, the rush for his signature was immediate. Offers came from Italy and West Germany and he entered substantial negotiations with Liverpool. Stapleton was having his wedding ceremony and did not want any disturbances but when Ron Atkinson made the call and said get back to Manchester immediately, Frank responded. The fact that his new wife was a Mancunian helped to persuade him to choose United over Liverpool. Atkinson was less successful in his effort to persuade Mark Lawrenson at the time to opt for Old Trafford rather than Anfield.

A major wrangle developed about the size of Stapleton's transfer fee. Arsenal valued him at £1.5 million whereas United claimed he was only worth £750,000. As the two clubs could not agree, the matter was arbitrated on by the Football League Appeals Committee, which valued Stapleton at £900,000.

Ironically, they could have signed him for nothing. As a sixteen-year-old he went on trial to the club but it did not really work out and while United demurred about signing him Arsenal's Irish scout, Bill Darby, alerted his employers and Stapleton was on his way to Highbury.

There is a famous photo of the very young Liam Brady, Frank Stapleton and David O'Leary and another youngster on the way to make it big in Highbury. The fourth man was future Irish rugby international Johnny Murphy. In the annals of Irish sport, 'Iron Toe' Murphy is unquestionably one of its most colourful characters. Irreverent is much too tame a word to describe his famous after-dinner speeches as captain of Leinster. He had a bus and hearse business and turned up for training one night in his hearse with a coffin inside. Some of the players found it to be disconcerting to be doing their press-ups beside a coffin and grumbled to Johnny. He is alleged to have just said: 'She's not going anywhere and doesn't mind waiting.'

In contrast, Stapleton was not known for his great sense of humour. The former Scottish centre-half Gordon McQueen, father of Sky Sports' Haley, and Stapleton's teammate at United once said of Frank that he gets up in the morning and smiles at himself in the mirror just to get it out of the way for the day.

SHOCKER

After Roy Keane's time at Manchester United came to an unhappy and controversial end, he moved to Glasgow's Celtic but injury curtailed his impact. A number of big names have had their reputations tarnished while at Celtic.

After he 'parted company' with Celtic, John Barnes was asked about the role the media played in his demise. He simply quoted Leo Tolstoy, 'All newspaper and journalistic activity is an intellectual brothel from which there is no retreat.'

John Barnes's brief reign as Celtic manager was doomed to a sad end when Celtic lost a cup tie 3–1 to First Division minnows Inverness Caledonian Thistle FC in 2000. It created a seismic shock in Scottish football. *The Sun* captured the moment brilliantly in its headline: *Super Caley Go Ballistic, Celtic Are Atrocious.*

BUM DEAL

Who said lightning doesn't strike twice? Three years later, and just four days after Martin O'Neill was a candidate for canonisation when his club beat Liverpool to qualify for the UEFA Cup semi-final, Inverness beat Celtic again in the fifth round of the Scottish Cup. In that moment O'Neill understood a statement Alex Ferguson had made the previous day, 'It's going to get very twitchy over the next few weeks; it's squeeze your bum time.'

A BIRD'S EYE VIEW

For many people in the UK, the voice of Scottish football is Roddy Forsyth because of his authoritative reports on BBC radio. Roddy was in full flow of a report on a Rangers match when he came to an abrupt halt. After a little expletive Roddy explained the cause of his problem, 'A pigeon just sh*t all over my notes and it's really big. It's on my coat as well.' Clearly the pigeon was a Celtic fan.

FLOWER OF SCOTLAND

In his playing career with Manchester United, Gordon Strachan's flower bloomed brightly. In his time managing Celtic and Scotland he found the soil more treacherous. He did have some interesting exchanges with the press though:

Journalist: 'What about Agustín Delgado?'
Strachan: 'I've got more important things to think about than

that. For instance, I've got a yoghurt to finish by today, the expiry date's today. That could be my priority rather than Delgado just now.'

Reporter: 'In what areas where they better than you today?'
Strachan: 'That big green one out there.'

Journalist: 'What is your impression of Jermaine Pennant?'
Strachan: 'I don't do impressions.'

Reporter: 'Gordon, can we have a quick word?'
Strachan: 'Velocity.'
Journalist: 'If you were English what formation would you play?'
Strachan: 'If I was English, I'd top myself.'

Reporter: 'So, Gordon, any changes then?'
Strachan: 'Naw, still five foot six, ginger and a big nose.'

16

IRELAND'S CALL

My kids always ask me, 'Are you happy, Dad?'
When I tell them I am they say,
'Would you ever tell your face?'

Roy Keane

For younger readers, the close links between Ireland and Manchester United may be puzzling. It is necessary to give some historical context to clarify this phenomenon. In the Great Irish Famine of the 1840s, two million Irish people died from hunger and sickness. Within a decade or so a further two million people were lost to emigration.

Paradoxically while most Irish immigrants were anxious to protect their national identity in foreign fields, they were also anxious to blend in their new environment. Sport, particularly football, provided the perfect outlet and, long before the term was coined, it was politically correct to do so. Other avenues at social integration such as joining the local branch of the Conservative Party would have incurred social leprosy. Thus, for Irish immigrants in Manchester at the end of the nineteenth century, football assumed a deep sociological significance.

For immigrants in particular, football was more than a game – it was an integral part of people's identity. The Irish immigrants were by and large a contented resourceful people enshrined in a devout and peaceful religious society, dwelling in an austere environment where, to be self-supporting, they had to work hard. Their tastes were simple and their needs modest. History endowed them with an amazing sense of community. This, in turn, nurtured a tradition of great goodwill and generosity and an awareness of other people's difficulties and readiness to help in times of adversity. They were patient up to a point but did not want the hostility that they experienced throughout the 1860s and '70s to continue.

The thirst for social inclusion was most keenly felt by those handfuls of Irish immigrants with aspirations to move in the upper echelons of Mancunian society. The first Irish were brought over to Manchester by the de Traffords, a Catholic family, who made the journey as a consequence of religious persecution during the Reformation. The de Traffords were the most influential land-owners in the area and owned the ground which would become the theatre of dreams, Old Trafford. They attracted the Irish intelligentsia in the shape of such professionals as doctors and lawyers who would almost without exception rise to prominence in their adopted city.

Manchester United fans, indigenous and imported, were united on the terraces in a common cause regardless of class, nationality or creed. Football was a badge of identity which enabled Irish immigrants to consider themselves as Mancunians. Attendance at a United fixture was a social rite of passage for any Irishman with ambitions to fit in to the local community.

The bonds of loyalty between the Irish and United were considerably strengthened as the Reds began to taste the fruits of success. In 1907/08 and in 1910/11 United won the league titles and in 1909 they beat Bristol City to win the FA Cup for the first time, courtesy of a goal from Sandy Turnbull and a fine performance from Billy Meredith. Five years earlier Turnbull had picked up his first FA Cup medal when he helped Manchester City defeat Bolton 1–0 as had Meredith who scored City's winning goal in the final. Turnbull was killed in action on the battlefields of France on 3 May 1917.

An important milestone occurred on Saturday 19 February 1910 when United moved into their new home at Old Trafford. United's previous grounds at North Road and Bank Street had both been well short of the desired standard and following their league and cup successes the club decided on a move to a new stadium, especially built for them, and that would match their footballing triumphs. The stadium was designed by Archibald Leitch, the acclaimed architect of a number of football grounds. It was intended to be the biggest ground in the country, with the most lavish of facilities for players and staff.

The site was purchased with a £60,000 grant from the chairman John Davies but as construction costs rocketed by an additional £30,000, some of the planned facilities had to be significantly scaled down. Instead of holding 100,000, the capacity was reduced to 70,000 and some of the planned office facilities had to be shelved. The first game was against Liverpool. An estimated 50,000 paid to see the match. It is said that a few thousand more were sneaked in free of charge when gatemen, unable to cope with the queues, simply opened the doors.

In 1911 the FA Cup final replay was played there in front of 56,000 spectators, when Bradford City defeated Newcastle 1–0. Four years later Old Trafford was chosen as the venue for the FA Cup final itself, with Sheffield United beating Chelsea, as Crystal Palace had been turned into a military camp. The 1915 final was called the 'khaki final' as so many soldiers in uniform were among the crowd.

The fact that Irish immigrants quickly identified so fiercely with United and so easily with their new neighbours on the terraces is something of a surprise – given that the historical enmity between Britain and Ireland continues to distort the sporting relationship between both countries right through to the present day.

For the Irish working class, watching football at Old Trafford provided an escape from their problems and anxieties. There were other distractions. Manchester had a thriving theatrical tradition. Samuel Beckett put on a number of his first nights in Manchester. Another enrichment of Manchester's rich cultural tapestry was Mike Costello of Irish extraction. He gained celebrity status as the great Blondini when he was buried in a coffin for seventy-eight days for a £500 bet. One of his favourite escapades was to place himself in an ordinary coffin blown apart by dynamite.

Football though was the battery that drove Irish immigrants' imaginations and dared them to see themselves in a very different light – as pillars of the Manchester community. It allowed them to dream of better days to come. Success, albeit by association, such as watching United winning the title increased their self-esteem. They walked that little bit taller, they talked just a little more boldly, and they mingled among their new neighbours with pride. Football was their passport to social inclusion. In this way, sport fulfilled its historic role of unifying people and acting as a counterweight to narrow sectional interests.

From the very beginning, Irish players were at the heart of United's playing staff. John Peden became Ireland's first professional footballer when he joined Newton Heath. Tommy Morrison made history on Christmas Day, 1902 when he became the first Irishman to wear the colours of Manchester United in a league derby match against City. The following day, Morrison went one better when he became the first Irishman to score a league goal for the club. Two years later Morrison earned the distinction of becoming the first Irishman to score for United (against Notts County) in an FA Cup tie.

THE KEANE EDGE

In the last football generation, no Irish player has got the acclaim of Roy Keane. In May 1993, Steve Bruce placed the crown-shaped lid of the premiership trophy on the head of Bryan Robson, on one of Old Trafford's most memorable nights – it was a fitting coronation for Captain Marvel. However, not even Robson could go on forever. A replacement would have to be found for him in midfield, but it was a formidable task.

In the summer of 1993, Roy Keane signed for United from Nottingham Forest for a then club record of £3.75 million. Keane then had the awesome task of replacing Eric Cantona as United captain in 1997, following the French star's shock decision to leave the club. That same year, on his video of his dream United team, Alex Ferguson described Keano as one of the best midfielders in the world.

His first season at Manchester United was not without its problems because of the burden of a record £3.75 million transfer fee and the inevitable comparisons with Bryan Robson whose mantle he was destined to inherit – the young pretender in the shadow of the master. At Old Trafford, Keane was called 'Damien' by the other players after the character in *The Omen*.

NO FLASH HARRY

As a pundit today, Keane has lost none of his edge. In their first game back in 'Project Restart' against Spurs in June 2020, United were trailing Spurs and Roy was 'fuming' at half-time. His main targets were Harry Maguire and David de Gea. So 'disgusted' was he with their performances that he said he would not allow either of them on the team bus after the game!

Team manager Ole Gunnar Solskjaer leapt to de Gea's defence. However, his excuse for the keeper's blunder which cost the team a goal was certainly original. It was because 'the ball was moving in the air'.

TEARJERKER

In June 2020 Roy Keane gave a lengthy interview to a newspaper journalist. At the end, the reporter apologised for taking so much time.

Keane replied, 'Yeah I know. My beard has grown much longer since this interview started.'

In the interview Keane was asked when he last cried. He replied: 'Watching a film.'

'What kind of films make you cry?'

'For f**k's sake. Sad ones.'

YOU DON'T KNOW JACK

In July 2020, the football world mourned the sad passing of Jack Charlton. The first thing you noticed when you met Jack was the speed with which he forgot your name. The conversation about football was peppered with comments like 'the boy with the great left foot' and 'that nippy little winger' which substituted for players names. What was equally clear was that Jack had a razor-sharp brain with an encyclopaedic knowledge of the game. He talked affably about all the issues and personalities in the game. Our conversation was not without incident.

The sun threw long, blood-red streaks of light into Jack's room in a Dublin Hotel. Big Jack was just out of the shower and was wearing only a bathrobe and, to be honest, when he crossed his legs, I saw a bit more of him than I would have wished!

In seeking his opinion on the Manchester United players who played for him when he managed the Ireland team, I had to compete with a nature programme or something to do with fishing on the television. As I got out my tape-recorder, he turned down the television to minimum volume and conducted the interview while keeping the corner of his eye on the screen. Occasionally he paused in mid-sentence when some arresting image caught his attention.

After an hour's conversation, I was anxious to let him watch his programme in peace. I quickly collected my gear in Jack's cluttered room and bade him goodbye. To my absolute horror I discovered outside that I had departed with one of Jack's stockings. My first reaction was to run like the devil. How many people can say they have a souvenir of Jack Charlton's sock? Then I discovered the bitter truth of Hamlet's observation that 'conscience doth make cowards of us all' and I meekly returned with my tail between my legs. I was afraid that the former Irish manager would choke with laughter. Although I returned home sockless at least I had the consolation of getting closer than any other journalist to the sole of Big Jack.

Listening to Jack talk, it was easy to feel overwhelmed by the sheer strength of his character. I wondered if he ever stepped down from this heightened plain of existence to, as it were, the world of mere mortals. The question amused him without providing the series of revelations I had half hoped for. Most of our conversation was about the boys in green and to the importance he attached to bringing pleasure to the Irish football public. In Jack's distinctive Geordie brogue most became 'moost' and goalkeeper becomes 'gullkeepah'.

His mind was as agile as an Olympic gymnast. When he talked about football he always seemed, quite simply, to hit the right note. You could not ask any more of a manager than that. It did not bother him unduly that not everyone accepted his football creed. He did not expect all his critics to be converted to the 'Jack Orthodoxy'.

A far cry from the hard man he was sometimes portrayed as, there were shafts of tenderness in all his comments. In conversation, he was a star performer. When he was on his game, as he was then, there was none better. He thought on his feet but, when necessary, kicked with his mouth. He was a complex character, commanding respect and signalling friendship in the one moment. Though he had no doubt been asked the same questions and had to tell the same stories again and again, his eyes shone, when I queried him about his glory days with Ireland.

I was afraid he would laugh when I suggested that he would be canonised by the Irish people because of the success he has achieved with the team. Instead, he said:

'Public attention is part of the job. I'm a miner's son from the North East of England, who's spent a life in football. They gave me a job to do over here – which was to produce a team which would get results and bring people into the game. I've been very successful in doing exactly that. The fact that the people of Ireland like me is great. I like being popular. I would be a liar if I said I didn't. It's got its drawbacks. There is very little privacy anymore. Canonisation? You couldn't have done that to me anyway. I'm a Protestant!'

Big Jack got very animated when I asked him his opinion of Roy Keane: 'He's not the greatest talker I ever met. There were times I wasn't really sure if he was listening to me but when he really got going, he was something special. He had the most amazing engine I've ever seen. In the World Cup in America, he put in a huge amount of work for us. The funny thing was that he never took any water in that heat during the match except at half-time. He could just run and run and run. He was a great battler and well able to put himself about. I know people say he's a bit hot-headed, but he never got into any trouble when I was in charge of him. I think people forget he was so young then 'cos he seemed to have been around for a long time. He was the sort of player you would want to have with you rather than against you.'

Disappointment was boldly stamped on Jack's face as he recalled one unhappy aspect of his association with Keane during his time as Irish manager:

'I know Alex Ferguson thought the world of him and to be honest that caused me a few problems 'cos he missed out on some vital games for us especially in the qualification for the European Championships in England. Our squad was so small that we couldn't afford to miss out on key players in vital positions. Roy's absence left us very thin in the middle of the park for some vital games and we paid a high price for it. I know Alex paid Roy's wages but maybe Roy could have played a few more big games for us. He is a very competitive lad and without him we weren't the force we could've been or should've been. But that's water under the bridge now. I'm glad he went on to even greater things for United.'

MISTAKE

When he was eighteen, Roy Keane signed for Nottingham Forest for a snip of £25,000. Brian Clough comments would prove to be well founded: 'It's a long time since I've been so excited by a young man... I'd quite happily have paid £500,000 for him.' Less than a month later he was making his league debut against Liverpool at Anfield. He was voted the Barclay's Young Eagle of Year for 1991/92.

Cloughie said of his young protégé, 'I couldn't understand a word he was saying. But his feet told me all I wanted to know.'

For most of his teenage years Roy was told he was too small to make it as a football player. The only comparable story I can think of such a misjudgement happened a century earlier. Two men, Mr Marks and Mr Smith, were talking. Mr Marks outlined his plans for a new shop and asked Mr Smith to be his partner. Mr Smith replied: 'Nah. It'll never work.' Mr Marks found a new partner – Mr Spencer. The rest is history.

THE LIFE OF BRIAN

Keane has consistently praised the importance of the then Nottingham Forest boss Brian Clough to his career. Not every player could say the same. Gary Megson's stay at Forest was particularly short. He had a habit of making himself sick before a match and at half-time. Megson was making his Forest debut in a friendly game before Dundee. Forest's manager Brian Clough came into the dressing room and heard retching noises coming from the toilets.

'What the hell is that noise?' he demanded.

'It's Megsy being sick,' replied one of the players.

Clough called Megson back into the room, 'Why are you being sick?'

'I'm always sick at half-time.'

'Not in my dressing room, you're not.'

Megson never played for Clough again. His career with Forest lasted one match.

HAIRS AND GRACES

Brian Clough did not seem to visit the barber very often, he just did his job with no hairs and graces. He had unusual motivational strategies. During a reserve match he was not very happy with his strikers, especially Nigel Jemson, who not surprisingly did not have a long stay with the club. At half-time, all the team were sitting down in the dressing room with their heads bowed low. Things had not gone well for Forest in the first half. Clough walked up to Jemson and forcefully instructed him to, 'Stand up.' Jemson obediently complied with Clough's demand.

'Have you ever been hit in the stomach, son?' Cloughie enquired.

As soon as Jemson had said, 'No,' Clough hit him hard in the midriff.

Jemson doubled up in pain and let out a scream of agony. 'Now you have, son!' said Clough calmly and with that he walked away.

OBEDIENCE

When Forest won consecutive European Cups in 1979 and 1980, their centre-half was Kenny Burns. Clough warned Kenny many times about passing the ball square across the front of his own goal. During the second half of a big match, he again defied Clough's orders and repeated the feat. The final whistle blew, and Burns walked back to the dressing room to find an envelope waiting for him at his changing place. He opened it. It was a typed letter on official club paper – he had been fined by the manager for disobeying orders.

THE FLOATING VOTE

Brian Clough was not a man to hide his opinions, 'Trevor Brooking floats like a butterfly and stings like one too.'

DOUBLE OR QUITS

During the late 1970s, Larry Lloyd was Forest's centre-half. Forest had played an evening match in Greece and were congregating in the hotel foyer before departing for the airport. Although the temperature was soaring, the manager had decreed that everybody was to report wearing the club blazer and slacks. The only rebel who did not conform was Lloyd, who was wearing a tracksuit.

Clough shouted over, 'Go and get your blazer on!'

Lloyd was having none of it, 'No, it's too warm. I'm wearing my tracksuit.'

The manager immediately replied, 'If you don't put it on, I will fine you £100.'

The answer was immediate, 'I don't care.'

'Right, that's £100. If you don't put it on now, I'll double it.'

'Go on, then.'

... and so it went on and on.

During the trip back, the fine was doubled many times over, until Larry reached home having lost about six months' wages.

HARSH WORDS

Lloyd had won three England caps at Liverpool but fell out of the international reckoning until he joined Forest. On his recall to the heart of the English defence, England were thrashed 4–1 by Wales. Shortly afterwards in the Forest dressing room, Larry was confronted by Clough.

'Larry, which England international got two caps on the same day?'

'I don't know, boss. Who was it?'

'You did. Your fourth and your last!'

DOG-GONE

When he managed Nottingham Forest Brian Clough was out walking his dog, and watched his team play a five-a-side in training. He called over his full-back Brian Laws and said, 'You're wasting your time doing this – take my dog for a walk.' Laws did – twice around the training ground.

TACTICAL SWITCH

Brian Clough was known for his decisiveness: 'I always tell directors and chairmen that they only have to make one decision – to pick someone to do the job they can't do.'

Once Cloughie bewildered a camera crew, who had been asked

to interview Gary Charles, by sending out a young apprentice who vaguely resembled the full-back.

NO RESPECT

At Forest, Clough was the uncrowned king. Despite his success with the club when he managed Derby, Cloughie was not always treated with reverence. One day he rang down to the dressing room for a cup of tea.

The apprentice who answered said simply, 'Bugger off,' and slammed down the phone.

Clough rang down again, asking: 'Do you know who I am?'

The apprentice answered with another question: 'Do you know who I am?'

'No.'

'Well, bugger off again, then.'

LOVE AND MATRIMONY

When he was a young man, Roy Keane got some advice from his local curate, 'Roy you need to take a wife.'

Roy replied, 'That's a great idea Father. Whose wife should I take?'

FANS' ZONE

The constant source of passion is the fans. Of course, fans often have polarised opinions. Take the case of Roy Keane. One of his supporters claims, 'If he was still playing, Roy Keane would have had more suitors than Kylie Minogue.' One of his many detractors, though, claims, 'It is not that Roy Keane is grumpy. It is just that if he found fifty quid on the ground he would be complaining about littering.'

A NUN'S STORY

Roy Keane was on the Ireland team for over fourteen years, including playing in the 1994 World Cup in the USA. After a bust-up with the then Irish manager Mick McCarthy in Saipan, Roy Keane did not play for Ireland in the 2002 World Cup.

Ireland's then goalkeeper was Packie Bonner. Packie's status as one of the top goalies in the world at the time did not come without a price. He attracted huge adulation from people of all ages – including nuns. Once, he had to go to hospital for a hernia operation. He had missed Mass on the Sunday and because he was in the Bon Secours – a nuns' hospital – it was a very holy place. He thought he would go to Mass during the week and he went down to the ten o'clock service. Everyone there were nuns, all but himself.

He was being very extra holy that day. In most churches people leave as soon as the priest is finished but he was making sure he was not going to make that mistake and he was going to stay as long as the nuns. As the priest said his final words, a little nun came up beside him and said, 'Excuse me Mr. Bonner I wonder if you could sign my Bible for me?' Packie's sure she is still doing penance somewhere for that!

Another time during his Celtic days he was in hospital for the cup final and Celtic were playing. He was all set to watch the match on television when a nun from an enclosed order came in to see him and sat down on the chair. She stood chatting to him for the whole afternoon. He had to switch off the telly and missed the whole match.

PRIDE COMES BEFORE A FALL

Another of Keano's Irish teammates was Andy Townsend. In 1990 Townsend was walking with his wife in Dublin. It was shortly after the World Cup and, everywhere they went, people were asking for Andy's autograph and requesting to have their photo taken with him. Eventually they decided to head for a quieter part of the capital. They were walking down a side street when Andy noticed a woman on the road with a camera. Instinctively, Andy stopped and posed for the camera. After a pregnant pause, the woman screamed, 'You stupid c**t. Will you get out of the f**king way.'

Andy turned around to see a beautiful statue behind him – the woman was desperate to take a photo of it!

SUCKER PUNCH

There was an expectation that age might cause Keano to mellow, particularly when he became manager in the more restful and rustic setting of Ipswich in the 2009/10 season. Not for the first time, Keane defied expectations: 'It's good to go a bit mad, but I don't throw teacups around. That's not my style – I'd rather throw punches.'

MAKING A MARK

Straight talking is Roy's forte.

ITV's Mark Pougatch: 'What is Ross Barkley's best position?'
Roy Keane: 'Probably on the bench.'

DENIS THE MENACE

Asked about his opinion of one of Manchester United's great full-backs Denis Irwin, Jack Charlton's words come thick and fast:

> Denis was a wonderful player. I can't think of any time he ever let Ireland down. He was a big plus for us when he came into the side. He gave us extra options 'cos he was a great crosser of the ball, a good tackler and he's great in dead ball situations. He's a quiet lad who is dependability itself – if that's the right word.
>
> To be a successful football side you need different types of players. There are players like our Bobby who have that bit extra, that can see things that other players couldn't see and make things happen for you and ensure you win big games.

Sometimes they can be a bit annoying, like Paul Gascoigne. They can be totally useless for eighty-nine minutes and then turn the game with one stroke of genius. But no matter how many flair players you have you need players like Denis Irwin who you know will always give you one hundred percent.

There are certain types of players who give managers headaches and I've come across a few in my time in the Ireland job. Denis though was a manager's dream, a class act, a nice guy and a player you could always bank on to come up trumps.

Irwin earned the nickname 'Mr Consistency' for his contribution to United's success. He never dated any of the Spice Girls nor Dani Behr, which was *de rigeur* for any footballer with pretensions to a star profile at the time. The French sports newspaper *L'Equipe* did a feature on him under the headline 'His name is Nobody.'

His temperament is such that he has been called 'the Ice Man'. If there was one incident which illustrates that it was a Wednesday night in May 1995 as United and Blackburn were neck and neck in the title race. United were struggling to overcome Southampton. It was 1–1 with eight minutes to go, when a hotly disputed penalty went United's way. All the United players started to look around. Who would have the bottle to take the kick that might secure the championship? Irwin stepped up as the star names went absent. The fear of failure can chill the blood of the most hardened professional – witness hard man Stuart Pearce's missed penalty in the World Cup semi-final in 1990, not to mention Chris Waddle's orbit-chasing, botched effort. When it mattered most, Irwin showed nerves of steel and made no mistake ensuring a nail-biting *denouement* on the final 'Super Sunday' of the season.

At Denis's testimonial dinner, Jack Charlton brought the house town with his unconventional tribute to Denis. Jack said, 'Denis was the consummate professional; the best full-back to play for Manchester United; the best full-back to play for the Republic of Ireland; he was always our most consistent player; he never made mistakes; he never gave the ball away; he was always on time for training; always first on the bus for training, he never let you down nor never once caused a problem .... What a boring, f**king b*stard?'

NO CHARGE

Denis kindly donated one of his United jerseys to a local charity. As a thank you for his efforts, the organisers later gave him some batteries that had been given out free of charge.

A MARKED MAN

After an underwhelming career at Manchester United, Don Givens's career only really took off when he moved to QPR. Givens scored one goal for United in his nine appearances, four as substitute, in his short stay with the club. He joined the club as a teenager in 1966. In 1970, at the age of twenty, he was called into Matt Busby's office and told he was no longer wanted at Old Trafford which was a devastating blow to the Irishman whose sole ambition was to play for United. He then moved to Luton for £15,000 before really establishing his reputation with QPR where he scored 76 goals in 242 games. He subsequently played for Birmingham City, Bournemouth, Sheffield United and Neuchatel Xamax in Switzerland. In 1997 he joined the coaching staff at Arsenal. He won fifty-six caps for the Republic of Ireland.

Former English captain and QPR manager Gerry Francis spoke to me of his admiration for his former teammate:

QPR had a great team in the mid-1970s. Liverpool only snatched the title from us by a point in the '75/76 season. Practically all our team were internationals from Phil Parkes in goal right up to Don at the front. We also had some wonderful characters in the side like Stan Bowles. It's only as I look back on it now, I realise how balanced we were and how much flair we had in the team. What we lacked that season was that our squad just wasn't as strong as Liverpool's and we had to pay a high price for that in the end.

Don Givens was an integral part of our success at the time. He got a lot of vital goals for us as he did for the Republic, though he was unlucky in the sense that he missed out on playing for you lot when you were going so well after Jack Charlton took over. He was a quality finisher with all the attributes of a top-class striker. I can tell you one thing, the Irish manager would have been much happier drawing up his plans for the future if he had a striker like Don in his side.

In 1974 Givens was given a rather unusual task. His teammate and fellow Irish international, Terry Mancini, was having such a run of scoring own goals that Givens was brought back to mark him every time QPR conceded a corner!

RADIO DAZE

Another teammate of Givens was the England striker Stan Bowles, who was as renowned as much for his gambling as for his mercurial talent. On the day of the Grand National, Stan (Bowles 'em Over) had backed Red Rum. During a home match that day he heard the commentary of the race on a transistor radio in the crowd as he was back defending a corner. He deliberately kept conceding corners for the next few minutes so that he could continue to listen to the commentary. As soon as he heard the result, he cleared the ball up field and went on to play the game of his life.

A DOG'S LIFE

Another time he was asked what he did after he lost a lot of money at the races. Bowles answered, 'I go home and play cards with my dog.'

'Good gracious. You must have a very clever dog?'

'Not really. Every time he gets a good hand, he wags his tail.'

THE DYNAMIC DUO

Manchester United has given Irish television two of its most famous faces. Those RTÉ viewers who lived in single channel land were first introduced to football analysis via *Match of the Day* which was shown after *The Late, Late Show* on Saturday nights. RTÉ has always been good at spotting a good idea and, by the 1978 World Cup in Argentina, was fast catching up with the stations across the water in the punditry stakes. It was the 1982 World Cup though that really showed a star was born in the way Eamon Dunphy went against the tide of virtual universal euphoria about the Brazil team. He claimed that the stylish Brazilians were flawed because they couldn't defend properly. Italy went on to prove Eamon right.

In the European Championships in 1984, Eamon was at it again. This time he consistently claimed that French superstar Michel Platini was 'a good player but not a great player'. This time though Platini proved Eamon wrong. The point though was that everyone was talking about Eamon and that is what a television station prays for.

Eamon has the inside knowledge of the game that a pundit needs.

He joined Manchester United as an apprentice in 1960 at the age of fifteen. After two years at Old Trafford he signed professional forms but never made it on to the first team. In August 1965 he moved to Third Division new boys York City. The following January he moved to Millwall for a fee of £8,000 where his career really took off and he helped the Lions to win promotion to Division Two in his first season with the club. In his seven seasons at the Den he made 274 league appearances but his Millwall career is also remembered for his classic book *Only A Game?*, a definitive work which chronicled a season in the life of Millwall FC and in the process furnishes a fascinating insight into what it is really like to be a footballer outside the top flight, with all its disappointments, humour, insecurities and petty politics. He subsequently went on to help Charlton win promotion to Division Two, and Reading win promotion to Division Three before his retirement. Capped twenty-three times for Ireland, he jokes, 'I won most of them because John Giles didn't turn up!'

A good quality in any pundit is irreverence. Dunphy scores highly in this category. In 2002 when speculation was rife as to who would replace Mick McCarthy, Dunphy was asked if he'd like the job. He replied, 'I'd love to do it, but I couldn't afford the wage cut.'

I think Eamon is better at football analysis than at self-analysis. I was more than a little surprised to hear him describe himself: 'I'm the simplest, most clean-living guy in this country.'

With Dunphy and his co-panellist John Giles there's no danger of blandness. Giles was part of the United team beaten 4–0 by Everton in the Charity Shield in 1963 and was dropped as a consequence. His response was to seek a transfer request which was reluctantly accepted. He joined Leeds for £37,000 and went on to establish himself as one of the great playmakers of the game. Matt Busby subsequently said selling Giles was his greatest mistake. Giles is universally recognised as one of the greatest players of his generation and was the midfield general at the heart of Leeds United's great success in the 1960s and '70s.

Following his retirement from management, Giles became a media pundit. He didn't have the same style of commentary as his former playing colleagues like Frank Stapleton, 'You've got to be careful. You're not sure if the ball is going to bounce up or down'; David O'Leary: 'Achilles tendon injuries are a pain in the butt' and 'The surprise for me and I'm delighted for Gary Kelly, but Steve Finnan for me has had an outstanding season for Fulham, but as I say that's the only surprise even though, as I say, I'm delighted for Gary' and Andy Townsend, 'There won't be a dry eye in the house.'

Giles and Dunphy became two of the most famous people in Ireland during the glory days of Jack Charlton's reign as Irish manager. In that period, they served one of the key functions of analysts, which is to provoke controversy. Ray Houghton's goal gave Ireland a 1–0 victory over the 'old enemy' England at Euro '88. The RTÉ switchboard was jammed following Ireland's victory with irate callers complaining about John Giles's less than glowing endorsement of the Irish performance. People expected Giles to go mad with delight. Giles has never gone mad about anything. He tried to be as professional as possible. He saw his role as an analyst and not a supporter. He is not the type to go wear a green and white scarf around his neck and shout his head off, though he felt as deeply about Ireland's victory as anybody. He gave an honest view, but some people thought that he was sour because Jack Charlton had struck gold – and he had not.

The debate inevitably seemed at times to be somewhat personalised but from an RTÉ perspective the important thing was that everyone was reacting to the analyst's comments. Of course, the 'civil war' about the controversy between Mick McCarthy and Roy Keane during the 2002 World Cup was 'pundit gold'.

The Giles partnership with Dunphy works because of the contrast in personalities, though Giles has got slightly more Dunphy-esque, in recent years. Take, for example, his comment on Paolo Di Canio: 'He's a legend in his own head.' Many people watched RTÉ's football coverage not mainly for the games but for the opportunity to see Dunphy saying or doing some dramatic, like appearing 'tired and emotional' as he did during the 2002 World Cup.

A huge part of the credit for their success must also go to the show's presenter of many years, Bill O'Herlihy. Bill was able to take Dunphy down a peg or two, like at a half-time in a Champions League match when Eamon said, 'I'm starting to wonder why I went for Stuttgart now.'

Bill replied, 'Well, there's always a gap between the logic and the statement with you, Eamon, isn't there?'

DEMOCRACY IS COMING

Eamon Dunphy was one of the leaders of the campaign to give Irish managers the power to personally pick the Ireland national team. Until the late 1960s, the side had been chosen by a selection committee with disastrous results. After Dunphy helped achieve this democratic revolution, Mick Meagan was appointed manager and Dunphy was chosen for Meagan's first game against Austria at Dalymount. Dunphy jokes that he asked Mick to substitute him at half-time because he was exhausted by the campaign and, frankly, he was an embarrassment to democracy!

KEEPING DOWN WITH THE JONESES

Dunphy's friend and former Wimbledon manager Joe Kinnear was asked what was the most outrageous thing he had ever bought. He replied, 'Vinnie Jones.'

THE MIDFIELD GENERAL

John Giles was only eighteen when he made his international debut in November 1959. Ireland trailed Sweden 2–0 at Dalymount Park when Giles made his debut and launched a rocket of a shot to score a wonder goal. Two further goals from Ipswich Town's Dermot Curtis enabled Ireland to win 3–2. Giles is unquestionably one of Ireland's greatest ever players, but he was also well able to take care of himself.

In June 2020, Graeme Souness described him affectionately as a great player but also 'a nasty little bast*rd'. Giles took it as the compliment, as was intended. Not sure the current generation of United players would react the same way to such a 'compliment'.

During his tenure as Irish manager, Giles was credited with finally dragging the Republic of Ireland into the professional era. There were some occasions though when the amateurism of Irish officialdom got him down, as his former Irish teammate Ray Treacy recalled for me:

'In 1978 we went out with a League of Ireland team to Argentina. It was, as usual, a real last-minute effort. We picked a team over the weekend and flew to London, where we stayed overnight. The next morning, we flew to Buenos Aires via Lisbon and half a dozen other places. I think it was on the trip I decided to become a travel agent!

'We had a 28-hour journey before we got to Buenos Aires. We were shocked to see posters on the way to our hotel advertising a full-scale international game between Argentina and Ireland. We got two or three hours' kip and then had a training session. After that we had a few hours kip before the match. The Manchester United legend Shay Brennan was in the party at the time and Giles said to him: "I'd sign a contract now for a 5–0 defeat."

'Shay said: "I'll settle for 6–0."

'Giles disagreed: "No, that would be a hiding." We played in the Bocca Juniors Stadium. Some of our players had never been out of the country before and they couldn't believe the size of the venue. It was probably Argentina's greatest team of all time and we were their final World Cup warm-up game. It really was a case of men versus boys. It was the most incredible result I've ever seen in all my playing days. We only lost 3–1.'

'Why so?'

'My mother.'

'Sorry?'

'My mother is a very religious woman and she prays a lot to St Anthony and all her prayers for me must have been answered that night! A much fairer reflection of the game would have been 23–1. At one stage I really thought they were taking the micky out of us when they started warming up this kid with a long hair. I was convinced he was a ball boy. When he came on, though, the things he could do with the ball were amazing. It was Maradona.'

Treacy had great respect for his former Irish boss:

'John Giles really changed things in Ireland and made things a lot more professional. However, he had one weakness. He couldn't say the words "specific" or "specifically". Instead he said "pacific" or "pacifically". When he gave his team talks, he would always get it wrong and I would start pretending to row a boat and start singing: "Row, row, row the boat, merrily down the stream."

'It always made him red in the face and he would get really annoyed and bark at me to shut up.'

Giles's ability to think of nothing but football often spilled over to family life, though there was one memorable occasion when he was brought back to earth with a bang:

'When I was manager of Shamrock Rovers, I forgot my wife was going to the clinic one day. We had four children then, the youngest was seven at the time, and that was going to be the end of it all. When I got home that evening, I said nothing. My wife said: "You never asked me how I got on at the clinic."

'"Oh, how did you get on?"

'You could have knocked me over with a feather when she said: "We're going to have twins!"'

A BUN DEAL

Politics intrudes into all facets of sport. In 1980 Giles resigned as Irish manager and a sixteen-man committee of the FAI was chosen to decide who would be the next Irish manager and were deliberating on the respective merits of Eoin Hand and Paddy Mulligan. Hand emerged victorious, 9–7 in the vote. One of the sixteen is reported to have said that the only reason he voted for Hand was that he thought Mulligan was the person who had thrown a bun at him on one of the foreign trips.

MATERNAL INSTINCT

Giles clearly enjoys his role as analyst: 'Analysis is not nearly as stressful as management. I haven't been shot yet!'

He feels that his partnership with Eamon Dunphy worked because of the contrast in personalities. Their partnership and Bill O'Herlihy's chairmanship was memorably celebrated by the late, great Dermot Morgan (who subsequently found great fame as Father Ted) in a sketch when O'Herlihy broke the news that Dunphy was to have a child by Giles:

BO'H: *Now here to give the update on his life and love indeed is Eamon Dunphy. Sitting beside him is the proud dad-to-be John Giles. Eamon, how's your pregnancy?*

ED: *Yes Bill, this is a great pregnancy. I feel, in a sense, very maternal.*

BO'H: *You're feeling presumably very paternal, John?*

ED: *He is, and I'll tell you something. Pregnancy is something that is great. Sperm has got guts and heart. They have the full DNA, chromosomes the lot. Pregnancy is like professional football. Fertilisation is akin to winning a first team place at Liverpool. Sperm is like professional footballers. They battle and they thrive,*

*but the uterus is probably a hostile environment but the sperm that
makes it through to the egg, that is a great sperm.*
BO'H: *You are blooming a mother-to-be and, if I may so, you are
showing a bit early . . . ha, ha, ha.*
JG: *Great foetus Bill, great foetus.*
ED: *As John says this is a great foetus . . . it's going to be another
Gilesie.*

Consternation emerged though after the birth of the baby. The
father was found not to be Giles but Bono.

RADIO GA GA

Seán Óg Ó Ceallacháin was the first presenter of *The Sunday
Game* in 1979, a rare programme on RTÉ television then devoted
exclusively to Gaelic Games. Seán Óg's contribution to Gaelic
Games is well known. In fact, so associated was he in the popular
mind with Gaelic Games that people had great difficulty thinking
that he had an interest in any other sports. This was memorably
demonstrated when a caller to RTÉ Radio Sport rang to ask about
a Manchester United result. The conversation went as follows:

'Is this Seán Óg?'
'It is indeed.'
'Seán Óg Ó Ceallacháin?'
'The one and the same?'
'Off the radio?'
'That's me!'
'Sure, what the f**k would you know about football.'

A HOLY SHOW

One of the most unusual stories of people who played for
Manchester United was Philip Mulryne. He was part of the 'Class
of 92' and made his only Premier League appearance for United

against Barnsley in 1998 before signing for Norwich. He won twenty-three caps for Northern Ireland. In 2017 he was ordained as a Dominican priest.

After his ordination he bumped into a well-known Manchester United player who was clearly the worst for wear because of alcohol. He went up to reproach him, 'I'm sorry to see you are back on the drink. Haven't I told you before that the drink is your worst enemy?'

'Yes, but remember, Philip, the Church is always telling us to love our enemies.'

'That's true. But I can't ever remember them saying to swallow them.'

PORRIDGE

Another time, Fr Philip went to the local prison to visit a former teammate who had fallen foul of the law. He asked the man what he was charged with.

'Doing my Christmas shopping early,' he answered.

'But that's no offence,' Fr Philip replied wide-eyed. 'How early were you doing this shopping exactly?'

'Before the shop opened,' admitted the convict.

While he was in the building Fr Philip remembered the words from Matthew's Gospel, 'I was in prison and you visited me.' So, he decided to visit some other inmates. He met the thief who stole a calendar and got twelve months.

One had such sad eyes and looked so lonely that he felt really sorry for him.

'Does your mother visit you often?' Fr Philip asked.

'Never.'

'Your father?'

'Never.'

'Your brothers or sisters?'

'Never.'

'Why is that?'

'I killed them all,' the prisoner said with a whisper.

At that stage, the Father made a hasty retreat.

LOVE AND MARRIAGE

Once Fr Philip's car broke down on the way to a wedding ceremony and he was an hour late on arrival. The wedding party was beginning to panic when he arrived, and he was so embarrassed he never forgot the incident. Two years later, he met the husband, a prominent former Manchester United player, at a function and said, 'I'm so sorry about that horrible fright I gave you on your wedding day.'

'So am I,' said the United star. 'I've still got her!'

His next wedding was that of a dentist and manicurist. They fought tooth and nail.

One of Philip's favourite stories was about the woman who went to confession. She asked, 'Father I was looking into a mirror and I decided I was beautiful. Was this a terrible sin?'

The priest answered, 'Certainly not. It was just a terrible mistake.'

Fr Philip claims to have broken the world record for running 100 metres. The circumstances were rather bizarre. He agreed to be a 'pretend Santa Claus' in a charity fund-raising event in the local school. He donned a white beard and red cloak in the normal way. He took his place beside a Christmas tree but was a bit puzzled to see that someone had decided to light a number of candles behind his chair.

He started giving out presents and was really getting into the spirit of things when a young girl started screaming hysterically,

'Santa's dress is on fire.' Fr Philip looked down to see his cloak had brushed against one of the candles and was indeed on fire. The footballing priest became the racing priest as he fled into the bathroom at great speed with a trail of smoke in his wake, leaving behind a hall of children in hysterics and his dignity in shreds.

HORSE SENSE

As a result of his fame as a player with Manchester United, Fr Philip is one of the most frequently invited guest speakers at conferences. One of his favourite stories to the faithful is the following:

One of the big events in Ireland every Christmas is the horse racing at Leopardstown, when the people come in their thousands to have a flutter at the races; the women in particular dressing in their best, most outrageous hats for the occasion.

There is a strong security presence after a previous sabotage attempt where a heating boiler nearly blew up after someone had inserted a dead mouse as a plug into a pipe of the safety system.

Frank the farmer went to the races on St Stephen's Day. Everyone was in thick, heavy overcoats with gloves, scarves and warm hats that sometimes covered the most ghastly Christmas jumpers but the odd hilarious one, too.

Frank's nervousness was clearly visible as he shifted his weight from foot to foot, unable to remain still for more than a few seconds. As the jockeys appeared from the weighing room and mounted their horses, they brought a burst of colour to the scene, their silks shining brightly.

Frank the farmer had brought five hundred quid with him to bet on the horses. He decided that he would not put a bet on the first race and instead watched the horses get ready. He noticed that there was a priest in the parade ring, blessing one of the horses called 'The Christmas Presence' on its head with holy water. The horse then went on to win the race by half a mile and at a price of fifty-to-one! Many in the crowd cheered and jumped up and down with excitement, slapping one another on the back.

Frank smiled as the owner's ruddy-faced image shown on the big television screen, his huge grin stretching almost from one side of the screen to the other. It was these moments that were essential to the success and popularity of racing. The owner was a small shopkeeper and his success gave others hope that they too might one day own the winner of a great race.

Frank decided not to bet on the second race until he had seen which horse the priest blessed next. Sure enough, the priest blessed one of the horses called 'The Christmas Miracle' and this time the horse won by a full mile.

Frank's adrenalin climbed to stratospheric levels. He was very impressed and decided to follow the priest before the third race, and saw him blessing a horse called Benedictus. The horse won at a canter at 100 to 1. Afterwards he thought the bookmaker was speaking Latin when he said, wryly: 'Jesus Benedictus wrecked us.'

Before the fourth race, he saw the priest blessing a horse called 'The Christmas Treasure' with holy water except this time he did not just bless the horse on the head but on his back, his four legs and his tail as well. Frank the farmer was certain that with such a blessing The Christmas Treasure was sure to win the race, so he bet the full five hundred on the horse.

Frank the farmer had a big smile on his face as he watched the race starting. The Christmas Treasure took off like a train and he had a big lead. Frank's heart was beating quickly, and he could ever hear the rush of blood in his ears above the sound of the crowd.

Then disaster.

The Christmas Treasure fell at the first fence.

A few minutes later the horse breathed his last. At that moment, the scuttling clouds spilled open and it started to pour.

Frank the farmer was sad and upset. He raced straight up to the priest and said: 'I don't understand. You gave a small blessing to the first three horses and they won their races easily. You gave a big blessing to the fourth horse and he fell and died. How could that happen?'

The priest shook his head and put his hand on Frank's shoulder and softly said: 'Ah, you poor man. You don't understand the difference between a blessing and the last rites.'

HOD AND GOD

Jean-Paul Sartre believed that a truly free man, who wants to use his freedom, will choose 'play' as the activity by which to express that freedom.

Sports and games have been an integral part of the human race for as long as there have been human beings. Through sport, people discover their strengths and find their limits. In games they discover their relationships to other people and how they shape their community. Sports and games have a special significance for the humanising of human beings.

Against this background it is not that surprising that football and religion have overlapped in significant respects. To take just one example, the late Pope John Paul II enjoyed a successful stint as a goalkeeper before a higher calling took him away from their goalmouths of Poland.

Another former goalkeeper, Coventry City's David Icke, went on Terry Wogan's television programme in 1991 and calmly told the British public that he was the son of God. The unique match of football and religion has generated some comic moments.

Of course, the most infamous link between football and religion was provided by Glen Hoddle whose controversial opinions on divine retribution for the sins of people's past lives caused shock waves. It all began innocently enough when Hoddle became 'a born-again Christian'. This inspired a classic comment from the comedian Jasper Carrott: *I hear Glenn Hoddle has found God. That must have been one hell of a pass!*

Back then Hoddle was restricting himself to some insightful comments about his chosen sport: *Football's about ninety minutes on the day; it's about tomorrows really.*

During his time as England manager things seemed to go off the rails when among other things Hoddle elevated his faith-healer Eileen Drewery to daughter of God status: *Jesus was a normal, run-of-the-mill sort of guy who had a genuine gift, just as Eileen has.*

HELLO. HELLO. HELLO

Sometimes star players do not get on together. One of Ireland's national treasures is Newstalk presenter and former lead singer with Something Happens, Tom Dunne. He is also the presenter of the popular tv series *The Zoo*. As a result, he is equally at home discussing the zoo and Yazoo.

Tom took Anthony as his confirmation name as a tribute to the late, great Tony Dunne, the Manchester United full-back from their European triumph in 1968. As an avid Manchester United fan, one of the highlights of Tom's life came when he was invited to do a public interview with some of the United legends. One of them was Peter Schmeichel. He had heard that the great goalkeeper did not get on well with Roy Keane and enquired how best to broach the subject. In response, he got a message saying that Schmeichel was no longer happy to do the interview and would stay in the dressing room. Eventually, a comprise was reached. Schmeichel agreed to do the interview as long as there were no questions about Roy Keane.

Tom really enjoyed the assembly line of trophies United won under Fergie. However, once Sir Alex left in 2013, he knew that things might not be the same again. In 2014 he started to get really excited with the rumour that Ángel di María would sign for United from Real Madrid. By his own admission, Tom has not the highest level of religious devotion in Ireland. Such was his desire for Di María to sign for the club that not only did Tom pray for the transfer to happen, he also got his daughters Eva and Skye to pray with him. Their prayers were answered. Di María signed for United for a then record fee for a British club of £59.7 million. The nicest term most United fans have for the Argentinian's short spell at the club is 'expensive flop'. The experience has done wonders for Tom's faith.

He is now a firm believer.

In unanswered prayers.

BLUSHING BERTIE

Former Taoiseach Bertie Ahern is another of Ireland's best-known Manchester United fans. In Ireland in the early 1970s, there was a few bob to be made in the summer football seven-a-sides. Because of that, it was a very serious business indeed. As a result, the cream of the League of Ireland players were involved, like Ben Hannigan and Eric Barber. One player who got in on the act was Bertie Ahern. It was shortly before he got married and he was working as an accountant in the Mater Hospital at the time. One evening, he did not have time to go home for his gear and all he had with him was a pair of squash shorts with a fly and a zip. Disaster struck in the dressing room. He got his zip stuck in his foreskin. He was in agony. (The wounded tone of his voice leaves no room for doubt about the veracity of this claim.)

There was a man from Cork in the dressing room called Barry. Bertie can't remember his surname, but he will never forget him to his dying day. He was a soldier and had served in Vietnam. At first, he suggested that Bertie go to the Mater but there was no way the man who would be Taoiseach would agree to that because he worked there. Barry rustled up a jar of Vaseline and a knife and went to work to untangle Bertie ... if that's the right word!

The saga of the zip, Vaseline and knife is not for the squeamish nor for those about to eat. Suffice to say that the delicate operation was completed successfully – if very painfully and the future Fianna Fáil leader was spared the nickname Bertie Bobbit!

He had taken part in the kickabout before the game and his team-mates had no idea why he hadn't taken his place on the pitch. They played on with ten men, but he came back on for the second half. That's dedication! They won 2–1 but the lads never knew why Bertie missed the first half.

Happily the procedure did not leave a lasting impression but it did leave an enduring conviction: 'The one piece of advice I would give an aspiring footballer is never, ever, ever wear a pair of togs with a zip!'

A CROWD FAVOURITE

To Manchester United's Irish fans, Old Trafford is the contemporary equivalent of Mount Olympus. In 2007 Sky Sports were asking people leaving the England match after their 1–1 draw to Brazil if they were disappointed.

Fan wearing a Manchester United jersey: Not at all, I'm Irish.

Reporter: 'But would you not support England when Ireland are not action?'

Fan: 'No way.'

Reporter: 'Why not?'

Fan: 'Eight-hundred years of oppression.'

Reporter: 'Is there ever any time you would support England?'

Fan: 'If they were playing Liverpool.'

PART II
Personal Perspectives

For many, Manchester United has been a fixed point in a fast-changing age. Those years have not been without their troubles but even when the storm clouds gathered as they did during the Covid-19 crisis the club has not withered before their blast. A better, stronger movement will come out into the sunshine when the tempest is past.

Our economic system values measurable outcomes but what is deepest about us, transcends what can be said and outstrips what can be analysed. There are moments when we know that there is more to life – and to us – than the grim and grasping existence of seeking and striving and succeeding. There are moments of wonder, hope and grace that give us hints of ecstasy and lift us out of ourselves. They are, in Yeats's phrase, 'the soul's monuments of its own magnificence'. These moments take us to the heart of the deep mystery of being a person, the subterranean stirrings of the spirit, the rapid rhythms of the human heart. They have to do with remembering who we are, enlarging our perspective, seeing ourselves whole.

Each of us has a unique relationship with the club. In this final section are three personal pieces – about my two favourite United stars and my most memorable Manchester United match.

17

OH, AH PAUL MCGRATH

It could be bad news for him. His knee
is locked up in the dressing room.
                    Sky Sports' George Gavin

In 1990, Nelson Mandela caused traffic chaos during his visit to receive the Freedom of the City of Dublin. Huge crowds flocked to see him and, as they waited for him to appear, the tens of thousands of people chanted in unison: 'Oh-ah Paul McGrath's da.'

Paul McGrath's story is the stuff of movies. Born in Ealing, west London in 1959, the future Black Pearl of Inchicore was brought to Monkstown, Dublin where his mother placed him in an orphanage when he was only two months old. He lived in the main in residential care until he was sixteen, then left the orphanage at the age of seventeen. He struggled to adjust to life outside the orphanage; in his teens he found his world dissolving beneath his feet and suffered two nervous breakdowns.

It is still difficult for him to talk about this time. He is taciturn, even reticent. He averts his eyes from mine and appears confounded to find himself the centre of attention. Although there are many reasons why he could be arrogant, he is the personification of modesty – the sort of man you want to instinctively protect. He speaks in a self-deprecatory and half-apologetic way:

'It was a funny time. I started to play for Dalkey United and things were going well on the pitch. We went on a tour of Germany. Things weren't so hot outside football, though. I was out in the real world for the first time and it was harder than I had expected. There was nobody there to pick up the pieces when I slipped up. I was not trained to fend for myself.'

He fights to disguise his annoyance with any show of weakness. In deep despair and despondency, he endured the hard times, with the hope they would eventually lead to a better life. He became one of the shining lights of those from humble origins, one of the very few men who had broken free and who had sought the rewarding adventures of the new life, with thanks to the help of people like Frank Mullen and Tommy Cullen.

He came under the eye of Charlie Walker and was signed by Saint Patrick's Athletic in 1981. McGrath's unique talents as a football player persuaded Manchester United to part with £30,000 for his signature. He was on his way to Old Trafford, having secretly nursed an ambition to perform on the highest stage plus additional payments for international and first-team appearances. The package also included a friendly between Pat's and United. Ron Atkinson described the deal as an 'absolute bargain'. Then came some of the happiest memories of his life; memories which have now dimmed the nightmare of those teenage years.

Success bred jealously and the full glare of media intrusion. Mercifully, he is no paragon. There were times when he sought solace in the bottom of a bottle. This led to a lot of press speculation about his lifestyle. But he never lost sight of his objectives. In the main he did not heed any rumours, he did not care for gossip, he was too busy tending his career and pursuing his ambitions to worry about what others thought. Although for years he was the undisputed star of the Irish football team and brought so much pleasure – he shines but he shines modestly.

In 1989 Graham Taylor brought him to Aston Villa for just £400,000 when injuries and problems related to alcohol had cast a cloud over his future. McGrath's career flourished at Villa Park – although amazingly without the benefit of regular training. In 1992/93 as Villa pushed United relentlessly for the title, McGrath was voted the Players' Player of the Year.

Having lost his place on the Aston Villa team at the beginning of the 1996/97 season, he moved to Derby County and helped them secure their premiership status. In the summer of 1997, he moved to Sheffield United but to the displeasure of most Irish football fans he was unable to make the Irish squad at the time.

In 1987 he played for the Football League in its centenary fixture against the Rest of the World. Against Maradona et al, McGrath bestrode the elite of world football like a Colossus. Most observers made him the man of the match. The performance spoke volumes about his genuine class.

From the dawn of time, identification with heroes has been an integral part of the human condition. Great sporting performances have always grabbed the imagination of the young as they fantasise about emulating the glorious feats of their heroes. Thanks in no small part to television, sports heroes occupy an even larger part of the imagination than in earlier generations. The fear that we had lost Paul McGrath to injury generated a sense of loss which far exceeded anything that would have been felt for any politician or media personality. The most casual fans took vicarious pride in the style, craft, courage and character the game that is among one of the finest creative manifestations of popular culture.

A few flaws have been revealed along the way, notably in a few falls. But perhaps this adds to rather than detracts from McGrath's popularity. Before his 'fall from grace' with an infamous episode in a toilet, George Michael, in a moment of exceptional, perhaps surprising, psychological insight said that a star is not a person who has a little bit extra but someone who has a little bit missing. Evidence to support this analysis can be found in the icons of the twentieth century, the ones who keep you staring into the television screen or the newspaper image, who dazzle you with the life and radiance in their faces even though you know they are dead; individuals such as Evita, Elvis Presley, Marilyn Monroe and James Dean.

It is significant that Ireland's favourite sporting hero over the last generation has been Paul McGrath: a footballer of sublime skill and a wonderful human being with a few blemishes.

Paul's story would have made Aristotle leap about in his sandals, it is such a brilliant illustration of the classic precepts of tragedy: the hero with his flaw and the audience torn between awe and pity. He has become Ireland's favourite hero because in some ways he is a mirror of our inward selves, but for that very reason the odd vulture would try nailing him like they have nailed all others.

I have always believed that everybody has 'their song'. Given Paul's battle with his demons I think Paul's song is the Ray Charles classic: 'Take these chains from my heart and set me free.'

FAMILIAR STRANGERS

As I sit down with Paul, he looked me steadfastly in the eye. His own eyes are soft and kind and so being stared at was not threatening for a stranger like myself. He spoke deliberately, thoughtfully, using his hands to help find and deliver the right words. His little asides were intimate, wry, and chatty by turns.

As we talked, two young children burst into the room unannounced to say hello to their hero. His eyes lit up when he saw them. On moments like those when he felt totally relaxed, he was much, much funnier than his grave, intense facial expression suggested. At times, his customary shy smile gave away to a delighted grin.

I have often tried to put my finger on why this soft-spoken man made such a lasting impression on me, but I can't.

In his parting words to me, he looked back on his United career with affection:

'I recall David Platt being let go at United, but he went on to make it huge with Aston Villa and England. Peter Beardsley joined United round the same time as me but only got one game with the club. I think back now to Billy Garton who was a very promising centre-half but he got injured and was forced to pack it in before his career ever got the chance to take off. When I think about it now, I was very lucky to last so long especially 'cos of my dodgy knees.'

THE BRADY BUNCH

McGrath's Irish teammate Liam Brady was not the most popular Celtic manager with the fans. However, Manchester City fans appear to hold him in higher esteem, as their parody of Oasis's hit single 'Wonderwall' indicates after Alan Ball was appointed their manager:

Maybe, just maybe, we should have gone for Liam Brady, 'cos after all we've got Alan Ball.

THE MASTER

In the beginning, God and Paul McGrath were seen as quite separate individuals. It was only later that confusion crept in.

One story illustrates Paul's status in the game. The All-Heaven final was taking place between Manchester United and the rest. The United team were powered by some of the giants of deceased footballers. The other team likewise had the pick of players who had gone on to their eternal reward and were captained by Sir Stanley Matthews. With just three minutes to go, the opposition were leading by three goals. Suddenly there was a gasp from the crowd as a sub appeared on the United team. In the final three minutes four balls were pumped into the replacement. The supersub got on the four of them and stuck each of them in the net. United won by a goal. After the game was over, St Peter went over to commiserate with the defeated stars. The players were stunned by the appearance of the sub and Sir Bobby Moore asked, 'I never knew Paul McGrath died. When did it happen?'

St Peter replied, 'Oh that's not Paul McGrath. That's God. He just thinks he is Paul McGrath.'

18

RAY OF LIGHT

Wilkins sends an inch-perfect pass to no one in particular.
Bryon Butler

Some people really like themselves. When Simon Cowell was a guest on *Desert Island Discs* and was asked to choose the luxury item he would like to take with him his reply left Sue Lawley, speechless, 'A mirror.'

Larry Ryan was lining out for Saint Johnstone and was marking Virgil van Dijk in his final game for Celtic. It was a humbling experience for Larry, 'The first ball, I tried to sprint with him and he just boshed me out of it. I was out of breath and blowing out of my backside and he just turned to me and said: "I wouldn't even bother, I'm just too good."'

GARDENER'S WORLD
I like people who have a sense of humility. Mick McCarthy captained Ireland to their greatest achievement, reaching the quarter-finals of the World Cup at Italia '90. He said at the time, 'The only thing is, I'm not quick, we all know that – I mean, I go out running and a woman with a pram passes me.'

In autumn 2002 after Ireland lost 4–2 to Russia the consensus was that Mick McCarthy was a shoo-in to replace Peter Reid as manager of Sunderland. To everyone's surprise, the job went to Howard Wilkinson.

Mind you, he did not have the stiffest competition for the job. One of the few other applicants was a fan whose application had two main planks, 'My spouse is willing to launder the football kits after each match and my uncle Jack, who has his own allotment and a petrol lawnmower, is willing to cut the grass once or even twice a week.'

LET'S BE BLUNT

When the Covid-19 crisis broke, every top singer – and sadly many less talented – took it on themselves to record concerts and upload them on various social media platforms.

My favourite response though was that of James 'You're Beautiful' Blunt: 'Everybody is recording special sessions for their fans. To help keep the world sane and healthy I have decided not to record one.'

In May five year-old Leeds united fan Daniel Auton wrote to Brighton offering the football club all his pocket money, fifteen pounds and seven pence to buy Ben White who was on loan at Leeds. I enjoyed White's reaction: 'I'm not worth £15.'

KISS

When Lee Trevino was winning one of his most famous golf tournaments the TV coverage picked up on the fact that he kept looking at one of his gloves and the fact that he had a word scribbled on it – which was indistinguishable. After he won the tournament he was bombarded with questions from the media about the word and he told them that it was the word 'Kiss'. They were all confused by his response, so he explained that it stood for: 'Keep It Simple Stupid'. This was the Ray 'Butch' Wilkins way.

Ray joined Manchester United from Chelsea in the summer of 1979 for £800,000. He went on to make 194 appearances with the club before signing for Italian giants AC Milan in 1984. He won eighty-four caps for England, ten as captain.

He was an incredibly gifted footballer. During the Covid-19 crisis I allowed myself a treat every evening. On alternate nights I watched Ray's stunning goal for England against Belgium in the 1980 European Championships and against Brighton in the 1983 FA Cup final.

The other United goal in their 2–2 draw with recently relegated Brighton was from Frank Stapleton, with whom Wilkins forged an excellent understanding, and who became the first player to score in the final for two different FA Cup winning teams. The first was his goal for Arsenal against United in 1979.

With only three minutes to go and Brighton seemingly down and out, United led 2–1 when Gary Stevens equalised. Extra time brought a moment of high drama. There were only seconds remaining when Brighton got a gilt-edged opportunity to steal victory. The late Michael Robinson broke through the defence and set up a chance for Gordon Smith. The radio commentator said: '...and Smith must score...' but Gary Bailey saved his weak shot with his legs. The moment was immortalised in the title of the Brighton fanzine *And Smith Must Score*.

DEAD CERTAIN

Many years later Ray was picking through the frozen turkeys at the local supermarket, but he couldn't find one big enough for the family for Christmas. He asked a passing assistant, 'Do these turkeys get any bigger?'

The assistant replied, 'I'm afraid not, they're dead.'

FIRST MEETING

The first time I met Ray was on the last Monday of October in 1992. At the time he was playing for QPR. It may be hard to imagine but that season, which was the inaugural Premier League season, QPR finished fifth and were the highest placed London team in the League. Ray was pulling the strings in midfield and Les Ferdinand was their star striker. Two days previously they had beaten the reigning league champions Leeds 2–1 in a pulsating game at Loftus Road. At the time QPR were managed by another of my childhood idols Gerry Francis, who kindly invited me to attend a training session with the bonus of a one-to-one conversation with Ray afterwards.

After he was appointed manager of Queens Park Rangers for the second time, Gerry Francis was asked about the barren state of the club's coffers. With a classic 'Coleman balls' he replied, 'It's not just money, there's financial problems as well.'

MANNERS MAKETH THE MAN

I never know what unique insights into football I might find in my conversation with Ray, as if he was a crime scene I was searching for the first time. His insights were not really for a book like this, but it was clear that he had a fine football brain. I asked if he would be willing to do a 'proper football book' with me.

He replied: 'Some top player should do a book, warts and all ... and even name the warts. But it is not for me.'

For all his appearance of accessibility, when it comes to the playing the media game there was something impenetrable about Ray. Sporting legends sometimes find their minds can wander in the presence of those who have not accomplished all they have. It may sound old fashioned but what stood out in the time I was with him was his manners. He would have fitted perfectly as a hero in a Jane Austen novel.

The QPR fans loved Ray because of his grace on the ball and

his keen intelligence on the pitch. In November 1994, Francis left QPR to manage Spurs and, by acclaim, Ray succeeded him as QPR manager.

AN UNUSUALLY TALL STORY

QPR were in the Premiership when Wilkins took them over. After they were relegated to Division One, they came up against Oxford United, who featured Kevin Francis, who was six foot seven inches tall. It gives a whole new meaning to the big league. Afterwards Wilkins gave his opinion of Francis, 'To be fair he's got quite a good touch, but he's quite daunting. If I ever need my guttering fixed, I'll give him a call.'

APPRAISAL

As the late Enoch Powell famously observed of politicians, so one might say of footballers that every career is bound to end in failure; or, if not failure, at least not complete satisfaction. Ray did not savour complete satisfaction.

Graeme Souness said, 'I have come to the conclusion that nice men do not make good managers.' Sadly, Ray was not the exception that proves the rule. The real problem Ray faced as QPR manager was that a few months later Les Ferdinand was sold to Newcastle United for £6 million and the team were relegated.

In April 2018 after suffering a cardiac arrest, Ray's time on Earth ended. Sporting heroes are people like us. They do what we do. They live our lives – in the sporting area better but in ordinary life they face the same struggles as we do. Ray Wilkins embodies this definition more fully than any sporting personality I can think of.

Ray personified what the late American sportswriter, Grantland Rice meant when he wrote: 'For when the great scorer comes to write against your name, He makes not how you won or lost, but how you played the game.'

Few players put the beauty into the beautiful game better than Ray Wilkins.

ROCKET MAN

My enduring memory of Ray is of the second time I met him – completely by chance in Heathrow airport about twenty years ago. He was on great form. We both had noticed a report in the newspaper that David Beckham was busy promoting his new fashion brand. Ray took me by surprise when he said, 'I launched my own clothing line this week. I shouldn't have lit fireworks so near the washing!'

HOPELESSLY DEVOTED TO YOU

Ray refused to name the best player he ever played with or against, but it was very evident that he was a huge admirer of Bryan Robson. He told me a story of Robson when he was manager of West Brom.

After training one day, a mobile phone on a bench rings and Robson engages the hands-free speaker function and began to talk. Although they were trying to pretend otherwise, all the players were listening in.

Robson: 'Hello.'

Robson's wife: 'Hi, honey, it's me?'

Robson: 'What a lovely surprise.'

Wife: 'I'm in the shop now and I have seen this amazing coat. It's only £5,000; is it okay to buy it?'

Robson: 'Sure, if you like it so much.'

Wife: 'Oh, I also stopped at the car dealer and saw their new cars. I saw one I absolutely loved.'

Robson: 'How much?'

Wife: '£75,000.'

Robson: 'Fine, but at that price make sure you get one with all the options.'

Wife: 'Wonderful. One last thing. I was talking to the estate agent and that house I wanted last year is back on the market. It has a lot of light.'

Robson: 'That will bring a touch of glass.'

Wife: 'The thing is they are asking £1 million for it.'

Robson: 'Well go ahead and make an offer of £950,000. They'll probably take it. If not, we can go the extra £50,000 if it's what you really want.'

Wife: 'Thanks. I love you so much. See you this evening.'

Robson: 'Love you, too.'

Then he hung up to find the eyes of every player on him – watching him like hawks.

It was then that Robson asked, 'Anybody know whose phone this is?'

19

THE CLASSIC

The scoreline didn't really reflect the outcome.
Tony Gubba

They say confession is good for the soul. I hope so. For forty years I have harboured a dark secret from my family. Many sleepless nights I have turned and twisted in my bed as the pangs of guilt racked my troubled conscience. No amount of counting sheep could shake off the tidal waves of remorse that swept over me.

In my defence, it wasn't really my fault. The real villain was Jimmy Magee. The great sports commentators share a magical capacity to raise and refresh the spirit and to heighten the quality of human perception. Jimmy Magee was one of them. His was a world of wonder, admiration and enchantment.

In the pantheon of Irish sport, a special place is reserved for Jimmy. No less a diplomat than a great broadcaster, he had a great flair for handling Manchester United fans. 'Jimmy,' an anxious United fan in the bleak days of the 1970s desperately seeking assurance enquired, 'Do you think we still have a great team?'

'Ah, my good man,' Jimmy replied with the utmost sincerity. '*Great* is not the word to describe it!'

MATCH OF A LIFETIME

It was the 'Five Minute Final', the 1979 FA Cup final between Manchester United and Arsenal. Around Old Trafford the club went into a dizzy state and tickets for the final were chased with a passion. An advertisement appeared in *The Manchester Evening News* a few days before the final: 'Young Manchester United supporter of good appearance and sound health offers hand in marriage to any young lady with two tickets to the final next Saturday. Please send photograph. Of the tickets.'

My family though were in a tizzy because my aunt Sheila was getting married two days later after a twelve-year courtship. Nobody could accuse her of marrying in haste. The match had thankfully permitted me to provide a pretext for missing the rehearsal. All I had to was to deposit the newly acquired three-tiered wedding cake into my uncle-in-law-to-be's Capri car while the rest of the family went to the church.

With five minutes to go Arsenal were cruising with a 2–0 lead and Jimmy assured me that the match was theirs. This was the moment to leave out the cake.

My decision seemed to trigger a domino effect. Arsenal manager, former Northern Ireland international Terry Neill had even decided to take the luxury of replacing his midfielder David Price with substitute, Steve Walford – apparently just to give the youngster a taste of the glory. Then Gordon McQueen scrambled a goal for United. Almost immediately Sammy McIlroy made a jinking run through the crowded defence before unleashing a bending shot past his Northern Irish colleague, Pat Jennings.

The Arsenal players looked totally baffled and dejected. Wembley suddenly seemed transformed into a sea of Manchester red and white. Somehow though Liam Brady found a last drop of energy to set up a movement which led to Alan Sunderland sensationally scoring a last gasp winner. McIlroy captured the mood of the United players: 'It was like picking eight draws and then finding the pools coupon still in your pocket.'

It was starting to rain. The rain slid, tapping, through the branches, and swept in windy puffs across the fields. As I carefully placed the cake on the back seat of William's Capri I could hear Jimmy recklessly abandoning his normal calm, mellifluous tones for a state of near frenzy. I raced back inside to see that United had scored. Jimmy could scarcely contain his excitement. A minute later United equalised. Jimmy's voice pulsated with enthusiasm. Then, with time almost up, another piece of wizardry came to sensationally set up the winning goal. By now Jimmy was in a state of near rapture.

At the final whistle, a feeling of panic descended on me. I raced outside. My worst fears were realised. I had left the car door open and our dog – imaginatively called Lassie – was licking the wedding cake.

Lassie was warm, brown and smooth-coated, with a cream arrow on her forehead and flecks of cream on her two front feet. She was a very knowing, friendly creature and I loved her with a passion. At that moment I could have killed her, especially as icing dripped off her whiskers like a snowman melting in a heatwave.

The damage to the cake was surprisingly small and a little surgery with a knife seemed to do the trick.

Blood may be thicker than water, but it is also a great deal nastier. I decided that news of Lassie's appreciation for the wedding cake was best kept to myself. Whoever said silence is golden knew what they were talking about.

Such was my acute anxiety that overnight I was attacked by a virulent form of acne. My mother thought that was the reason that during the wedding I sought the shadows as resolutely as the Phantom of the Opera.

A look of adoration passed into my aunt's face as she cut the cake, like the look of the mother of a child who has just won first prize. To my eyes the icing looked as buttery and soft as white custard. So acute was the sensation of panic across my chest I felt I might explode.

Everyone agreed they had never tasted a nicer wedding cake.

THE LAST WORD

Their away record is instantly forgettable –
the 5–1 defeat and 7–0 defeat spring to mind.

Ian Payne

Sky News have just had a newsflash.

A Manchester City fan had his car smashed.

The thief took everything his wallet, his credit cards, his laptop, his passport, his books and even his picture of his wife and children.

The only thing he left behind was the owner's Manchester City's season ticket.

But in act of cruel and unusual punishment he left ... a second Manchester City season ticket.

He also left a handwritten note which said:

Q: What do you call fifty Manchester City Season tickets at the bottom of the sea?

A: A good start.

THE VERY LAST WORD

*I was surprised, but I always say
nothing surprises me in football.*

Les Ferdinand

Is there a serious purpose to the humour in these pages? *The Book of Ecclesiastes* tells us that there is 'a time to weep and a time to laugh'.

Blessed are those who can laugh at themselves.

They shall never cease to be amused.

I have tried to keep the stories as politically correct as possible. I received a timely reminder of the importance of this recently when one of my best friends lost his job. You would imagine there is nothing wrong with asking: 'Smoking or non-smoking?'

It becomes a real problem though when you are an undertaker and the choice is: 'Cremation or burial?'

Discretion permits me from naming the former Manchester United star, who was spotted in great distress crying at a graveside and screaming hysterically, 'Why did you have to die?'

'And when did your wife die?' asked a passer-by sympathetically.

The sobbing footballer shook his head. 'That's not my wife's grave. It's her first husband's.'

NO PRIME MINISTER

As I finish this book, Boris Johnson is on the radio telling us 'that the worst is over'. I should feel reassured but instead I am experiencing acute intimations of mortality.

What does posterity need me for? Nothing.

But what would I like said about me at my funeral? I'd like someone to say, 'Look! He's moving!'

As I sit here at my laptop, my publisher rings.

He is the last one laughing.

He thinks my writing is all over.

It is now.

IN MEMORIAM

Football is my passion. Golf less so. But during the writing of this book I was very saddened to hear of the death of Peter Alliss. He became the 'voice of golf' after a successful playing career. Peter won more than twenty tournaments during his career and played on eight Ryder Cup teams. His move into broadcasting came about after he was overheard by the BBC's Ray Lakeland talking to a friend on a flight back from a tournament in Ireland in 1960. Just as John Motson's voice defined my introduction to football, to me Peter simply 'was golf'.

Like many of the personalities featured in this book he is famous for his funny quotes including the following gems:

'It's like turning up to hear Pavarotti sing and finding out he has laryngitis.' (After Tiger Woods shot 81 at the 2002 Open.)

'One of the good things about rain in Scotland is that most of it ends up as Scotch.'

'Look at that. Faldo looks a young man again, and poor old Greg, well he looks ready for his bus pass.' (On Faldo versus Norman at the 1996 Masters.)

'Looks a bit like *Jurassic Park* in there.' (On the rough during the 2003 Open.)

'He has been a giant in a land of pygmies.'

'Some of the fans there, fuelled by the local giggle-juice' (On noisy spectators.)

'If he could just get over this shy part of his nature ...' (As Sergio Garcia leaped and jumped around after holing a 60-yard approach shot at the 17th in the third round of the 2003 British Open.)

'He used to be fairly indecisive, but now he's not so certain.'

'I can't see, unless the weather changes, the conditions changing dramatically.'

'We can now have that new kitchen you promised me.' (Peter's interpretation = possibly requiring a male chauvinism alert – of what Mike Weir's wife is saying as she hugs her hubby after Weir's victory.)

I had the good fortune to have some dealings with Peter. I once asked him to select his ten top golfers of the twentieth century. He said:

> It's a virtually impossible task to pick your ten greatest and of course the further back you go, you have to consider the equipment they had to use and the degree of time it took to travel anywhere. I think all of the following players showed tremendous character, all won the world's major champion-ships and although I'm sure someone else would suggest different names, this list covers seventy years and is formi-dable. I think it's impossible to go back too far but I do think we must start with Bobby Jones.

Peter's list read as follows:

IN MEMORIAM

1. Bobby Jones.
2. Sam Snead
3. Ben Hogan
4. Jack Nicklaus
5. Arnold Palmer
6. Gary Player
7. Bobby Locke
8. Peter Thompson
9. Walter Hagen
10. Gene Saracens

Thanks for the memories, Peter.

ACKNOWLEDGEMENTS

I am very honoured that Ken Doherty wrote the foreword. Ken is Irish sporting royalty and is one of the few sports stars to have brought a world championship to Old Trafford. His great love of Manchester United is very evident in this piece.

I am profoundly thankful to lifelong Red Devil Simon Delaney for his support of this book. Simon is Ireland's combined answer to Matt Damon, Michael Parkinson and ... Nigella Lawson! He is some man for one man.

Pat Crerand is a true United legend. I am very gratified by his generous support for this book.

Alex Gordon's practical assistance has been invaluable.

I am very grateful to the many people who shared their stories and jokes with me. I am particularly thankful to Paul McGrath, John Giles, Eamon Dunphy, and Gerry Francis for their time and wisdom. The late Jack Charlton will always command a special pace on my affections and I really appreciated his insights.

I am grateful to and always entertained by another massive United fan Tom Dunne. When Something Happens Tom always rises to the occasion.

On the field Chloe Mustaki has played the beautiful game with grace. Off the field she has been an inspiration for all seasons because of her courage.

This book has mercilessly poked fun at Manchester City. And rightly so! That said I found Pep Guardiola in my thoughts during the Covid-19 crisis because of the sad passing of his mother, Dolors Sala. May she rest in peace.

In its rich and distinguished history, Manchester United have produced generations of amazing fans. Tom Hogan is the number one United fan of all time. He carries the team like a fire in his heart. May he know only good days. Tom's dad Cian had a big birthday this year. May the road (to Cork) rise to meet him and may the wind always be on his back.

My deepest gratitude for the friendship of another huge Manchester United fan, Rob Canning.

Amyas Butler entered the world to the delight of his parents Siobhan and Gordon and sister Claire. May he only know health and happiness.

The great Gareth O'Callaghan has been much in my thoughts as this book was written. May the sun always shine brightly on your face. *Audere est facere*.

Thanks to all at Black & White Publishing, particularly Campbell Brown, for backing this book so enthusiastically. My thanks also to Simon Hess and Declan Heeney for their support.

ABOUT THE AUTHOR

JOHN SCALLY is the author of over forty books, including a series of bestselling books about sport. His most recent titles include *100 Great GAA Teams*, *The People's Games* and *101 Great Irish Rugby Moments*.

John has made a lifelong study of Footballing Foot and Mouth disease, and he has been clinically diagnosed as suffering from SAD: Sporting Anecdotes Disorder.

ALSO BY JOHN SCALLY

100 Great GAA Teams
The People's Games
Great GAA Rivalries
Blood, Sweat, Triumph & Tears
101 Great Irish Rugby Moments
100 Great GAA Moments
The GAA Immortals

Inspiration for All Seasons
My Miracle Cure